THE
PLAYBOY
BOOK

FORTY
YEARS

THE
PLAYBOY
BOOK

FORTY
YEARS

By Gretchen Edgren

GENERAL PUBLISHING GROUP, INC.

Publisher: W. Quay Hays
Art Director: Kurt Wahlner
Production: Maria Mandis, Nadeen Torio
Production Assistants: Lisa Barnes, John Valenzuela

The publisher wishes especially to thank Hugh M. Hefner, Arthur Kretchmer and Tom Staebler;
also Jonathan Black, Gary Cole, Bill Farley, Lee Froehlich, Peter Glassberg, Tim Hawkins, Christie Hefner, Eileen Kent, Bruce
Kluger, Maria Mandis, Barbara Nellis, Mary O'Connor, Michael Perlis, Cindy Rakowitz, Stephen Randall, John Rezek, Howard
Shapiro, Chet Suski, Marcia Terrones, Terri Tomcisin, Michelle Urry and Joyce Wiegand-Bavas along with the following for their
kind contributions to this book: Colby Allerton, Wilma Barnett, Joe Bein, Hilary Bein, Sharon Lynn, Charlie Raab,
Irene Robinson, Kassandra Smolias, Bernie Steinhouse, Trici Venola and Suzanne Weaver

CONTENTS

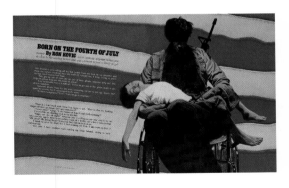

INTRODUCTION

his book isn't intended for those who "only buy PLAYBOY for the articles," because this is a book of images—the award-winning art, photography, cartoons and covers of the magazine that changed America—that literally transformed the social-sexual climate of the country in the second half of the 20th century and became the most popular and most influential men's magazine in the world.

The images collected in this book serve to explain both PLAYBOY's popularity and its influence. In a time of repression and conformity, PLAYBOY presented a revolutionary perception of life that was both sophisticated and playful. The editorial point of view—that life was more than a vale of tears, that play and pleasure were important parts of being alive—was reflected in the words and pictures of every issue.

In a very real sense, the Playmate of the Month was just as important a political declaration as *The Playboy Philosophy*, and it made a similar statement in far fewer pages. Inspired by the pinup art and photography of the Thirties and Forties, PLAYBOY presented an all-American dream come true, the girl next door transformed into an erotic icon. What this said about female sexuality—that nice girls like sex, too—is as important as any feminist polemic.

In their own way, the art and illustrations in PLAYBOY were as revolutionary as the centerfold. Before PLAYBOY was published, commercial art and fine art existed in two different worlds. Arthur Paul, PLAYBOY's founding Art Director, changed that by using fine artists to illustrate PLAYBOY's fiction and nonfiction, encouraging them to use a variety of styles and techniques. There is good art and bad art, Paul believed, and it doesn't matter whether good art is reproduced in the pages of a magazine or hangs on a gallery wall.

We changed the world of cartoons as well, allowing them the freedom to be more sophisticated and innovative. Exposing the humor in the human condition, the magazine satirized sex and society, men and women, work and play, lust and lament. We sent a cartoonist (Shel Silverstein) to discover the old world, and created a cast of characters—from Little Annie Fanny to Buck Brown's Granny—that are a permanent part of the American family tree.

The service features—which emphasized food and drink, fashion, grooming, gear and gadgetry—helped to define the PLAYBOY lifestyle. These articles demystified those accessories that became synonymous with "the Good Life." But it was always obvious that gear and gadgetry were only accessories to the more important point of it all: an optimistic, romantic exploration of all the possibilities life had to offer.

There was a time, at the turn of the century, when the Sears, Roebuck catalog was known as the "wish book," because it provided rural America with an illustrated source for merchandise of every imaginable description. It offered a world otherwise unknown to people living outside the major cities. Similarly, PLAYBOY became the wish book of the second half of the century. From the pictorials to the articles to the service features, PLAYBOY was a handbook and a book of dreams for young, urban American males.

Looking back over the five decades captured in these pages, I feel a real nostalgic rush—a sentimental journey shared with a major part of my generation and the generations that followed. We all grew up with this magazine, myself included. Most of you probably remember the first time you saw PLAYBOY—you remember the covers, cartoons and centerfolds from those issues. The magazine had that sort of impact on many of our lives.

Turning these pages is a trip down memory lane for me and, I hope, for you as well. They capture moments in my life and the life of the magazine that are unforgettable. They capture, in an especially evocative way, the personalities of each of the five decades reflected here.

Hugh M Hefner

Editor and Publisher

FOREWORD

For over 40 years PLAYBOY has been one of the most powerful voices in American culture. People have a serious reaction to the magazine because it is a magazine people take seriously. They know it's an integral part of the fabric of male life, and it has always enjoyed mass circulation, mass audience and mass acceptance. It's as much an American institution as it is a magazine.

All that some people know about PLAYBOY are the pictures, and a segment of this group completely misunderstand them. They infer—from their own view of the pictorials—that men's interests as PLAYBOY presents them couldn't possibly be compatible with women's interests.

From day one, PLAYBOY has demystified the battle of the sexes. The idea of improving relationships by improving communication is nothing new to the magazine. It is now, and has always been, about decent behavior between men and women. PLAYBOY approaches its portrayal of women from an idealized, romantic and respectful point of view. While far different and less idealized portrayals of women are indeed available in society, men continue to turn to PLAYBOY in recognition of their romantic curiosity—a curiosity that doesn't exploit women or objectify them. Sex is not sexism. Women have been and always will be objects of male desire, and men of female desire. PLAYBOY recognizes that.

PLAYBOY also recognizes that women may be bosses or beer buddies or mentors or colleagues. It writes about that—it writes about both the possibilities and complexities in male-female relationships. And 3.5 million people buy the magazine every month, and 12 million read it and that says something, too. Readers trust PLAYBOY to draw the line—to define the boundaries and standards of popular acceptance of public sexuality. It says that an interest in beauty and the erotic is a natural and healthy instinct.

It also proves what we've always said about the magazine: Men buy PLAYBOY for the women, and read it for the package. Readers see in it a man's vision of romance and fantasy, and they continue to learn from it all the lifestyle possibilities open to men in this century.

Christie Hefner

Chairman and Chief Executive Officer

For everyone

who

helped make

an

impossible

dream

come true.

"Affairs of state will be out of our province. We don't expect to solve any world problems or prove any great moral truths. If we are able to give the American male a few extra laughs and a little diversion from the anxieties of the Atomic Age, we'll feel we've justified our existence."

—Hugh M. Hefner
in his introduction to the
first issue of PLAYBOY

THE FIFTIES

n late summer of 1953, a skinny guy in khaki slacks, sweat socks and penny loafers, working at a card table in his living room, put together a new magazine for men. The young man was 27-year-old Hugh M. Hefner, and creating a magazine was his lifelong dream. He planned to call his magazine *Stag Party,* but at the last minute, he changed the name, fatefully, to PLAYBOY. By the time he finished that first issue, he had no idea that he had created what was to become the most successful magazine for men in history, influencing the sexual attitudes of a nation and introducing the concept of a new lifestyle to a world that sorely lacked one.

For his 44-page first issue Hefner wrote a defining statement: "Affairs of state will be out of our province. We don't expect to solve any world problems or prove any great moral truths. If we are able to give the American male a few extra laughs and a little diversion from the anxieties of the Atomic Age, we'll feel we've justified our existence."

It was one of the last understatements he ever made about PLAYBOY. That issue was a virtual sell-out, as was the next one, and the one after that. Within a year, it was the hottest new magazine on the market. Within two, it outsold *Esquire.* Before the end of the Fifties, it had precipitated what one commentator called "a generational prison break," with more than a million young readers lining up to buy it every month.

It was a magazine whose time had come. Chilled by the prudish moral climate of the Fifties, *Esquire* had toned down its racy ways, and the rest of the men's monthlies were celebrating the exploits of macho types who preferred huddling with their buddies in a duck blind to cuddling with a soft companion in front of the fireplace at home. Guns were in; girls were out. But not at PLAYBOY. In his introduction to the premiere issue, Hefner had compared his magazine's debut to the recently published *Kinsey Report.* The sexual revolution was being born, and if Kinsey was its researcher, Hefner would be its pamphleteer. And nothing would ever be quite the same again.

But sex wasn't the only thing PLAYBOY offered. Hefner's plan from the beginning was a rich mix of a magazine: first-rate fiction and articles, provocative cartoons and ground-breaking features about the latest male fashion, food and drink, cars and stereos that offered young readers a glimpse of "the good life," making it a handbook for the urban male. "Hefner's genius," said Dr. Paul Gebhard of the Kinsey Institute, "was to associate sex with upward mobility."

The magazine in those early days was crude but vital, flawed by occasional blunders but also full of freshness and wide-eyed enthusiasm. There was a go-to-hell zaniness about it, a healthy disregard for convention, that began to attract writers as well as readers who shared the same taste for irreverence and outspokenness.

In those formative years, PLAYBOY published Ray Bradbury's now-classic sci-fi thriller *Fahrenheit 451,* a powerful indictment of censorship set in a dark future, when all books were burned. And Shepherd Mead's delightful satire *How to Succeed in Business Without Really Trying*—a spoof of the gray-flannel mindset of the Fifties—was serialized in several issues. Walter Tevis' *The Hustler* went from the pages of PLAYBOY onto the movie screen—and into American mythology—with its riveting tale of a hotshot young pool player who had the chutzpah to believe he could ace the champ. And

The very first issue of PLAYBOY had Marilyn Monroe on the cover and a headline that promised a look at her famous nude. The magazine came out in November 1953. Its cover was undated so the issue could remain on the newsstands as long as possible, because there was no certainty of a second issue. Astonishingly, the new title sold more than 50,000 copies.

PLAYBOY

ENTERTAINMENT FOR **MEN**

50c

FIRST TIME
in any magazine
FULL COLOR
the famous
MARILYN MONROE NUDE

VIP ON SEX

1st ISSUE

Hefner planned to call his magazine *Stag Party*, but before the first issue came out, *Stag* magazine claimed trademark infringement. Unwilling to lose time in litigation, he changed the name to PLAYBOY and chose a new symbol. Cartoonist Arv Miller transformed his stag into a rabbit (above) and the hare began leading the way to the good life. Founding Art Director Arthur Paul then created the world-famous Rabbit Head logo.

George Langelaan's *The Fly*, published in 1957, created quite a buzz in two successful film versions.

At a time when most magazine art was representational and predictable, PLAYBOY graphics were an inspired innovation that influenced the direction of commercial illustration. Cartoonists Jack Cole, Jules Feiffer and Gahan Wilson were second to none. And then, in 1956, a young genius named Shel Silverstein walked in off the street with a sheaf of drawings. He would later travel the world as PLAYBOY's Innocent Abroad, armed with nothing but his wits and a sketch pad, keeping a cartoon diary of his misadventures from Tokyo to Moscow.

But the primary appeal of the magazine, certainly in those days, was its Playmate of the Month. Before PLAYBOY, the tradition of pinup photography was stylized and impersonal, but PLAYBOY's Playmates were presented like, well, like real live girls. When Janet Pilgrim, the magazine's Subscription Manager, was introduced as the first "girl-next-door" centerfold, she caused a sensation. Reappearing in subsequent issues throughout the decade, Janet joined the ranks of celebrity sex stars uncovered by PLAYBOY in the Fifties: Marilyn Monroe, Jayne Mansfield, Brigitte Bardot, Gina Lollobrigida, Sophia Loren, Anita Ekberg and June "The Bosom" Wilkinson.

By the end of the decade, PLAYBOY had become more than a magazine. With an all-star cast, the historic first Playboy Jazz Festival, staged in the summer of 1959 for 70,000 fans in Chicago Stadium, was the largest and most stellar gathering of its kind. And the fall of that same year, Hefner himself stepped out from behind his desk into the limelight as host of *Playboy's Penthouse*, a popular hour-long weekly television variety show with a guest list that included Lenny Bruce and Carl Sandburg.

Hefner had come a long way from the card table. And now that the dream was reality, he lived it to the fullest.

When PLAYBOY began, the entire editorial department could be captured in a snapshot of Hefner at his typewriter (above). Working alone, he created a magazine and a new life for American men. Although his name appeared nowhere in the first issue, Hefner wrote much of the text, including an editor's note in which he laid out a vision of PLAYBOY as a "pleasure-primer styled to the masculine taste." With this opening salvo, the young man began one of the most remarkable personal sagas in publishing history.

After his initial inspiration of featuring a nude pictorial in 3-D proved impossibly expensive, Hefner bought this celebrated but previously unpublished shot of Marilyn Monroe from the John Baumgarth Calendar Company, a suburban Chicago outfit that produced sexy calendars. This photo became the centerpiece of the premiere issue of his new "handbook for the urban male." With Marilyn au naturel as his magazine's "Sweetheart of the Month," all Hefner needed to do was create the rest of the magazine.

ILLUSTRATED BY BEN DENISON

"Come on, woman!" Montag cried.

PLAYBOY's literary and artistic ambitions were an unexpected bonus to readers who bought the magazine just for the pictures, and were among the most important defining factors in distinguishing PLAYBOY from the girlie magazines of the day. Its high standards of editorial and design excellence were established with its first major piece of fiction, Ray Bradbury's now-classic science-fiction novel *Fahrenheit 451*, serialized in the spring of 1954 (and later turned into a film by François Truffaut). Franz Altschuler's illustration for *Bird of Prey*, a fantasy by John Collier that ran in that year's January issue, won PLAYBOY its first major graphics award.

The house they call the engineer's house is now deserted. The new man from Baton Rouge gave it up after living less than a month in it, and built himself a two-room shack with his own money, on the very farthest corner of the company's land.

The roof has caved in, and most of the windows are smashed. Oddly enough, no birds nest in the shelter of the eaves, or take advantage of the forsaken rooms. An empty house is normally fine harborage for rats and mice and bats, but there is no squeak, or rustle, or scamper to disturb the quiet of this one. Only creatures utterly foreign, utterly remote from the most distant cousinhood to man, only the termite, the tarantula, and the scorpion indifferently make it their home.

All in a few years Edna Spalding's garden has been wiped out as if it had never existed. The porch where she and Jack sat so happily in the evenings is rotten under its load of wind-blown twigs and sand. A young tree has already burst up the boards outside the living-room

Hurry! Run! It's one of those cats from the men's camp has got hold of poor Tom!"

Jack sprang out of bed, but caught his foot in the sheet, and landed on his elbow on the floor. Between rubbing his elbow and disentangling his foot, he wasted a good many seconds before he was up again and had dashed through the living room and out upon the porch.

All this time, which seemed an age, the squawking and fluttering increased, but as he flung open the door it ceased as suddenly as it had begun. The whole porch was bathed in the brightest moonlight, and at the farther end the perch was clearly visible, and on the floor beneath it was poor old Tom parrot, gasping amid a litter of his own feathers, and crying, "Oh! Oh! Oh!"

At any rate he was alive. Jack looked right and left for traces of his assailant, and at once noticed the long, heavy trailers of the vine were swinging violently although there was not a breath of wind. He went to the rail and looked out and around, but there was no sign of a cat.

by JOHN COLLIER

Bird of Prey

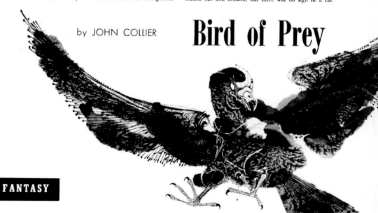

window, so that they fan out like the stiff fingers of someone who is afraid. In this corner there still stands a strongly made parrot's perch, the wood of which has been left untouched even by the termite and the boring beetle.

The Spaldings brought a parrot with them when first they came. It was a sort of extra wedding present, given them at the last moment by Edna's mother. It was something from home for Edna to take into the wilds.

Of course, it was not likely there would be. Jack was more interested in the fact that the swaying vines were spread over a length of several feet, which seemed a very great deal of disturbance for a fleeing cat to make. Finally he looked up, and he thought he saw a bird — a big bird, an enormous bird — flying away; he just caught a glimpse of it as it crossed the brightness of the moon.

The temperature at which book-paper catches fire, and burns...

FICTION

by

RAY BRADBURY

This is the first part of a 3 part novel. PLAYBOY doesn't usually print continued stories, but this is too good to cut to a single issue. FAHRENHEIT 451 will become, we believe, a modern science fiction classic. It is more than fantasy — it is a frightening prediction of a future world we are creating NOW.

PART ONE

IT WAS A PLEASURE TO BURN.

It was a special pleasure to see things eaten, to see things blackened and *changed*. With the brass nozzle in his fists, with this great python spitting its venomous kerosene upon the world, the blood pounded in his head, and his hands were the hands of some amazing conductor playing all the symphonies of blazing and burning to bring down the tatters and charcoal ruins of history. With his symbolic helmet numbered 451 on his stolid head, and his eyes all orange flame with the thought of what came next, he flicked the igniter and the house jumped-up in a gorging fire that burned the evening sky red and yellow and black. He strode in a swarm of fireflies. He wanted above all, like the old joke, to shove a marshmallow on a stick in the furnace, while the flapping pigeon-winged books died on the porch and lawn of the house. While the books went up in sparkling whirls and blew away on a wind turned dark with burning.

(continued on next page)

THE MONSTROUS EGG HELD A STRANGE AND FRIGHTENING SECRET.

"No," said Jack. "He's had a bit of shock, though. Something got hold of him."

"I'll bring him a piece of sugar," said Edna. "That's what he loves. That'll make him feel better."

She soon brought the sugar, which Tom took in his claw, but though usually he would nibble it up with the greatest avidity, this time he turned his lackluster eye only once upon it, and gave a short, bitter, despairing sort of laugh, and let it fall to the ground.

"Let him rest," said Jack. "He has had a bad tousling."

"Maybe," said Edna. "On the other hand — I don't know. blacks that the men have at the camp."

"It was a cat," said Edna. "It was one of those beastly blacks that the men have at the camp."

"It couldn't be an eagle," said Edna. "There are none ever seen here."

"I know," said Jack. "Besides, they don't fly at night. Nor do the buzzards. It might have been an owl, I suppose, but —"

"But what?" said Edna.

"But it looked very much larger than an owl," said Jack.

"It was your fancy," said Edna. "It was one of those beastly cats that did it."

This point was discussed very frequently during the next few days. Everybody was consulted, and everybody had an opinion. Jack might have been a little doubtful at first, for he had caught only the briefest glimpse of the creature crossed the moon, but opposition made him more certain, and the discussions sometimes got rather heated.

"Charlie says it was all your imagination," said Edna. "He says no owl would ever attack a parrot."

"How the devil does he know?" said Jack. "Besides,

shoulder without even thinking about it, and nobody minded.

"I should not have said that," said Jack.

"No, indeed you shouldn't," said Edna, and she was right.

The parrot said nothing at all. All these days he had been moping and ailing, and seemed to have forgotten even how to ask for sugar. He only groaned and moaned to himself, ruffled up his feathers, and every now and then shook his head in the most rueful, miserable, despairing way you can possibly imagine.

One day, however, when Jack came home from work, Edna put her finger to her lips and beckoned him to the window. "Watch Tom," she whispered.

Jack peered out. There was the old bird, lugubriously climbing down from his perch and picking some dead stalks from the vine, which he carried up till he gained a corner where the balustrade ran into the wall, and added his gatherings to others that were already there. He trod round and round, twisted his stalks in and out, and, always with the same doleful expression, paid great attention to the nice disposal of a feather or two, a piece of wool, a fragment of cellophane. There was no doubt about it.

"There's no doubt about it," said Jack.

"He's making a nest!" cried Edna.

"He!" cried Jack. "He! I like that. The old imposter! the old male impersonator! She's going to lay an egg. Thomasina — that's her name from now on."

Thomasina it was. Two or three days later the matter was settled beyond the shadow of a doubt. There, one morning, in the ramshackle nest, was an egg.

"I thought she was sick because of that shaking she

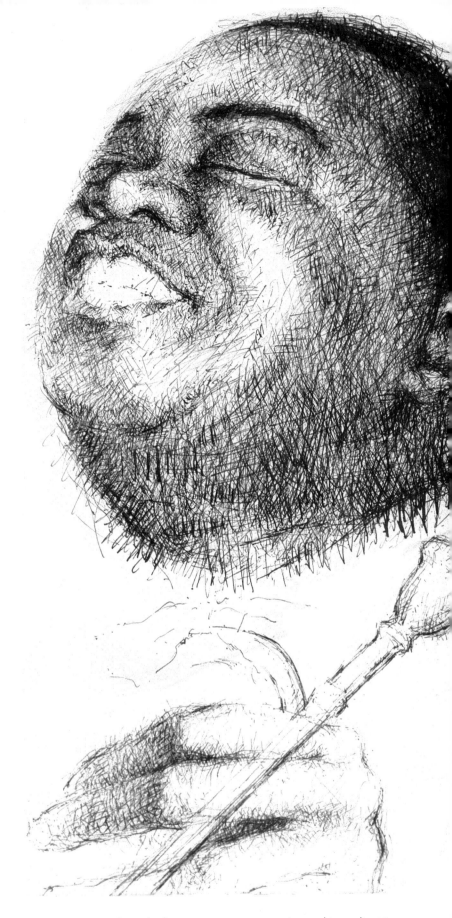

From the beginning, jazz was an integral ingredient in PLAYBOY's editorial mix. The ebullient persona of Louis Armstrong was captured in Art Lerner's illustration (above) and in author Charles Beaumont's profile *Red Beans & Ricely Yours* (February 1955).

The Playmate feature evolved quickly in the magazine's first year. In the second issue, Margie Harrison (opposite), became the first to be designated "Playmate of the Month" and granted the title Miss January. Her pinup picture—purchased, like the Monroe nude, from the Baumgarth Calendar Company—ran on a single page; the double-page Playmate spread did not make its bow until the third issue.

Miss May 1955, Marguerite Empey (above), was photographed by Hal Adams, who was famous in the Fifties for his Hartog shirt ads, which always included a seminude girl and a pipe. A California model and practicing nudist, Marguerite was to reappear as Miss February 1956. Author Gay Talese interviewed her under her married name, Diane Webber, for *Thy Neighbor's Wife,* his landmark 1980 study of the sexual revolution.

The first Playmate shots were purchased from pinup photographers, who followed the cheesecake conventions of the day: voluptuous women posed in front of colored backgrounds in a studio setting. All of that changed with Miss June 1955, Eve Meyer (above), the first Playmate photographed specifically for the magazine. The pose and setting, with two wine glasses suggesting an erotic moment and an unseen male presence, were planned by PLAYBOY's editors and executed by Eve's then-husband, photographer Russ Meyer. If that name sounds familiar, it should. With 1960's *The Immoral Mr. Teas,* Meyer created "nudies," a new genre of low-budget, hugely profitable sexploitation movies famous for featuring magnificently endowed women.

Early on, some potential Playmates were too shy to pose for male photographers. Bunny Yeager, however, easily recruited nude models—including herself (below and right). One of her most famous subjects was Miss January 1955, Bettie Page (opposite), who became a cult legend.

The Playboy Rabbit has appeared on every cover since the magazine's second issue. In the beginning, the covers featured photography and art work as well as rabbit collages designed by Art Director Arthur Paul's wife, Bea. The August 1955 issue (bottom left) achieved notoriety when a strategically placed strand of seaweed mysteriously slipped out of place sometime during the printing process.

PLAYBOY

ENTERTAINMENT FOR MEN

MAY 50 cents

PLAYBOY's cartoons have always epitomized the magazine's irreverent personality. An aspiring cartoonist himself, Hefner was soon publishing the likes of Jack Cole, Gahan Wilson, Erich Sokol, John Dempsey and Gardner Rea—whom PLAYBOY offered unprecedented freedom of expression.

"I ain't got no bod-eee…"

"I'll tell you why I hate this island—I'm a leg man."

"You mean if I sow liquor and dames,
I'll reap liquor and dames?"

"I'd rather not. That's how all my troubles got started."

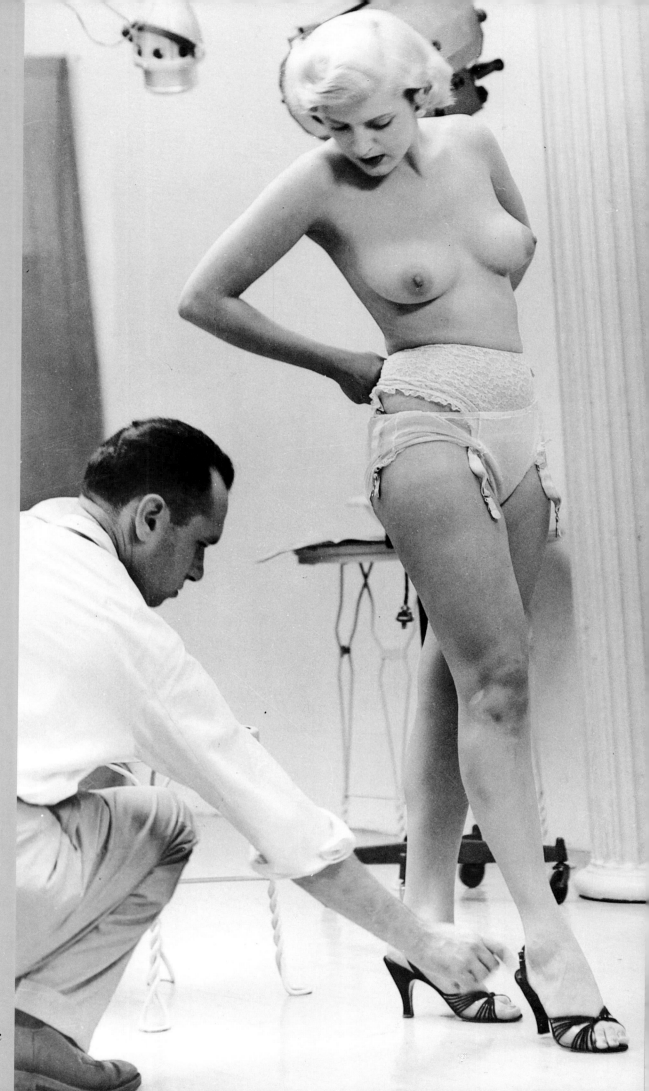

An early feature called *Photographing a Playmate* took readers behind the scenes during the shooting of Miss December 1954, Terry Ryan. Art Director Arthur Paul appeared in the layout, bringing the magazine's readers into the fantasy of life at PLAYBOY.

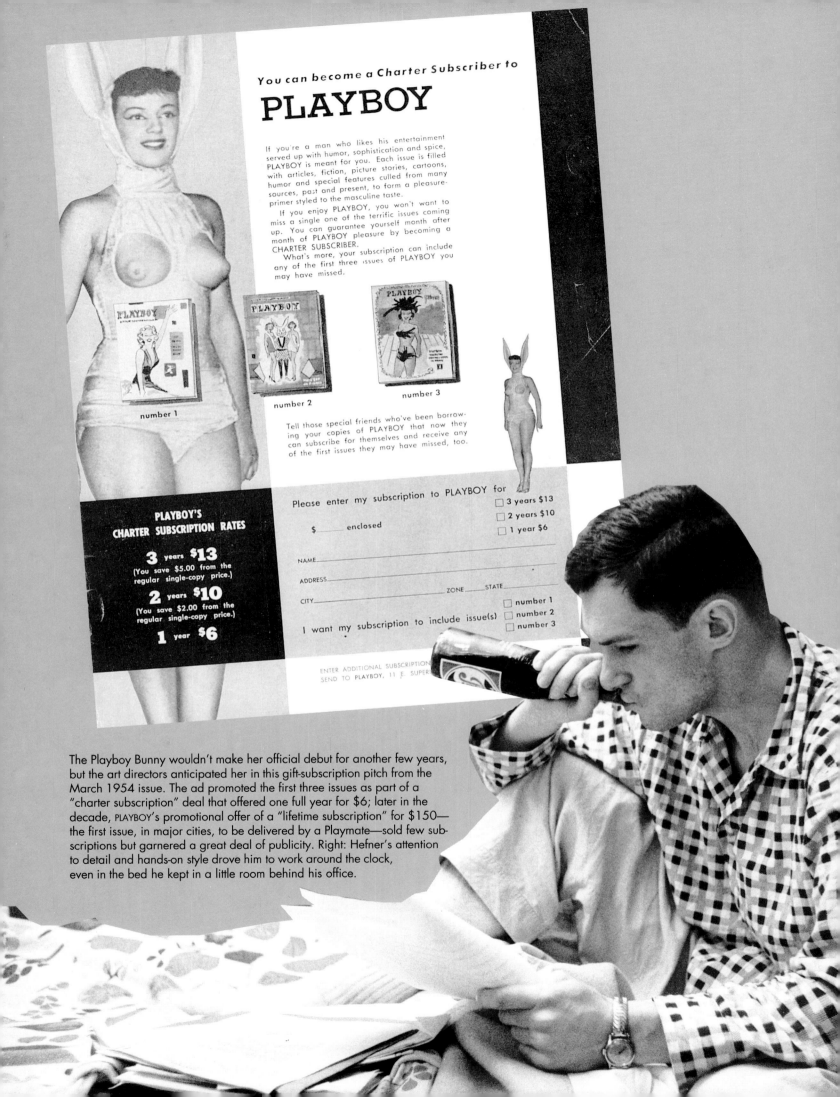

You can become a Charter Subscriber to

PLAYBOY

If you're a man who likes his entertainment served up with humor, sophistication and spice, PLAYBOY is meant for you. Each issue is filled with articles, fiction, picture stories, cartoons, humor and special features culled from many sources, past and present, to form a pleasure-primer styled to the masculine taste.

If you enjoy PLAYBOY, you won't want to miss a single one of the terrific issues coming up. You can guarantee yourself month after month of PLAYBOY pleasure by becoming a CHARTER SUBSCRIBER.

What's more, your subscription can include any of the first three issues of PLAYBOY you may have missed.

number 1

number 2

number 3

Tell those special friends who've been borrowing your copies of PLAYBOY that now they can subscribe for themselves and receive any of the first issues they may have missed, too.

PLAYBOY'S CHARTER SUBSCRIPTION RATES

3 years **$13**
(You save $5.00 from the regular single-copy price.)

2 years **$10**
(You save $2.00 from the regular single-copy price.)

1 year **$6**

Please enter my subscription to PLAYBOY for

☐ 3 years $13
☐ 2 years $10
☐ 1 year $6

$_____ enclosed

NAME_____

ADDRESS_____

CITY_____ ZONE____ STATE_____

I want my subscription to include issue(s) ☐ number 1
☐ number 2
☐ number 3

ENTER ADDITIONAL SUBSCRIPTION
SEND TO PLAYBOY, 11 E. SUPERI

The Playboy Bunny wouldn't make her official debut for another few years, but the art directors anticipated her in this gift-subscription pitch from the March 1954 issue. The ad promoted the first three issues as part of a "charter subscription" deal that offered one full year for $6; later in the decade, PLAYBOY's promotional offer of a "lifetime subscription" for $150—the first issue, in major cities, to be delivered by a Playmate—sold few subscriptions but garnered a great deal of publicity. Right: Hefner's attention to detail and hands-on style drove him to work around the clock, even in the bed he kept in a little room behind his office.

The "girl-next-door" Playmate was born when Hefner persuaded his subscription manager, Charlaine Karalus, to pose for PLAYBOY. Laughingly, she agreed to do it if he'd buy an Addressograph machine to lighten her duties. She had a deal. As Janet Pilgrim, she became Miss July 1955—and was a sensation. Because she was an actual employee of the magazine, she was even more real to readers, who responded so favorably that—in a record still unequaled—the magazine brought her back as Playmate in December 1955 and October 1956. It was Hefner's idea to pose her in a man's pajama top for her second appearance—suggesting that she liked men's pajamas, at least after she threw away the bottom half. This prompted several readers to send in their p.j. tops for her to wear. In her first Playmate appearance, photo opposite, the slightly out-of-focus fellow in the tux is the editor and publisher himself. Overleaf: Janet sparkles in December 1955's Christmas centerfold.

MISS DECEMBER PLAYBOY'S PLAYMATE OF THE MONTH

The magazine's unprecedented momentum convinced Hefner that he couldn't continue as a solo act. Above, he presides over a meeting with his editorial staff in PLAYBOY's original four-room space at 11 East Superior Street. From left are Art Director Arthur Paul, Assistant Art Director Joe Paczek, Hefner, Executive Editor Ray Russell and Managing Editor Jack Kessie.

Hefner's duties as Editor-Publisher kept him hopping—over layouts, artwork and cartoons—as desktops overflowed and work piled up on the floor, even in the more spacious offices at 232 East Ohio Street to which the magazine moved in 1956. "I used the rug as a giant desk," Hefner recalls, "and frequently held meetings with artists, cartoonists and editors while kneeling on the floor looking at their work."

From the outset, Hefner was selective about the kind of advertising PLAYBOY would accept. He knew it would be fatal in the long run to carry the kind of schlock ads that appeared in most girlie magazines. Although money was short, he rejected 80 percent of the magazine's would-be advertisers, who were trying to use the magazine's pages to peddle guns, hair restorers, trusses and correspondence courses of dubious worth. Not until February 1955 did PLAYBOY land its first major advertising—this sexy ad for Springmaid sheets. It would still be another year or two before important mainstream advertising appeared regularly in the magazine's pages.

"Certainly we're taking it...they're Springmaid sheets and I have a full chest too."

THE SPRINGS COTTON MILLS

Adding to Hefner's challenges in running the magazine were his battles with would-be censors. PLAYBOY had started taking subscriptions with the second issue, but was forced to send the magazine first class. When the Post Office denied his application for a second-class mailing permit, Hefner went to court. He won, securing PLAYBOY the mailing privileges other publications enjoyed, starting with the June 1956 issue. Hefner could now concentrate on subscription promotion. In this April 1956 pitch (right), staffer Ray Russell turned the anti-PLAYBOY attack into a brilliant promotional appeal, with a ringing affirmation of the title Hefner had chosen for his magazine—and his way of life.

WHAT IS A PLAYBOY?

Is he simply a wastrel, a ne'er-do-well, a fashionable bum? Far from it: he can be a sharp-minded young business executive, a worker in the arts, a university professor, an architect or engineer. He can be many things, providing he possesses a certain *point of view*. He must see life not as a vale of tears, but as a happy time; he must take joy in his work, without regarding it as the end and all of living; he must be an alert man, an aware man, a man of taste, a man sensitive to pleasure, a man who—without acquiring the stigma of the voluptuary or dilettante—can live life to the hilt. This is the sort of man we mean when we use the word *playboy*. Does the description fit you? If so, we imagine you will agree that PLAYBOY belongs in your life. And we suggest that you enter your subscription at the first opportunity.

1. Pour gin freely.… but accurately. 250 cubic centimeters should do as a starter.

PLAYBOY took seriously its role as a handbook for the urban male, but that didn't stop it from wedging its editorial tongue firmly in cheek with such features as *Mixing the Perfect Martini,* a September 1955 satire featuring an impossibly fastidious bartender.

2. The gin is poured into a mixing glass that is thoroughly chilled and filled to the top with crystal clear ice cubes. The gin is poured in first.

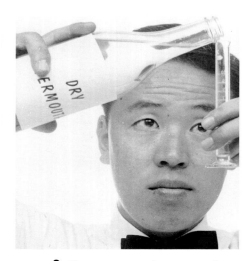

3. Pour vermouth accurately…

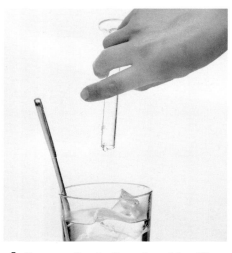

4. But not freely. 2 cc should suffice.

5. Stir concoction no less than 25 revolutions. Wrist action is very important here; keep head well back to avoid inhaling intoxicating fumes.

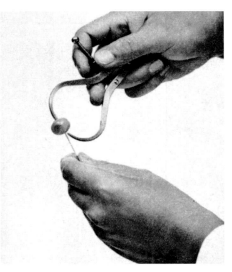

6. Wiping lemon peel gently around the edge of the glass adds to the flavor of the cocktail and the cleanliness of the glass.

7. The size of the olive is very important as one that is too large displaces too much gin. 20 mm diameter is suggested.

8. Pour carefully into glass. Try to avoid spilling mixture on table cloth as it will disintegrate linen fibers.

9. Twist lemon peel over glass. This has no effect on the cocktail, but impresses onlookers.

10. The perfect Martini can only be followed by another, another, and…

11. . . . *WOW!*

Playboy's Penthouse Apartment, a lavish 12-page vision of the ultimate bachelor pad, looked pretty neat to the readers. Published in the September and October issues of 1956, it was the most popular feature up to that time—even surpassing the Playmates—and it drew hundreds of letters from readers requesting information on where they could buy the furnishings pictured in the layout.

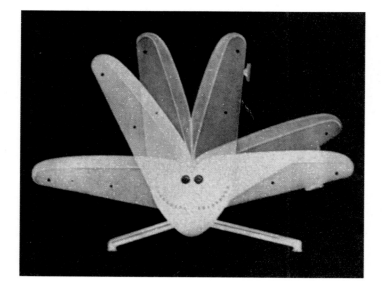

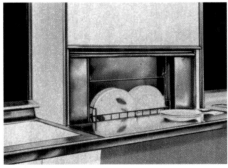

Among the accoutrements in the futuristic *Penthouse Apartment* kitchen (above) were an "ultrasonic dishwasher" that cleans with "inaudible hi-fi sound" and a glass-domed oven that cooks with "its luscious viands in tantalizing view." The resulting meals were served in a sleekly modern Scandinavian-style dining room (below).

LeRoy Neiman (below), a friend of Hefner's since the publisher's days as a department-store ad copywriter, began his PLAYBOY career with illustrations for fiction and fashion. Soon he became the magazine's prolific artist in residence, creating the cartoon Femlins for the *Party Jokes* page (above) in July 1956. But what really made his name was *Man at His Leisure*, a series begun in 1958 that celebrated such night spots as Chicago's Pump Room (opposite).

PUMP ROOM

In the A... ...ner ...oeth... ...the Gold Coast, Chicago

T

Imported Bismarck Ha... ...Spinach,
Imported Freſh Beluga Cav... ...eat Naſh in Caſserol...
...arrots Bourguignonne... ...ght Turkey ...h ...
...s Ambaſſador (Prepa... ...uſtard ...
...d Pate de Foie Gra... le S... ...de, W...
...Crabmeat, Wra... ...Gia...
...e Juice Co...
...mp G... ...tes i...
...Broi...
...of...

Kentuck...
Caeſar Salad (...re are...
Pump Room Bowl (on Wag...
Avocado Pear, Half 1...0
Hollywood Bowl 2.25 ...F...ng
Tomatoe Stuffed with Chicke... Sal...
Imported White Coloſſal Aſparagus Vi...
Lobſter Salad 5.25
Ruſſian Dreſſing 1.25 Roquefort...

Actress Marian Stafford made history in March 1956 when the Playmate feature was expanded from a double-page spread in the center of the magazine to a triple-page centerfold. Opening up the pinup picture in the center of the magazine became a ritual so familiar that it has since been immortalized in countless movies and TV shows. The word "centerfold" quickly became so synonymous with PLAYBOY's Playmate of the Month that it entered the language as a generic term for pinup photography itself. The Rabbit monitors Marian's television career (right), providing a connection between the cover and the pictorial.

PLAYBOY personalized sexuality with the concept of the "girl next door." By running a nude centerfold along with photos of a Playmate in everyday life, the magazine conveyed the message that the wholesome, attractive women the readers encountered in real life were also interested in sex. A PLAYBOY ad salesman persuaded a client's secretary, Jacquelyn Prescott (above and below), to pose as Miss September 1957.

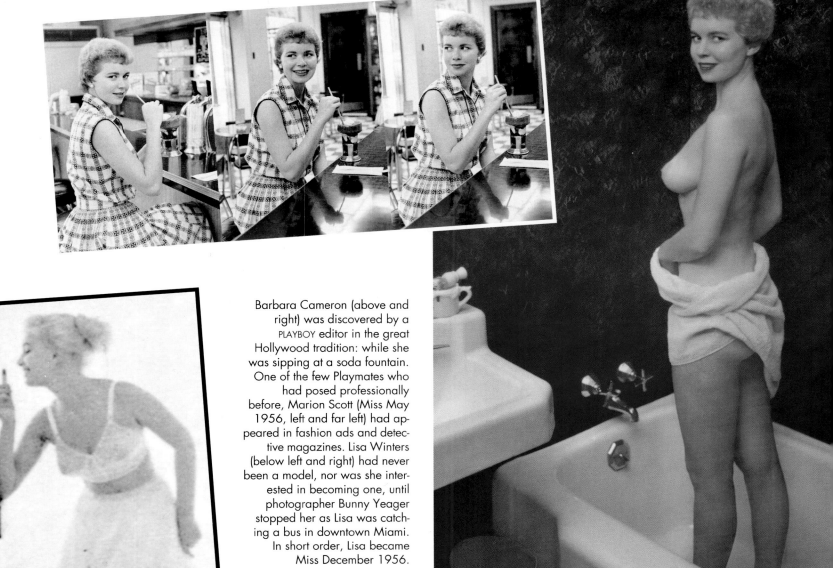

Barbara Cameron (above and right) was discovered by a PLAYBOY editor in the great Hollywood tradition: while she was sipping at a soda fountain. One of the few Playmates who had posed professionally before, Marion Scott (Miss May 1956, left and far left) had appeared in fashion ads and detective magazines. Lisa Winters (below left and right) had never been a model, nor was she interested in becoming one, until photographer Bunny Yeager stopped her as Lisa was catching a bus in downtown Miami. In short order, Lisa became Miss December 1956.

Figure studies of actress Anita Ekberg (left), the first of PLAYBOY's movie-star pictorials, made waves in 1956. Even though they were cropped to eliminate the pubic hair that violated the prevailing American standards of decency, the Ekberg photos were daring enough for *Time* magazine to note that "*Esquire* still cannot keep abreast" of PLAYBOY, since *Esquire*'s shots of Ekberg had "a few clothes on." Three features on Brigitte Bardot (below) focused on Europe's favorite sex kitten. One of the first American actresses to get a boost from exposure in PLAYBOY was Kim Novak (above), introduced in 1959.

PLAYBOY readers saw more of Sophia Loren (left) than usual in this shot from an Italian film in the November 1957 issue. Above, La Loren eyes the even more spectacular cleavage of Jayne Mansfield in a shot editors labeled "some feud for thought, in the Hollywood tradition." The magazine's fans already knew Jayne (below right), who'd been a relative unknown before becoming Miss February 1955. Another Italian eyeful, Gina Lollobrigida (below left), turned up in a 1954 PLAYBOY feature on a film called *Beauties of the Night*.

Shel Silverstein, a free-spirited young cartoon talent discovered by PLAYBOY in the early Fifties, took his act on the road and around the world in a series of satiric cartoon adventures. Returning as a kind of national folk hero, he went on to become a celebrated songwriter, playwright and best-selling author of children's books.

JAPAN

"Contrary to popular Western beliefs, the Geisha girl confines her entertainment to singing, dancing, playing a musical instrument ...."

RUSSIA

"So you see, Olga, with world tension as high as it is ... with humanity threatened with total destruction through an atomic war ... with Russian-American diplomatic relations strained almost to the breaking point, it's up to people like you and me to cooperate!"

ITALY

"It's really a very simple dish ... you take a flat piece of dough ... cover it over with tomato sauce ... chop in chunks of Italian sausage, mushrooms and anchovies ... top it all with provolone cheese and bake."

AFRICA

"It just wouldn't work out, Mzaba—you have your world and I have mine!"

PARIS

"You let Gene Kelly dance in the street ... you let Fred Astaire dance in the street ... you let Audrey Hepburn dance in the street ... you let ...."

SPAIN

"OK, but now let's look at it from the *bullfighter's* point of view!"

SWITZERLAND

"I've heard of hypothetical situations like this, Sylvia, but I certainly never thought I'd be faced with the actual decision!"

LONDON

"I believe I can say with assurance, sir, that Princess Margaret will not be interested in appearing as January's Playmate of the Month."

THE VARGAS GIRL

The wondrous long-limbed dream girls of Alberto Vargas captivated men's hearts for nearly a century. Vargas began his career in the Twenties as a poster artist for Flo Ziegfeld and his Ziegfeld Follies, and married one of his first models. When the Follies closed in the Thirties, Vargas switched to Hollywood and began illustrating movie-studio posters. Being blacklisted for union activity, he turned his hand to World War Two pinups for *Esquire* that became world-famous. His introduction to PLAYBOY's readers came with this March 1957 pictorial, and his Vargas Girls appeared exclusively in nearly every issue of PLAYBOY from 1960 to 1978. It was the happiest and most productive relationship of his career. The artist died in December 1982 at the age of 87.

A couple of curvaceous cartoon characters came to life when Al Capp's *Li'l Abner* was staged as a 1957 Broadway musical starring two of PLAYBOY's favorite femmes fatales in conspicuous cameo appearances. Capp created these drawings specifically for PLAYBOY.

On Broadway, Hollywood's Tina Louise (left) vamped as Appassionata von Climax, a big-city siren who does her best to seduce Abner, and Julie Newmar (above) played the aptly named Stupefyin' Jones.

THE FLY *fiction* By George Langelaan

*if she looked upon the horror any longer
she would scream for the rest of her life*

TELEPHONES AND TELEPHONE BELLS have always made me uneasy. Years ago, when they were mostly wall fixtures, I disliked them, but nowadays, when they are planted in every nook and corner, they are a downright intrusion. We have a saying in France that a coalman is master in his own house; with the telephone that is no longer true, and I suspect that even the Englishman is no longer king in his own castle.

At the office, the sudden ringing of the telephone annoys me. It means that, no matter what I am doing, in spite of the switchboard operator, in spite of my secretary, in spite of doors and walls, some unknown person is coming into the room and onto my desk to talk right into my very ear, confidentially — and that whether I like it or not. At home, the feeling is still more disagreeable, but the worst is when the telephone rings in the dead of night. If anyone could see me turn on the light and get up blinking to answer it, I suppose I would look like any other sleepy man annoyed at being disturbed. The truth in such a case, however, is that I am struggling against panic, fighting down a feeling that a stranger has broken into the house and is in my bedroom. By the time I manage to grab the receiver and say: "*Ici Monsieur Delambre. Je vous ecoute,*" I am outwardly calm, but I only get back to a more normal state when I recognize the voice at the other end and when I know what is wanted of me.

This effort at dominating a purely animal reaction and fear had become so effective that when my sister-in-law called me at two in the morning, asking me to come over, but first to warn the police that she had just killed my brother, I quietly asked her how and why she had killed Andre.

"But, Francois! . . . I can't explain all that over the telephone. Please call the police and come quickly."

"Maybe I had better see you first, Helene?"

"No, you'd better call the police first; otherwise they will start asking you all sorts of awkward questions. They'll have enough trouble as it is to believe that I did it alone . . . And, by the way, I suppose you ought to tell them that Andre . . . Andre's body, is down at the factory. They may want to go there first."

"Did you say that Andre is at the factory?"

"Yes . . . under the steam-hammer."

"Under the what!"

"The steam-hammer! But don't ask so many questions. Please come quickly Francois! Please understand that I'm afraid . . . that my nerves won't stand it much longer!"

Have you ever tried to explain to a sleepy police officer that your sister-in-law has just phoned to say that she has killed your brother with a steam-hammer? I repeated my explanation, but he would not let me.

"*Oui. Monsieur, oui,* I hear . . . but who are you? What is your name? Where do you live? I said, where do you live!"

It was then that Commissaire Charas took over the line and the whole business. He at least seemed to understand everything. Would I wait for him? Yes, he would pick me up and take me over to my brother's house. When? In five or 10 minutes.

I had just managed to pull on my trousers, wriggle into a sweater and grab a hat and coat, when a black Citroen, headlights blazing, pulled up at the door.

"I assume you have a night watchman at your factory, Monsieur Delambre. Has he called you?" asked Commissaire Charas letting in the clutch as I sat down beside

The more you relax . . . the better.

BE AN IDEA MAN!

it is the man with ideas who succeeds in business without really trying

BY SHEPHERD MEAD

*on this level — is best done under
forced draft.*)

Each little notion will no doubt be worthless, but by exercising your own Vision, you may be able to combine or develop them into something that will work, and something which, again, will be truly Your Own.

3. *Use Your Advertising Agency.* If you have kept your agency properly on its toes you may find it of occasional help in producing ideas. Agencies employ people who do nothing but sit around and think up ideas. Use them!

Here again you will have to take their dreamy notions and Whip Them into Shape, stamp them with your own brand. The agency will not mind. In fact, the agency is used to it. They may even try to make you think that an idea that is wholly theirs is yours. Do not be deceived! Fiddle with it. It is your duty to improve everything.

4. *Use Your Subconscious.* When all else fails, you may have to use your own brain — for the original processes, that is.

Remember, your brain is like an iceberg. Only an insignificant part shows above the surface. The rest is submerged. This submerged part is your subconscious mind, and wise indeed is the businessman who makes his subconscious work for him.

Simply feed the facts to your subconscious and then relax. The more you relax, the better. Forget the problem. The answer will come to you. Sometimes it will come while you are shaving, or while you're sinking a putt. But it will come!

For example, let us say you have assembled a set of facts carefully, sparing no effort. Then as your high-caliber subconscious goes to work on them, strange things can happen.

"Oh, uh, Mr. Finch, you know all those figures and things I spent the last few nights getting up for you?"

"Yes, son?"

"Well, it just happened to occur to me that a solution might be simply to give the wickets a left-hand thread."

"Amazing, isn't it! I knew it would

come to me!"

"Uh, beg pardon, sir?"

"Ways of the subconscious are mighty strange, aren't they, son? Thanks for reminding me."

You will have many other manifestations of the true power of your subconscious, able as it is to come to incredible solutions and even to implant them in other and lesser minds. It is difficult to explain this power to others, and many feel it is best not to try.

"It just came to me, Mr. Biggley. There I was, sitting in my office and it just came to me."

"Magnificent, Finch, really magnificent!"

Make it clear, however, that the Idea Man is always working. You may not *look* as though you are working. To the untrained eye you may be drinking a Martini, or improving relations with the secretarial staff, but the big wheels are turning in your subconscious, the real work is going on in the great sunken iceberg of your mind the source of your true power.

29

PLAYBOY stories that have made their way to stage and screen are legion. Among the earliest were George Langelaan's *The Fly* (June 1957), Shepherd Mead's series *How to Succeed in Business Without Really Trying,* which spanned several issues in 1954 and 1955, and Walter Tevis' *The Hustler* (January 1957). Other prominent voices in the magazine's early years were those of Ray Bradbury, whose *A Sound of Thunder* (June 1956) was a science-fiction keeper, and Jack Kerouac, whose *The Origins of the Beat Generation* chronicled one of the decade's leading social movements.

Out of the mist, one hundred yards away, came *Tyrannosaurus rex*. "Jesus God," whispered Eckels.

A Sound of THUNDER

one of the greatest science fiction thrillers ever written

BY RAY BRADBURY

THE SIGN ON THE WALL seemed to quaver under a film of sliding warm water. Eckels felt his eyelids blink over his stare, and the sign burned in this momentary darkness:

TIME SAFARI, INC.
SAFARIS TO ANY YEAR IN THE PAST.
YOU NAME THE ANIMAL.
WE TAKE YOU THERE.
YOU SHOOT IT.

A warm phlegm gathered in Eckels' throat; he swallowed and pushed it down. The muscles around his mouth formed a smile as he put his hand slowly out upon the air, and in that hand waved a check for ten thousand dollars to the man behind the desk.

"Does this safari guarantee I come back alive?"

"We guarantee nothing," said the official, "except dinosaurs." He turned. "This is Mr. Travis, your Safari Guide in the Past. He'll tell you what and where to shoot. If he

says no shooting, no shooting. If you disobey instructions, there's a stiff penalty of another ten thousand dollars, plus possible government action, on your return."

Eckels glanced across the vast office at a mass and tangle, a snaking and humming of wires and steel boxes, at an aurora that flickered now orange, now silver, now blue. There was a sound like a gigantic bonfire burning all of Time, all the years and all the parchment calendars, all the hours piled high and set aflame.

A touch of the hand on this burning would, on the instant, beautifully reverse itself. Eckels remembered the wording in the advertisements to the letter. Out of chars and ashes, out of dust and coals, like golden salamanders, the old years, the green years, might leap; roses sweeten the air, white hair turn Irish-black, wrinkles vanish; all, everything fly back to seed, flee death, rush down to their be-

30

ILLUSTRATED BY FRANZ ALTSCHULER

COLOR WOODCUT BY RICHARD TYLER

THE HUSTLER

fiction **BY WALTER S. TEVIS**

all games are dangerous when the stakes are high

THEY TOOK SAM out of the office, through the long passageway, and up to the big metal doors. The doors opened, slowly, and they stepped out.

The sunlight was exquisite; warm on Sam's face. The air was clear and still. A few birds were circling in the sky. There was a gravel path, a road, and then, grass. Sam drew a deep breath. He could see as far as the horizon.

A guard drove up in a gray station wagon. He opened the door and Sam

got in, whistling softly to himself. They drove off, down the gravel path. Sam did not turn around to look at the prison walls; he kept his eyes on the grass that stretched ahead of them, and on the road through the grass.

When the guard stopped to let him off in Richmond he said, "A word of advice, Willis."

"Advice?" Sam smiled at the guard.

"That's right. You got a habit of getting in trouble, Willis. That's why they

didn't parole you, made you serve full time, because of that habit."

"That's what the man told me," Sam said. "So?"

"So stay out of pool rooms. You're smart. You can earn a living."

Sam started climbing out of the station wagon. "Sure," he said. He got out, slammed the door, and the guard drove away.

It was still early and the town was nearly empty. Sam walked around, up and down different streets, for about an hour, looking at houses and stores, smiling at the people he saw, whistling or humming little tunes to himself.

In his right hand he was carrying his little round tubular leather case, carrying it by the brass handle on the side. It was about 30 inches long, the case, and about as big around as a man's forearm.

At ten o'clock he went to the bank and drew out the 600 dollars he had deposited there under the name of George Graves. Only it was 680; it had gathered that much interest.

16

Late last year, at the Brandeis University seminar at Hunter College, Jack Kerouac, coiner and captain of Beat, delivered an address on the topic of Beat and its beginnings. In the address, he sounded depths hitherto not plumbed, dispelled widespread misconceptions, debunked what he considers the phonies of the Beat movement and reaffirmed his faith in the basic principles of true Beat. At our request, he has written for PLAYBOY an article based on this speech. It is our pleasure and privilege to publish this statement here.

THE ORIGINS OF THE BEAT GENERATION

opinion **By JACK KEROUAC**

THIS ARTICLE necessarily'll have to be about myself. I'm going all out.

That nutty picture of me on the cover of *On the Road* results from the fact that I had just gotten down from a high mountain where I'd been for two months completely alone and usually I was in the habit of combing my hair of course because you have to get rides on the highway and all that and you usually want girls to look at you as though you were a man and not a wild beast but my poet friend Gregory Corso opened his shirt and took out a silver crucifix that was hanging from a chain and said "Wear this and wear it outside your shirt and don't comb your hair!" so I spent several days around San Francisco going around with him and others like that, to parties, arties, parts, jam sessions, bars, poetry readings, churches, walking talking poetry in the streets, walking talking God in the streets (and at one point a strange gang of hoodlums got mad and said "What right does he got to wear that?" and my own gang of musicians and poets told them to cool it) and finally on the third day *Mademoiselle* magazine wanted to take pictures of us all so I posed just like that, wild hair, crucifix, and all, with Gregory Corso, Allen Ginsberg and Phil Whalen, and the only publication which later did not erase the crucifix from my breast (from that plaid sleeveless cotton shirt-front) was *The New York Times*, therefore *The New York Times* is as beat as I am, and I'm glad I've got a friend. I mean it sincerely. God bless *The New York Times* for not erasing the crucifix from my picture as though it was some-

out of king kong
and krazy kat

In 1957 PLAYBOY set sail on a cruise for *Playboy's Yacht Party,* a combination travelog and pictorial that gave readers the ultimate hedonistic adventure. Another feature, *Playboy's House Party* (May 1959, opposite), was prompted by Hefner's first visit to Miami. The Florida mansion in which it was photographed inspired him to buy one of his own, equip it with an indoor swimming pool and adopt a similar fantasy lifestyle back home in Chicago.

Just as the Sears, Roebuck catalog had been a "wish book" for rural Americans earlier in the century, PLAYBOY fulfilled the material fantasies of the urban male of the Fifties. "Our food and drink features were, in reality, a form of foreplay," explains Hefner. "But they also helped to define a new breed of man—more chivalrous and romantic than before, as comfortable in the kitchen as in the bedroom or out on the road. The gadgetry and other gear we featured were a part of that romanticized perception of manhood." PLAYBOY illustrated that perception with regular articles on food and drink by Thomas Mario, roadworthy features such as automotive authority Ken Purdy's April 1957 *Compleat Sports Car Stable* and a January 1958 layout on equipping a basic home bar.

food **By THOMAS MARIO**

quick, easy, happy holiday eating

AT THE OUTSET, let anyone who still looks upon the casserole as merely a trencher for bulky peasants' food remind himself of squab *en casserole, coq au vin*, breast of chicken with broccoli *Mornay* or *cassoulet* of duckling. For holiday chefs who, each year, rebel more and more against oversize roasting pans, tough giblets and mountainous bread dressings, such dishes are the staunchest sort of ally, because they combine the heights of both elegance and ease.

In turning to the casserole, the wise cook simply avails himself of the oldest utensil in the entire *batterie de cuisine*. Earthenware casseroles were used by men in the earliest times, and you'll still find brown earthenware casseroles in restaurants specializing in French provincial cooking, or in stores displaying imported cooking ware. But these honorable relics have generally been replaced by the porcelain cast-iron casserole, a utensil which is ovenproof, flameproof and almost foolproof.

There are two ways in which the sturdy new casserole makes gala cooking easier. First of all, it disencumbers the pot-washer of countless pots and pans that would otherwise pile up in the kitchen sink: a large casserole is versatile enough to take the place of a mixing bowl, a sauté pan, saucepan, stew pot, baking dish, roasting pan, serving dish and storage dish for either refrigerator or freezer. Secondly, a casserole opens the door to the most comfortable kind of informal serving.

Even at those tables where the conventional roast turkey *must* appear on the menu at any cost, the casserole can come to the aid of the carver. It works like this: the turkey is roasted so that it's finished a few hours before the guests arrive. At his leisure the carver walks into the kitchen, rolls up his sleeves and gets down to work. First of all, like any professional cook, he uses his bare hands to separate leg and thigh from the breast. In the same way he removes the tailpiece and the two tender chunks called the oysters. He carves the meat at his own pace. When the bird becomes awkward to handle, he grabs a side of the cavity, with his left hand, and, with his right hand, slices alongside the keel bone, wings and back. After the carving is completed he fills a large shallow casserole with mounds of bread dressing, separated comfortably from each other. On the dressing he first places dark meat, then crowns it with slices of white meat. He pats each portion into a hemisphere, and covers the casserole.

THE CHRISTMAS CASSEROLE

About 20 or 25 minutes before the festal rites begin, he pours into the casserole a half cupful or full cup of chicken or turkey stock (the amount depending on the number of portions), places the casserole in a moderate oven and returns to his double martini. Just before the turkey is borne to the table, he pours piping-hot gravy over each appetizing mound in the casserole. At the table, the placid host comfortably lifts each portion from the casserole to the serving dish. The proceedings are urbane, but — infinitely more important — the turkey is hot, moist and actually seems more fresh-tasting than when it's carved at the table. Second helpings are kept in the covered casserole resting over a candle flame, where they remain hot throughout the meal.

If this kind of formulary strikes you as somewhat too mechanized, be assured that it won't seem so to your diners. The kind of husky and charming casserole that's come into vogue in recent years is impressive when it's brought to the table. And it's practical. It's so tough that you can take it from the hottest oven and place it in the coldest water, and it won't crack. Models of this type of kitchenware now range from tiny little cocottes for drawn butter to huge round or oval casseroles big enough for a rich brown gosling or three or four guinea hens.

The following yuletide dishes are (continued on page 108) 53

BASIC BAR

The 1956 introduction of licensed merchandise such as cufflinks helped the Rabbit logo become one of the world's most recognized symbols. Other PLAYBOY items included neckties, tie tacks, bracelets, sport shirts, sweaters, matches, playing cards, a variety of bar accessories and magazine binders in which devoted readers saved every issue. To this day, some have complete collections. PLAYBOY also sold felt emblems for sweaters like those worn by Playmates Lisa Winters, Linda Vargas and Janet Pilgrim (below), promoting PLAYBOY styles at a national clothing convention.

PLAYBOY ACCESSORIES FOR YOU AND YOUR PLAYMATE

PLAYBOY's familiar rabbit in bright rhodium on gleaming black enamel, attractively packaged in felt bag.

Earrings **$4.50**	Bracelet **$3**	The Set **$7**
Cuff Links **$4.50**	Tie Tack **$2.50**	The Set **$6.50**

Send check or money order to:

PLAYBOY PRODUCTS, Dept. 108 • 232 East Ohio Street, Chicago 11, Illinois

"Hefner's genius," observed Dr. Paul Gebhard of the Kinsey Institute, "was to associate sex with upward mobility." In few aspects of the magazine was this more apparent than in fashion and lifestyle features, in which the affluent men in the illustrations were often accompanied by attractive women. Before long, menswear manufacturers were finding PLAYBOY exposure for their products a surefire sales booster. To maintain a close contact with its growing market of collegiate readers, PLAYBOY set up a corps of campus representatives who surveyed their classmates on various issues, including tastes in fashion.

Bradley

Texas Christian

Southern Methodist

Bowling Green

George Washington   Drake

University of Iowa

UCLA

University of Kansas City

Northwestern

Syracuse

Beloit

University of Chicago

University of Illinois   Minnesota

Rutgers

Georgia Tech

Columbia

As the magazine's campus presence increased, PLAYBOY-themed parties flourished. With PLAYBOY paraphernalia bedecking college proms, hops, cotillions and fraternity bashes on campuses around the country, it appeared the magazine was beginning to speak not only to, but for, a new generation. In the process, it was able to recruit readers who would remain loyal for years to come.

What Sort of Man Reads Playboy? was the inspired theme of a long-running and highly successful series of ads designed to overcome the sales resistance of mainstream advertisers to appearing in the new men's magazine. Starting in September 1956, the campaign's promotion of PLAYBOY's uniquely young, ambitious, upscale, fun-loving, free-thinking and college-educated readership did much to gain Madison Avenue's acceptance.

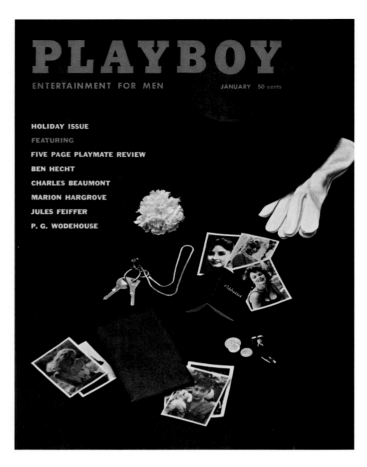

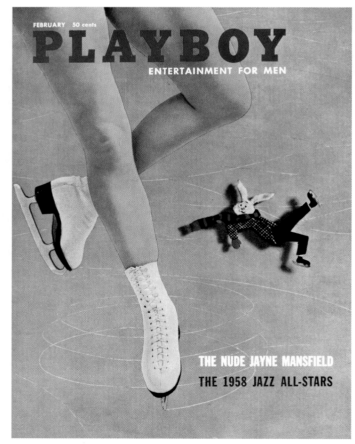

By the late Fifties, PLAYBOY was celebrated for the playful sophistication of its covers, as always featuring the popular Rabbit—by then so well known that the magazine could sell in excess of a million copies with nothing but a pair of Playboy cufflinks on its cover. The hare was apparent as both bikini fabric and background on the cover opposite featuring Miss December 1958, Joyce Nizzari.

PLAYBOY

ENTERTAINMENT FOR MEN

JULY   50 cents

PICNIC CAPERS

Eleanor Bradley's February 1959 Playmate appearance (below and right) caused such a sensation in her home town of Waukegan, Illinois, that she moved to the more cosmopolitan Chicago, where she worked as a Playboy receptionist when she wasn't doing Playmate promotions. Eleanor was a prominent regular on Playboy's first syndicated television show, *Playboy's Penthouse*, hosted by Hefner.

Recruited over espresso in a coffeehouse, uninhibited Yvette Vickers (top) became PLAYBOY's "beatnik Playmate" in July 1959. Company lawyers thought her centerfold too hot for publication, but Hefner disagreed. Another of Bunny Yeager's finds, Florida's Joyce Nizzari (far left) became Miss December 1958 as well as a personal playmate of the publisher. Vikki Dougan was aptly nicknamed "The Back" when the picture at near left appeared in the June 1957 PLAYBOY. "I'm not busty," said Vikki, "so what's a girl to do?" Miss January 1957, June Blair (below), went on to become a regular on TV's *Ozzie and Harriet* after marrying the Nelsons' son David.

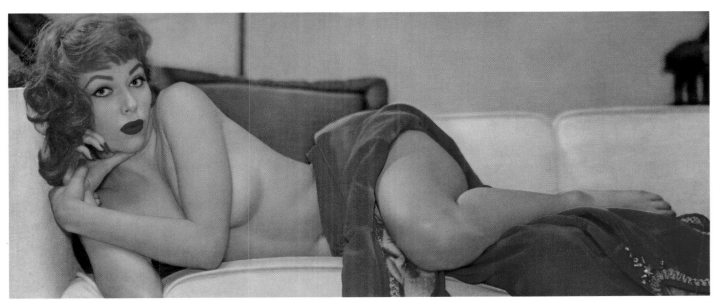

Elizabeth Ann Roberts (above and left) was featured as January 1958's *Schoolmate Playmate* with the naive notion that a girl in college—who had her mother's written permission—could appear nude in PLAYBOY. The fact that she hadn't yet turned 18 seemed unimportant at the time, but it caused a major furor. Hefner considered pointing out publicly that the model for *September Morn* (below) was also a nymphet, but he didn't have to when the charge of contributing to the delinquency of a minor was thrown out for lack of evidence. Thereafter, PLAYBOY policy demanded that all the magazine's models be at least 18 years old.

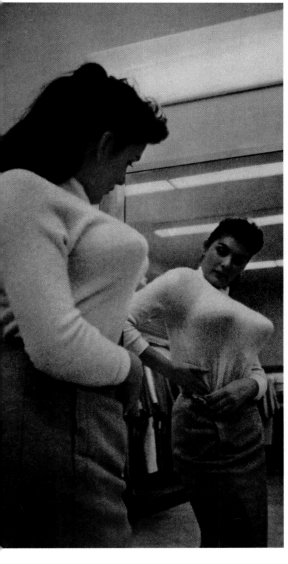

Another teenager, the awesomely endowed British model June Wilkinson, stopped by PLAYBOY's offices on a public-appearance visit to Chicago. A cautious Hefner waited until after her 18th birthday to photograph a provocative spread of June, which was shot in his office bedroom. PLAYBOY promoted her as "The Bosom." As a result of her September 1958 appearance (below) and subsequent pictorials in the magazine, she became a celebrity.

The Seduction by Jules Feiffer

Author-playwright Jules Feiffer has been going behind—and between—the lines in the battle of the sexes with satiric social commentaries in PLAYBOY since January 1959.

Gahan Wilson

"Sorry to keep you so late, but I'm determined to get to the bottom of this werewolf fixation of yours."

"Sherwood Forest…Robin Hood speaking."

"Er…have you a king size?"

"Ethel, why are you always wandering away from the boat crowd?"

In a sexy sequel to its popular *Penthouse Apartment* feature from 1956, PLAYBOY published *And So to Bed* in November 1959. This state-of-the-art design was a posh playpen whose many uses even included sleeping. This early prototype, with its controls to call up music, TV, drinks and snacks, presaged the legendary round, rotating model—perhaps the most famous bed in the world—that was especially designed for Hefner and featured in the magazine in 1965.

THE PIOUS PORNOGRAPHERS

article

BY IVOR WILLIAMS

FOR YEARS I have been bumbling along in the naive belief that the women's magazines were devoted solely to such matters as how to chintz up the living room and get a cake to rise. But it seems I was wrong—the most worrisome problem facing milady's monthly gazettes is how to muss up the marriage bed and keep one's mate aroused.

This belated discovery was as accidental as it was painful, and resulted from my having bitten down on a stray piece of shell in the lobster Newburg, cracking the filling out of my favorite molar. My face throbbed like an empty

sex and sanctimony in the ladies' home jungle

Although it considered itself primarily a vehicle for entertainment, PLAYBOY often courted controversy. October 1959's *The Pious Pornographers* pointed a satirical finger at self-righteous women's magazines that merchandised their own brand of sniggering sexuality. February 1959's *Rebel with a Caustic Cause* profiled the irreverent comic Lenny Bruce. Bruce, who first came to national prominence in the pages of PLAYBOY, became a personal friend of the publisher. The magazine commissioned the comic's autobiography, *How to Talk Dirty and Influence People,* and published it afterward in book form by Playboy Press. The autobiography and PLAYBOY's posthumous tribute *Lenny Lives!* helped turn Bruce into a legend—and the subject of a Broadway play and Hollywood movie—after his death.

KENTON

ARMSTRONG

"Readers dig hot and cool, progressive and bop, in PLAYBOY's first jazz poll," read the headline as the first Playboy Jazz All-Stars were announced in the February 1957 issue. Reflecting the musical tastes of the publisher and millions of other fans, this Academy Awards of jazz recognized the giants of an American art form. Above, Playmate Janet Pilgrim presents a Playboy Jazz Poll medal to All-Star bandleader Benny Goodman.

DESMOND

BROOKMEYER

MULLIGAN

JOHNSON

KESSEL

SINATRA

FITZGERALD

DAVE BRUBECK QUARTET

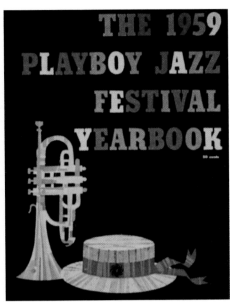

THE 1959 PLAYBOY JAZZ FESTIVAL YEARBOOK

Satch and Miles, Duke and Bean, Dizzy and the Count—almost every jazz star in the country—answered the call to perform when Hefner staged a three-day Playboy Jazz Festival in August 1959 celebrating PLAYBOY's first five years of publication. Critic Leonard Feather called it "the greatest single weekend in the history of jazz." The idea proved so enduring that the festival staged a comeback—20 years later and across the continent. The Playboy Jazz Festival now fills Hollywood Bowl every June.

PLAYBOY • JAZZ • FESTIVAL

SPONSORED BY PLAYBOY MAGAZINE

AIR-CONDITIONED
CHICAGO STADIUM ☞

aug. 7-8-9 fri. sat. sun.

INDIVIDUAL PERFORMANCE TICKETS
Saturday & Sunday / Matinees and Evenings
Reserved Seats at.......... $5.50 and $3.30
General Admission at................ $1.10

MAIL ORDERS NOW

PLAYBOY JAZZ FESTIVAL
PLAYBOY BUILDING
232 E. OHIO STREET
CHICAGO 11, ILLINOIS

Premiere Benefit Performance Friday Night at 8 00

Miles Davis Sextet
Count Basie Band
Joe Williams
Dizzy Gillespie Quintet
Dave Brubeck Quartet
Kai Winding Septet
Dakota Staton
Mort Sahl, Emcee

✮✮✮✮✮✮✮✮
Friday Night Prices
Proceeds to the Chicago Urban League
Reserved Seats at: $25, $15, $10, $7.50, $5
General Admission (1st Balcony)—$3.30
General Admission (2nd Balcony)—$2.20

(Benefit Prices Apply to Fridays Only)

Saturday Aft. at 2

Duke Ellington Band
Jimmy Rushing
Oscar Peterson Trio
Dukes of Dixieland
Jimmy Giuffre 3
Bobby Darin
The Signatures
Mort Sahl, Emcee

Saturday Eve. at 8

Count Basie Band
Joe Williams
Lambert, Hendricks & Ross
Ahmad Jamal Trio
Jack Teagarden All Stars
Don Elliott
Earl Bostic Sextet
Mort Sahl, Emcee

Sunday Aft. at 2

Stan Kenton Band
Four Freshmen
June Christy
Sonny Rollins Trio
Nina Simone
Austin High Gang
David Allen
Mort Sahl, Emcee

Sunday Eve. at 8

Louis Armstrong All Stars
Red Nichols and His 5 Pennies
Stan Kenton Band
Chris Connor
J. J. Johnson Quintet
Coleman Hawkins
Mort Sahl, Emcee

Georg Brunis' Dixieland Band in Residence at all Performances

On October 24, 1959, the magazine came to life on television when Hefner made his debut as host of *Playboy's Penthouse,* an hour-long variety show set in a bachelor pad. Over its two seasons on the air, the program featured jazz, hip humor and lively conversation. Guests included (right) Stella Stevens, who was to become Miss January 1960, and four Hollywood starlets; June "The Bosom" Wilkinson (below); jazz great Ella Fitzgerald (bottom), and poet Carl Sandburg (center right).

Other episodes featured bongo-boarding Playmate Donna Lynn (left) and humorist Lenny Bruce (above) grimacing at a stagehand's bare arm in a fish tank. Although *Playboy's Penthouse* was syndicated nationally, stations in the South refused to air the show because it featured black performers in an integrated social setting.

As the decade came to a close, PLAYBOY was prospering. In 1969 circulation passed the 1 million mark, and the HMH Publishing Company, Inc. boasted a hundred employees. Although others were predicting the coming of a new Victorianism, Hefner and his publication had most certainly jump-started the sexual revolution. With the success of PLAYBOY assured and the launch of *Playboy's Penthouse* underway, the Editor-Publisher was ready to begin moving beyond the pages of the magazine into other ventures and began living the good life reflected in his magazine. In so doing, Hugh M. Hefner re-created himself as "Mr. Playboy."

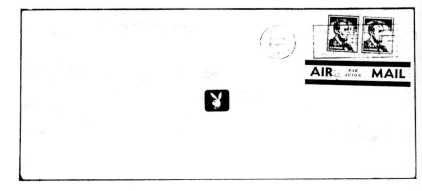

One of Hefner's first moves toward a more opulent lifestyle was his purchase of the Playboy Mansion on Chicago's Gold Coast (above left). On its front door he mounted a plaque with a Latin inscription that translated as: "If you don't swing, don't ring"—a gift from his Associate Publisher, A.C. Spectorsky. As proof of PLAYBOY's increasing fame, a letter addressed with nothing more than the Rabbit logo found its way straight to the company's offices. The foundation had been laid for Hefner to become more than a publisher, and PLAYBOY more than a magazine.

THE SIXTIES

The Sixties began with a freshening wind. After the stifling Fifties, change was in the air. Ike was still president, but there was an election nearing and a handsome, vigorous young man stood poised to win the hearts and minds of the American public. His name was Bond—James Bond.

When the popular new president, John F. Kennedy, announced that his favorite spy writer was Ian Fleming, 007 became a national phenomenon. That came as no surprise to the editors of PLAYBOY, who had already introduced him to readers with a story in the March 1960 issue. Bond was their kind of guy: exciting job, got the girls, knew how to dress, licensed to kill—what else could one want? In the next few years, the magazine published four serialized novels, several pictorials of James Bond's girls, even a flinty interview with Sean Connery himself. Hefner would have run a spread on Miss Moneypenny if she'd been willing.

Fleming was only one of the names on a Sixties fiction roster that read like the guest list for a writers' awards banquet. Reigning giants such as Carl Sandburg, Henry Miller, Nelson Algren, Lawrence Durrell and Vladimir Nabokov graced the pages of the magazine, as did the most promising literary lights of a new generation: Philip Roth, John Cheever, Truman Capote and John Updike. For comedy relief, there were talents like Woody Allen, Jonathan Winters, Mort Sahl and Mike Nichols, and the autobiography of tragicomic Lenny Bruce, *How to Talk Dirty and Influence People*, was first published in the pages of PLAYBOY.

In 1962, Hefner had a few words of his own to say. Fed up with being misrepresented in the press, he sat down to answer his critics in an outspoken editorial. Warming to his subject as he denounced the uptight sexual attitudes that catalyzed the creation of PLAYBOY, he turned out a tidy 150,000 words of social commentary in 25 installments for the next two and a half years. *The Playboy Philosophy* touched off a moral debate that raged from campus to pulpit. Reader reaction was so overwhelming that a new department, *The Playboy Forum*, was added to make room for the editorial dialogue it inspired.

With the debut of the *Playboy Interview* feature that same year, the magazine began generating—and attracting—heat across a spectrum of social issues: most dramatically by airing the race struggle in interviews with Alabama's segregationist Governor George Wallace, American Nazi George Lincoln Rockwell, militant Muslim minister Malcolm X and civil rights leader Dr. Martin Luther King Jr. The last three were conducted by a young freelancer named Alex Haley, who would himself become the subject of a *Playboy Interview* after his monumental best-seller *Roots*.

The Sixties nearly wrenched America apart, pitting crew-cut dads against long-haired sons, bourbon-sipping Legionnaires against pot-smoking pacifists, cops against flower children. A striking image of the conflict was Herb Davidson's depiction of the threat posed to liberty by a group of right-wing militants called the Minutemen. Within weeks of *The Paramilitary Right's* June 1969 publication in PLAYBOY, FBI agents arrested the Minutemen's top leadership and confiscated thousands of pounds of arms and ammunition.

His magazine now attracting more than a million readers each month, Hefner began living the fantasy he'd created on its pages—and invited like-minded men to join him. "We wanted a place where we could hang out," Hefner recalls. So he created the Chicago Playboy Club, the cornerstone of what was to become an empire. Within a year of its opening on Leap Year night, February 29, 1960, the Club had enrolled more than 50,000 keyholders; so great was its popularity that lines formed outside nightly, even in the bitter cold of a Windy City winter. Above, Mr. Playboy with a group of early Bunnies, several of whom were also Playmates. Note the collarless, cuffless style of the early Bunny Costumes. By the early Sixties, PLAYBOY magazine had reached the farthest corners of the world; below, an Australian aborigine peruses the May 1963 issue.

As the clamor of social protest and political dissent grew louder, PLAYBOY sounded off: Supreme Court Justice William O. Douglas decried abuses to the environment, Ralph Nader argued for consumer protection, Senator Stephen Young called for curbs on the CIA and Senator William Fulbright appealed for a reordering of our priorities. But it was on the issue of Vietnam that the magazine spoke out most strongly—with essays and reportage by Kenneth Tynan, Nat Hentoff and John Kenneth Galbraith that reflected the antiwar views of a prophetic minority and, increasingly, those of our servicemen in Southeast Asia. PLAYBOY became the unofficial magazine of the war. Barracks from Saigon to the Mekong Delta were plastered with Playmate centerfolds—including that of 1965 Playmate of the Year Jo Collins. When a young second lieutenant stationed in Bien Hoa wrote Hefner a poignant letter asking for a Playmate to deliver a lifetime subscription in person, Hefner sent "GI Jo."

PLAYBOY kept the hearth warm at home with pictorials showcasing the leading sex goddesses of the day: Catherine Deneuve, Stella Stevens, Kim Novak, Ursula Andress and the empress herself, Elizabeth Taylor, in a peekaboo scene from the bomb of the decade, *Cleopatra*.

The party at PLAYBOY, meanwhile, overflowed the pages of the magazine—and the television screen—to come alive on Walton Street in

Chicago's Near North Side nightlife district. It was standing room only on the night of February 29, 1960 as crowds lined up in the freezing cold to sample the fare and enjoy the live entertainment—especially those cotton-tailed Bunnies—at the opening of the flagship Playboy Club. Within a year, more than 50,000 men—lured by shapely Bunnies, name entertainers and attractive prices (dinner or cocktail for the same $1.50)—had signed up as Playboy "keyholders," and by 1963 there were Clubs in Miami, New Orleans, St. Louis, New York, Phoenix and Detroit. This was just the beginning of what was to become the most famous and most successful nightclub chain in history, with two dozen Clubs and resorts spanning half the globe, from London to Osaka, employing more than a thousand Bunnies and attracting more than a million keyholders. "A Disneyland for adults," reported *Newsweek* magazine, admiringly.

The continuing battle for racial equality found the Playboy Clubs on the front lines. On January 13, 1961, the Chicago Club provided the stage upon which an unknown comic named Dick Gregory became the first black performer to break the color barrier in a mainstream nightery. Later, on hearing that the owners of the Miami and New Orleans Playboy Clubs were discriminating against black keyholders, Hefner bought back their franchises.

The real party, of course, went on in Hefner's new home: an opulent 70-room edifice on Chicago's Gold Coast that soon became the most famous private residence in the world. The legendary Playboy Mansion became a favorite destination for visiting celebrities, a posh dorm for Bunnies and Playmates and home-sweet-home for Hefner in this pivotal period of transformation from mild-mannered Editor-Publisher to "Mr. Playboy," a living embodiment of the swinging-single lifestyle celebrated in his own publication.

All in all, from Camelot to Aquarius, this decade of frenetic energy propelled the explosive growth of Playboy Enterprises, and gave both Hefner and his magazine the chance to demonstrate the wisdom of that Sixties rallying cry: Make love, not war.

Psychedelic designs showed up everywhere—from Volkswagen vans to dinnerware—in the mid to late Sixties, but it took Mario Casilli, one of PLAYBOY's favorite lensmen, to think up the notion of painting and photographing nudes in that style for a 1968 pictorial. The first *Playboy Interview*, in which a budding journalist named Alex Haley interviewed jazz great Miles Davis, appeared in September 1962. Through the years, Haley conducted many more *Playboy Interviews*, one of the most provocative of which was with George Lincoln Rockwell, self-appointed Führer of the American Nazi Party. Rockwell, who espoused white supremacy and anti-Semitism, agreed to sit for the interview after assuring himself that Haley wasn't Jewish. "I didn't tell him I was a Negro," Haley admitted. The question-and-answer session (left), which was published in April 1966, took place in the presence of an armed guard and with a pearl-handled revolver within Rockwell's reach.

the chronicle of a man and his genius

By CHARLES BEAUMONT

It's hard to tell which of Charlie Chaplin's proclivities—his left-of-center politics or his uninhibited sexuality (although proven innocent, he lost a 1944 paternity case)—got him in more trouble with FBI chief J. Edgar Hoover and other authorities. When the British-born comedian-turned-movie-director left the U.S. for the premiere of *Limelight* in 1952, his re-entry permit was revoked. Charles Beaumont's March 1960 PLAYBOY profile, accompanied by an Art Paul illustration that's still a favorite of magazine staffers (above), did Chaplin more justice and helped turn the tide of public opinion in his favor. The chilling scene from Louis Buñuel's *Un Chien Andalou* (left) illustrated Arthur Knight's *Far-Out Films*, a 1960 piece that drew more mail than any PLAYBOY article before it—and was the precursor of *The History of Sex in Cinema*, the long-running series written by Knight and fellow critic Hollis Alpert.

As the decade opened, PLAYBOY's editorial mix—reflecting the times—became more and more eclectic. A British writer and former intelligence agent named Ian Fleming introduced his fictional superspy, James Bond, to PLAYBOY readers in a novella, *The Hildebrand Rarity* (March 1960). The story later showed up as a plot device in the Bond film *License to Kill*. The magazine also plunged headlong into the decade's most stirring debates. Its publication of Nat Hentoff's July 1962 examination of black Americans' new militancy, *Through the Racial Looking Glass*, was but one of many examinations of civil rights issues. In 1962, when Dan Wakefield's *The Prodigal Powers of Pot* was published, penalties for simple possession of marijuana were harsh. Wakefield's article examined the history of cannabis from its first recorded mention, in a 2737 B.C. Chinese treatise on pharmacy, through its adoption as the drug of choice for the Beat Generation and the hippies of the Sixties.

miss november · PLAYBOY'S PLAYMATE OF THE MONTH

Petite brunette Joni Mattis (above) was Playmate of the Month for November 1960. She enjoyed a long career with the company, having filled just about every job from Bunny in Chicago to Hefner's social secretary at Playboy Mansion West. Two friends from Europe—Austrian-born Heidi Becker (left) and Germany native Christa Speck (below)—became Playmates in 1961. Heidi had been a hair stylist in Milwaukee and Christa, a former bank secretary, went on to marry Hollywood producer Marty Krofft.

In 1960 PLAYBOY encouraged readers to write to the magazine supporting their choices for a new honor, the title of Playmate of the Year. The winner, announced in the June issue, was legal secretary Ellen Stratton (right). Her successor, 1961 Playmate of the Year Linda Gamble (above), had been a Pittsburgh secretary before moving to Chicago and becoming a Playboy Bunny.

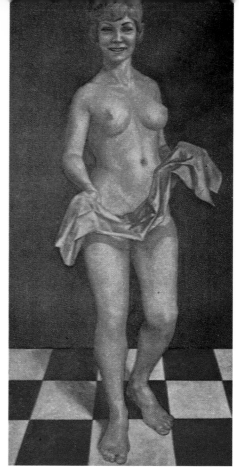

PLAYBOY sought in 1960 to merge art and photography by inviting 11 talented contemporary artists to portray Miss September, Ann Davis, for that month's feature *Painting a Playmate*. That's Ann's centerfold at left; above, Herb Davidson's interpretation; below, Richard Frooman's. Opposite, clockwise from top left: LeRoy Neiman's painting; Seymour Rosofsky's portrait in watercolor and pen; a sketching session with Ann, PLAYBOY Art Director Art Paul, Herb Davidson and Bob Christiansen; and the resulting portraits from Christiansen and Paul.

The first three Playboy Clubs, in Chicago (top left), New Orleans (center left) and Miami (bottom left), inspired some 120,000 men to sign up as keyholders by the end of 1961.

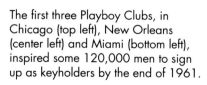

The Playboy Clubs were the most popular night spots of their time, featuring quality food and drink, excellent service and top-drawer entertainment. Liza Minnelli (opposite bottom right) was but one of the hundreds of stars who appeared on the Playboy circuit. Themes from the magazine were picked up in Club decor: The Chicago hutch boasted a Cartoon Corner (opposite top) and every Club had a Playmate Bar like the one below, decorated with illuminated transparencies of centerfolds. The New York Club, which opened in December 1962 at 5 East 59th Street—across from the Plaza Hotel, where hansom cabs lined up nightly for trips through Central Park—also featured a circular Piano Bar (above). But the Clubs' greatest attractions were the Bunnies, such as June "The Bosom" Wilkinson, on the phone opposite. Surpassing mere waitresses, the Bunnies were chosen for their personality, beauty and style. The three at top and right—Kelly Collins, Kitty Kavany and Bea Payton—doubled as sophisticated Chicago fashion models. Instructions for disco dancing (bottom) came from *VIP*, the magazine for keyholders that debuted in 1964.

KEY   THE BIRD   THE PONY   THE WATUSI   THE UNCLE WILLIE   THE SWIM   THE BUN

The Playboy Club concept quickly caught the public's imagination, soon spreading across the Atlantic to London, where Playboy's casino on fashionable Park Lane (top) drew an international clientele. For a quarter of a century, the Bunny was a pop culture icon, widely imitated on TV by the likes of Steve Allen (practicing the Bunny Dip, above left) and Johnny Carson (above right). Gloria Steinem (below left) even went undercover as a cottontail to write an exposé for *Show* magazine. Future stars as diverse as Lauren Hutton (below center) and Debbie Harry (below right) hopped tables en route to showbiz success, while countless other celebs such as Beatle John Lennon and then-wife Cynthia (opposite, bottom right) frequented the Clubs simply for the fun of it. Cottontails at the flagship Chicago hutch enjoyed a special perk: a chance to live in the Bunny Dorm at the Playboy Mansion (opposite, bottom left). Early on, there had been talk of dressing the waitresses in sexy nightgowns. Fortunately, it was decided to play on the magazine's Rabbit imagery and call the girls Bunnies. The Bunny Costume was registered with the U.S. Patent Office and displayed in the Smithsonian. Opposite, Chicago Bunnies model outfits in a new fabric for Hefner's approval.

Eldon Dedini's 1964 cartoon resurrects Carry Nation, the notorious temperance crusader who wielded an ax against Kansas saloons.

"Hi!"

PLAYBOY INTERVIEW: **MILES DAVIS**

a candid conversation with the jazz world's premier iconoclast

The technical and emotional brilliance of the trumpet played by Miles Davis has made him one of the most provocative influences in modern jazz. We spent two days with Miles not long ago in his rather unusual five-story home, a converted Russian Orthodox Church on West 77th Street near the Hudson River in New York City. Miles was between gigs at the time and we accompanied him on his restless daily home routine, asking questions at propitious moments while he worked out in his basement gymnasium, made veal chops Italian style for his family, took telephone calls from fellow musicians, his lawyer and stockbroker, gave boxing lessons to his three sons, watched TV, plucked out beginner's chords on a guitar and, of course, blew one of his two Martin trumpets, running up and down the chromatic scale with searing speed. Spending time with Miles in the refuge of his own home, and seeing him surrounded by the activities and people he loves, it was hard to reconcile this reality with his sometimes flinty and truculent public posture. It was on this facet of his personality that we first queried him.

PLAYBOY: Linked with your musical renown is your reputation for bad temper and rudeness to your audiences. Would you comment?

DAVIS: Why is it that people just have to have so much to say about me? It bugs me because I'm not that important.

Some critic that didn't have nothing else to do started this crap about I don't announce numbers, I don't look at the audience, I don't bow or talk to people, I walk off the stage, and all that.

Look, man, all I am is a trumpet player. I only can do one thing — play my horn — and that's what's at the bottom of the whole mess. I ain't no entertainer, and ain't trying to be one. I am one thing, a musician. Most of what's said about me is lies in the first place. Everything I do, I got a reason.

The reason I don't announce numbers is because it's not until the last instant I decide what's maybe the best thing to play next. Besides, if people don't recognize a number when we play it, what difference does it make?

Why I sometimes walk off the stand is because when it's somebody else's turn to solo, I ain't going to just stand up there and be detracting from him. What am I going to stand up there *for?* I ain't no model, and I don't sing or dance, and I damn sure ain't no Uncle Tom just to be up there grinning. Sometimes I go over by the piano or the drums and listen to what they're doing. But if I don't want to do that, I go in the wings and listen to the whole band until it's the next turn for my horn.

Then they claim I ignore the audience while I'm playing. Man, when I'm working, I know the people are out there. But when I'm playing, I'm worrying about making my horn sound right.

And they bitch that I won't talk to people when we go off after a set. That's a damn lie. I talk plenty of times if everything's going like it ought to and I feel right. But if I got my mind on something about my band or something else, well, hell, no, I don't want to talk. When I'm working I'm concentrating. I bet you if I was a doctor sewing on some son of a bitch's heart, they wouldn't want me to talk.

Anybody wants to believe all this crap they hear about me, it's their problem, not mine. Because, look, man, I like people. I *love* people! I'm not going around telling everybody that. I try to say that my way — with my horn. Look, when I was a boy, 10 years old, I got a paper route and it got bigger than I could handle because my customers liked me so much. I just delivered papers the best I could and minded my business, the same way I play my horn now. But a lot of the people I meet now make me sick.

PLAYBOY: What types of people do you find especially irritating?

DAVIS: Well, these people that's always coming up bugging me until they get me to act like this crap they heard. They ask you things, you say what you think, and if it ain't what they want to hear, then something's wrong with you and they go away mad and think you don't like them. I bet I have had that happen 500 times. In this last club I played, this newspaper reporter kept after me when I told him I didn't have

"I don't pay no attention to what critics say about me, the good or the bad. The toughest critic I got is myself...and I'm too vain to play anything I think is bad."

"In high school I was best in music class on the trumpet, but the prizes went to the boys with blue eyes. I made up my mind to outdo anybody white on my horn."

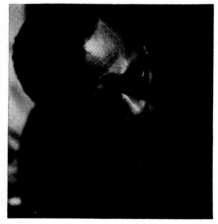

"I don't dig people in clubs who don't pay the musicians respect. You ever see anybody bugging the classical musicians when they are on the job and trying to work?"

57

THE PLAYBOY PHILOSOPHY

on our ninth anniversary playboy's editor-publisher spells out—for friends and critics alike—our guiding principles and editorial credo

editorial By Hugh M. Hefner

EXACTLY NINE YEARS AGO this month, the first issue of PLAYBOY was published, with a personal investment of $600 and $6000 begged or borrowed from anyone who would stand still long enough to listen to "a new idea for a men's magazine." Now something of a collector's item, that issue—forged with much youthful zeal by a small group of dedicated iconoclasts who shared a publishing dream—seems almost childishly crude when compared with the magazine you hold in your hands. We have come a long way since then, in editorial scope and polish as well as in circulation, and we are mightily pleased whenever we are complimented on the fact. But when well-wishers sometimes praise us for the way in which our magazine has changed, we must shake our head in disagreement. The fact is that in its basic concepts and its editorial attitude, in its view of itself and its view of life, its feelings about its readers and—we believe—their feelings toward it, the magazine called PLAYBOY is the same today as it was nine years ago. Improved—yes, we like to think. Altered in its aims and outlook—definitely no.

Recently, and increasingly in the past year, PLAYBOY's aims and outlook have been given considerable comment in the press, particularly in the journals of social, philosophical and religious opinion, and have become a popular topic of conversation at cocktail parties around

the highly prolific playwright-critic was an all-play-and-no-work sybarite. He certainly did not mean to suggest that Shaw led a pleasure-seeking life of indolent ease, nor that the platonically inclined vegetarian was leading a secret life of the seraglio. He did mean—and he told us so when he visited our offices on the occasion of the founding of the Shaw Society in Chicago—that Shaw was a man who approached life with immense gusto and relish. As a word, *playboy* has suffered semantic abuse: Its most frequent usage in the press is to characterize those functionless strivers after pleasure whom Federico Fellini, in *La Dolce Vita*, showed to be so joylessly diligent in their pursuit of self-pleasuring as to be more deserving of sympathy than righteous condemnation. PLAYBOY, the magazine, has been sometimes tarred with the same brush—usually by those who are more zealous in their criticism than in their reading of it. We have been accused of leadership in a cult of irresponsibility and of aiding in the decline of the Western world. We deny it.

With PLAYBOY's ever-increasing popularity, it would be foolish for us to pretend that the publication doesn't exert a considerable influence upon our society. But what kind of influence? Opinions vary. We first became aware that

fraternity, or a special business or social association. By the time we were ready to open the first Playboy Club in 1960, we fully appreciated the impact that PLAYBOY, in its many forms, was having upon the urban community (for by then we'd witnessed the success of the Playboy Jazz Festival, Playboy records, Playboy Tours and our nationally syndicated television show, *Playboy's Penthouse*).

The professional critics and commentators on the contemporary scene could not too long resist supplying a personal analysis of the PLAYBOY phenomenon. In *Commentary*—"A journal of significant thought and opinion on Jewish affairs and contemporary issues," Benjamin DeMott, professor of English at Amherst, wrote an article on the subject, "The Anatomy of 'Playboy,'" which he sums up as "the whole man reduced to his private parts."

But in "*Playboy's* Doctrine of Male" by Harvey Cox, first published in *Christianity and Crisis*—"A Christian Journal of Opinion," and reprinted in *The Intercollegian*—"A Journal of Christian Encounter," and the editorial pages of a number of college newspapers, PLAYBOY is criticized for being "basically antisexual," Cox describes PLAYBOY as "one of the most spectacular successes in the entire history of American journalism," but stamps us "dictatorial taste-makers,"

PLAYBOY has had few peers as a vehicle for the interchange of ideas. The December 1962 issue introduced the first of 25 installments of *The Playboy Philosophy*, written by Hefner partly in response to what he saw as misguided criticism of his magazine's principles, but, even more importantly, as an attempt to define what came to be known as the new morality—placing the responsibility for social and sexual activities in the hands of individuals instead of government. The *Philosophy* was a thoughtful consideration of morality, censorship, sexuality and related issues—some of them visible in the file folders above. The *Philosophy* was soon drawing so much mail that in July 1963 the magazine established *The Playboy Forum*, home to a reader–editor dialogue on issues raised by the *Philosophy*. Two years later, the Playboy Foundation was launched as *The Playboy Philosophy*'s action arm, leading the way for successful legal challenges not only to censorship but to restrictive sex laws. Foundation funding supported a series of court cases that culminated in the Supreme Court's *Roe vs. Wade* decision legalizing abortion. The Foundation also supported sex research—by Masters and Johnson and the Kinsey Institute—and educational efforts such as those conducted by the Sex Information and Education Council of the United States.

THE PLAYBOY FORUM

an interchange of ideas between reader and editor on subjects raised by "the playboy philosophy"

No feature previously published by PLAYBOY *has produced so much reaction and debate—both in and outside the* [magazine]*—as "The Playboy*

My hat is off to Mr. Hefner—he has taken a stand. Whether the rest of us agree or disagree, at least we have a position from which to start—a reference point to differ about.

make a mockery of all laws, and should be eliminated, because they tend to breed disrespect for all laws. Some people seem to feel that mere antiquity makes laws useful or valid, but it seems to me that we should learn from the

The doors of the palatial Playboy Mansion swung open to readers for the first time with the December 1961 publication of *Playmate Holiday House Party*. In the photos opposite and above, Hefner is flanked by Playmates; at near left, Joni Mattis and Susie Scott join Mort Sahl at the buffet. One of the magazine's most memorable photos—reproduced in most of PLAYBOY's anniversary retrospectives—shows Christa Speck getting a friendly shove into the Mansion pool (right). Among the guests dancing at the party (below): Hefner's brother Keith (far right), who was in charge of Bunny training; comic Jackie Gayle (fourth from right), who headlined more Playboy Club openings than any other performer; and Tony Curtis (bottom far right). The Mansion boasted many fascinating features: secret panels, an underwater bar (below right) that afforded a unique vantage point for watching bathers and a trap door in the ballroom floor through which one could look into the waterfall-curtained cave dubbed by *Time* magazine the "woo grotto."

PLAYBOY ARTISTS PAINT A PLAYMATE • PLAYBOY'S PIGSKIN PREVIEW •
GREENWICH VILLAGE AS VIEWED BY HERBERT GOLD AND SHEL SILVERSTEIN

THE PLAYMATE OF THE YEAR • SINATRA'S MEETING AT THE SUMMIT

ment or diversion; amusement; sport; frolic. pla´boi). **1.** A sporty fellow bent upon pleasure seeking; a man-about-town; lover of life; a *bon vivant.* **2.** The magazine edited for the edification and enter-tainment of urban men; i.e., in the June issue; "You Can Make a Million Today" by J. Paul Getty; a psychological portrait of Reno by Herbert Gold; five pages of color photography on the Grand Prix in Monaco with description by Charles Beaumont; cartoonist Shel Silver-tein visits Hawaii.—**played out** (plād out), *p.* Performed to the end; also, exhausted; used up.—**player** (plā´ēr), *n.* One who plays; an ac-or; a musician.—**playful** (plā´fool; -f'l), *adj.* Full of play; sportive; also, humorous.—**play-mate** (plā´māt), *n.* A companion n play.—**Playmate** (Plā´māt), *n.* A popular pictorial feature in PLAYBOY magazine depicting eautiful girl in pin-up pose; shor-ening of "Playmate of the Month"; i.e., Austrian beauty Heidi Becker in June issue; ence, without cap., any very ttractive female companion to a layboy.—**playock** (plā´ŭk), *n.* Prob. dim. of *play. n.*] Plaything.

JUNE PLAYMATE

Variety and innovation were the hallmarks of early Sixties PLAYBOY covers, which ran the gamut from the first appearance of LeRoy Neiman's play-ful Femlin to an erudite riff on the dictionary. Playmate Sheralee Conners starred in the front-and-back opener to the December 1962 issue.

ENTERTAINMENT FOR MEN   DECEMBER ONE DOLLAR

PLAYBOY

SPECIAL CHRISTMAS GIFT   ANNIVERSARY ISSUE

CHRISTMAS FEATURES
FACT & FICTION BY
JAMES THURBER
RAY BRADBURY
LUDWIG BEMELMANS
RUDY VALLEE
NELSON ALGREN
RICK RUBIN
GARSON KANIN
ART BUCHWALD
SHEPHERD MEAD
ERNIE KOVACS
HUGH M. HEFNER
PLUS "PLAYBOY'S
HOLIDAY PUNCH"
& "THE CHRISTMAS
DINNER FLAMBE"
BY THOMAS MARIO WITH
NINE COLOR PAGES
OF CHRISTMAS GIFT
SUGGESTIONS FOR MEN

CHRISTMAS CARTOONS
HUMOR & SATIRE BY
JULES FEIFFER
SHEL SILVERSTEIN
ELDON DEDINI
ALBERTO VARGAS
GAHAN WILSON
E. SIMMS CAMPBELL
ERICH SOKOL
JOHN DEMPSEY
PHIL INTERLANDI
PLUS A SIX-PAGE
PLAYBOY PICTORIAL
ON ARLENE DAHL &
A PHOTO UNCOVERAGE
OF "PLAYBOY'S OTHER
GIRLFRIENDS"—
SOPHIA LOREN
KIM NOVAK
BRIGITTE BARDOT
ANITA EKBERG

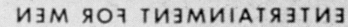
ENTERTAINMENT FOR MEN · DECEMBER ONE DOLLAR

PLAYBOY

SPECIAL CHRISTMAS GIFT... TH ANNIVERSARY ISSUE

CHRISTMAS CARTOONS
HUMOR & SATIRE BY
JULES FEIFFER
SHEL SILVERSTEIN
ELDON DEDINI
ALBERTO VARGAS
GAHAN WILSON
E. SIMMS CAMPBELL
ERICH SOKOL
JOHN DEMPSEY
PHIL INTERLANDI
PLUS A SIX-PAGE
PLAYBOY PICTORIAL
ON ARLENE DAHL &
A PHOTO UNCOVERAGE
OF "PLAYBOY'S OTHER
GIRLFRIENDS"—
SOPHIA LOREN
KIM NOVAK
BRIGITTE BARDOT
ANITA EKBERG

CHRISTMAS FEATURES
FACT & FICTION BY
JAMES THURBER
RAY BRADBURY
LUDWIG BEMELMANS
RUDY VALLEE
NELSON ALGREN
RICK RUBIN
GARSON KANIN
ART BUCHWALD
SHEPHERD MEAD
ERNIE KOVACS
HUGH M. HEFNER
PLUS "PLAYBOY'S
HOLIDAY PUNCH"
& "THE CHRISTMAS
DINNER FLAMBÉ"
BY THOMAS MARIO WITH
NINE COLOR PAGES
OF CHRISTMAS GIFT
SUGGESTIONS FOR MEN

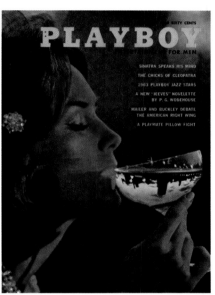  

  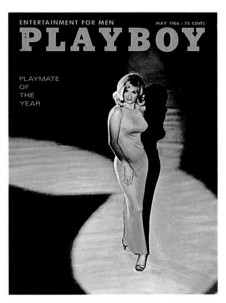

During the Sixties, PLAYBOY started playing a new game with its fans: hiding the Rabbit Head somewhere on the cover. Often, it was easy to find; when it wasn't, plaintive "where is it?" letters filled editors' IN boxes. Enterprising readers discovered that placing a hand over the top half of the June 1962 cover (top middle) gave it a racier perspective.

Bond was only 50 yards behind the girl at the town's outskirts but, with his big Bentley, he couldn't overtake the Lancia on the twisting, cobbled streets.

in perilous quest of spectral prey, james bond finds friends

MAJESTY'S SECRET SERVICE novel By IAN FLEMING

in a malevolent brotherhood, tenderness in compulsory love

Bond had no difficulty in keeping up with the twinkling feet and the twin white mounds of her behind.

YOU ONLY LIVE TWICE

it was a ten-thousand-to-one bet that james bond would not make it — but he was willing to take that chance

Part II of a novel **By IAN FLEMING**

SYNOPSIS: *The end of the career of James Bond on Her Majesty's Secret Service seemed to have arrived. After the death of his bride at the hands of Ernst Stavro Blofeld, mastermind of SPECTRE, the malignant cartel of international crime, Bond went downhill, gambling and wenching to excess and eventually becoming, at least in the view of his chief, the infallible M, a dangerous security risk. Reluctantly, M decided to discharge Bond, but eventually he was prevailed upon to give him a final chance. With a frosty* smile, M assigned Bond to a mission in which the latter's chances of success were ironically exposed as "totally improbable." In essence, Bond was told to acquire for the British the secrets of MAGIC 44, an infernal machine used to decode Soviet dispatches, now in the hands of Japan. This machine was controlled by Tiger Tanaka, chief of the Japanese Secret Service, whom Bond would contact through the aid of Dikko Henderson, top Australian agent in Japan.

In Tokyo, Bond met Tanaka and was informed that the secrets of MAGIC 44 would come at so high a price that the British Foreign Office could not conceivably afford it. At that point Tanaka launched into a description of the activities of a mysterious Doctor Guntram Shatterhand, who had established an exotic park on Kyushu island embellished with a castle and a priceless collection of plants and shrubs. But the park was actually a garden of death; its woods stocked with poisonous vegetation and crawling with snakes, scorpions and spiders; and its lakes alive with the deadly piranha. It a

---

THE MAN WITH THE GOLDEN GUN

there was little question about it; james bond was a sick man—yet there was a final, deadly mission for him to perform

Part One of the final novel

By IAN FLEMING

They threw themselves on Bond and even as they seized him his head fell forward on his chest.

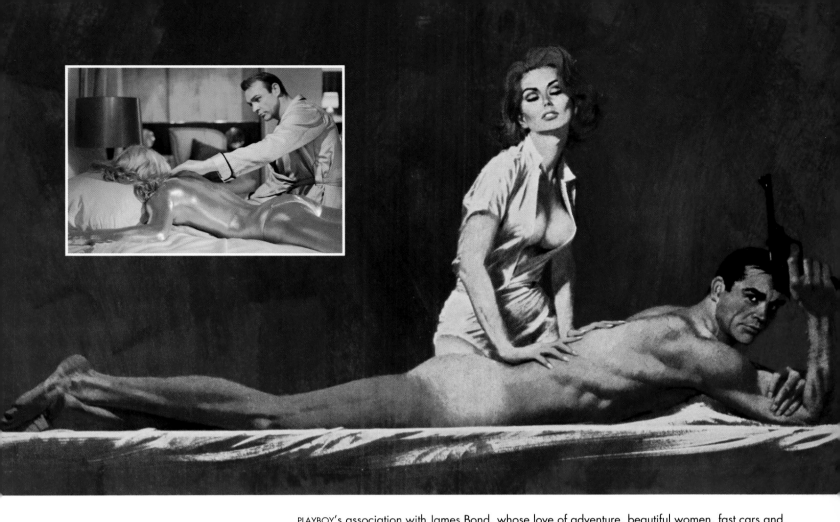

PLAYBOY's association with James Bond, whose love of adventure, beautiful women, fast cars and sophisticated gadgetry embodied the fantasies Hefner and his readers shared, was cemented as the decade progressed. For a time, the magazine serialized a new Bond adventure annually, starting with *On Her Majesty's Secret Service* (preceding spread). *You Only Live Twice* and *The Man With the Golden Gun* followed. Over the years, PLAYBOY has published ten Bond-related pictorials, showcasing scenes such as Sean Connery's discovery of Shirley Eaton's gilded corpse in *Goldfinger* (inset) and the classic poster for *Thunderball* (above), in which Claudine Auger treats Bond to a backrub. Connery had made his Bond debut in *Dr. No*, along with a woman who was to become a PLAYBOY pictorial favorite, Ursula Andress (below).

Romance was the essential ingredient in PLAYBOY's service features of the early Sixties. *Playboy on the Town in Paris* (April 1962), one of a series of guides to the world's great cities, featured "a guy and his gay *amie*" climbing to new heights in Montmartre (left); a piece on airplanes advocated the North Star Airparks Riviera amphibian as "the answer to a harried exec's need to get away from it all"—with a female companion (above). In *Thanksgiving Dinner à Deux* (right), Thomas Mario showed bachelors the way to a woman's heart through oysters, roast squab and champagne. And the BSA Rocket 3 from *Vroom at the Top* (below) is "powered for high-performance pleasure." Picnics, too.

When Hefner asked for a staff volunteer to become the magazine's football expert, Anson Mount raised his hand. From 1958 until his death in 1986, Smokey (as everyone called him) wrote *Playboy's Pigskin Preview* and, later, other sports forecasts—while also working in the promotion department and serving as religion editor. In the *Wyatt Summary*—the Nielsen ratings of college football forecasting—Mount finished first among the nation's sportswriters five times and second six times. It was "the best record of anyone in the country," said *Summary* publisher W. Judd Wyatt. For *Playboy's* 1962 Preview All-America Team, Mount picked Michigan State's Duffy Daugherty (bottom row, far left) to coach a squad that consisted of, among others, TCU quarterback Sonny Gibbs (top row, left).

George Bernard Shaw's play *Candida*—better known today as the foundation for Leonard Bernstein's musical *Candide*—celebrates the exuberance of innocence. Terry Southern's underground novel *Candy*, with its irresistible heroine constantly defending her virtue, updated the concept. But it was Harvey Kurtzman and Will Elder, collaborators at *Mad* magazine, who brought the fully developed character to life in the pages of PLAYBOY with the October 1962 debut of the adventures of *Little Annie Fanny*. Kurtzman, who died in 1993, was cited in *The New York Times* as "one of the most influential figures of postwar America; a man who helped create a sea-change in American humor."

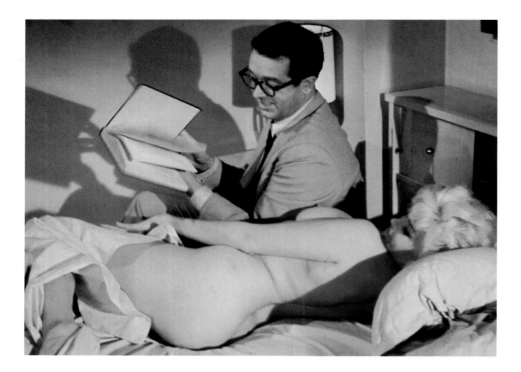

A cinema buff since his teenage days as an usher in a Chicago theater, Hefner loved to incorporate movie pictorials in his magazine. One of them, *The Nudest Jayne Mansfield* (June 1963, left) earned him an obscenity arrest from the Chicago police. The episode ended in a hung jury, but Hefner was convinced the authorities' real motive was their objection to his criticism of their Lenny Bruce bust in *The Playboy Philosophy*. A December 1962 pictorial showcased Arlene Dahl (left center); Tina Louise (below) appeared in several pictorial features, as well as in *Gilligan's Island*. Stella Stevens' appearance as Miss January 1960 (bottom) gave a boost to her budding movie career. When a Tennessee preacher railed against her PLAYBOY appearance, she replied: "It was my decision and mine alone. If it was a mistake, I'll learn from it. If it was not, and I don't think it was, I'll profit by it." She did. Her fan mail went up 1000 percent and she became an established Hollywood actress.

LIZ AS CLEO

*an exclusive unveiling
of a queen
in a taylor-made role*

WHEN ELIZABETH TAYLOR applied a six-inch Egyptian asp to her snowy bosom in Rome last summer, and thereby brought to a close the celluloid life of Cleopatra, the gesture was fraught with symbolic irony: While she dispatched the Nile Queen, Liz was also writing finis to the costliest movie opus in history, 20th Century-Fox's nearly calamitous *Cleopatra*. Bedeviled by Elizabeth's illnesses, hamstrung by pyramiding production costs and plagued by the offscreen antics of its principals, the epic will start its run this spring a hefty $37,000,000 in the red, with the future of Fox's fortunes riding squarely on its box-office take. When the first flack-happy press releases appeared announcing that Queen Liz had been signed to play Queen Cleo, the role-call struck most observers as an

Above: a clutch of Little Egypts puts on a floor show for banqueting Cleopatra (Liz) and her Latin lover, Mark Antony (Richard Burton), in a typically sumptuous scene from the Fox extravaganza. Liz and Richard's affectionate offscreen ad liberties stirred up an international ruckus that became a cause célèbre in gossip columns. Left and far left: looking like a million (considerably less than what she'll earn for her portrayal of the Sphinx lynx), crowned princess Elizabeth Taylor is every inch Cleopatra as she poses in two of 60 regal gowns created for her use in the film. It was Liz' lack of costume in the bath scene, however, that provoked the most publicity coverage.

It was the movie that nearly bankrupted Twentieth Century Fox, broke up two marriages and led to the tempestuous union of Elizabeth Taylor and Richard Burton. For PLAYBOY, however, the filming of *Cleopatra* brought the irresistible opportunity to publish exclusive behind-the-scenes photography by actor Roddy McDowall.

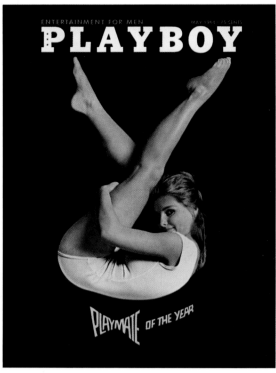

An important lady in the life of the magazine—and its publisher—was Donna Michelle, Miss December 1963 and Playmate of the Year in 1964. Her Playmate appearance earned her a part in a Warren Beatty movie, but in her later career she stationed herself on the other side of the lens, as a photographer. Of all the Rabbit Heads that have appeared on PLAYBOY's covers, Donna's May 1964 turn is by far the most athletic. She was still in fabulous shape 21 years later, when she posed for the magazine again.

Well before the daily work-out became part of the routine for every California girl, Miss October 1965 (and 1966 Playmate of the Year) Allison Parks (left) was preaching the gospel of physical fitness, giving swimming lessons to preschoolers. Dinah Willis, a professional poodle breeder and clipper from Hobbs, New Mexico, wrote to the magazine in 1965 asking if she had what it took to become a Playmate. She did, and PLAYBOY put her on its December centerfold (below)—along with a picture story chronicling her arrival at Chicago's O'Hare International Airport, where she experienced the first escalator ride of her life. China Lee (right), PLAYBOY's August 1964 Playmate, won a role in the Woody Allen film *What's Up, Tiger Lily?* and married hip satirist Mort Sahl.

RED RYDER NAILS THE HAMMOND KID
NOSTALGIA BY JEAN SHEPHERD

two renowned good guys, santa claus and iona pearl bodkin, combine forces to teach that deadeye gunslinger of warren g. harding elementary school an unforgettable yuletide lesson

IN ANGRY RED block letters, the slogan gleamed out like a neon sign from the big white button: DISARM THE TOY INDUSTRY. That's what it said. There was no question about it. The button was worn by an indignant little old lady wearing what looked like an upturned flowerpot on her head and, I suspect, a pair of Keds on her feet, which were primly hidden by the Automat table at which we both sat.

Toying moodily with my chicken pot pie, which is a *spécialité de la maison*, I surreptitiously examined my fellow diner. Wiry, lightly powdered, tough as spring steel, she dug with gusto into her meal: succotash, baked beans, creamed corn, side order of Harvard beets. Bad news—a vegetarian type. No doubt also a dedicated cat fancier. Silently we shared our tiny table and shoveled it in as the great throng of pre-Christmas quick-lunchers eddied and surged urgently around us. Finally I could contain myself no longer.

"Disarm the toy industry?" I asked.

She sat unmoved, her bright pink and ivory dental plates working over a mouthful of beets, attacking them with a raven-ousness usually associated with the larger carnivores. The red juice ran down over her chin and stained her white lace bodice. I tried another opener:

"Pardon me, madam, you're dripping."

"Eh?"

Her ice-blue eyes flashed angrily for a moment and then softened.

"Why, thank you, sonny."

She dabbed at her chin with a paper napkin and I knew that contact had been made.

"Disarm the toy industry?" I asked again.

"It's an outrage!" she barked, causing two elderly gentlemen at the next table to spill soup on their vests.

"It's an outrage the way the toymakers are forcing the imple-ments of blasphemous war on our innocent children, on tiny babes who are helpless and know no better! It's all a Government plot! I know what they're up to! Our committee is on to them, and we intend to expose this degenerate Communist conspiracy!"

She spoke in the ringing tones of a true believer, her whole life obviously an unending fight against the forces of evil. Stand-ing suddenly, she spun on her left Ked and strode militantly out into the crisp, brilliant Christmas air—and back into the fray.

I sat rocking slightly in her wake for a few moments, stirring

Roy Schnackenberg's first of many PLAYBOY illustrations was the painting of the banjo artist at left, accompanying *Folk, Folkum and the New Citybilly*, Nat Hentoff's June 1963 critique of folk singers. Jean Shepherd's *Red Ryder Nails the Hammond Kid* was adapted by Hollywood into the 1983 movie hit *A Christmas Story*. The piece, like most of Shepherd's tales, mixed equal parts of nostalgia and wicked humor drawn from the author's Indiana childhood. The accompanying illustration is by Gordon Kibbee. Supreme Court Justice William O. Douglas took the U.S. Army Corps of Engineers to task in *The Public Be Dammed* for its riding roughshod over requirements for conservation and ecology. German-born artist Robert Von Neumann created the sculpture (right).

THE PUBLIC BE DAMMED

In 1960, PLAYBOY published what it thought was a spoof on the direction of fashion and called it *The Nude Look*. Designer Rudi Gernreich's eventual introduction of the topless bathing suit turned the joke into reality, as noted in a 1965 *Nude Look* feature (left and opposite). Other features such as *No Cover, No Minimum* (November 1966, above and below) introduced similar fashions.

"That starter is fresh!"

"That's the note I was telling you about."

"Where are the others?"

"First of all, you must learn to be preoccupied with sex!"

MARTIN LUTHER KING JR.: *"The Nobel award recognizes the amazing discipline of the Negro. Though we have had riots, the bloodshed we would have known without the discipline of nonviolence would have been frightening."*

FRANK SINATRA: *"I'm not unmindful of man's seeming need for some kind of faith; basically I'm for anything that gets you through the night, be it prayer, tranquilizers or a bottle of Jack Daniel's."*

MALCOLM X: *"Christ wasn't white. Christ was black. The poor, brainwashed Negro has been made to believe Christ was white to maneuver him into worshiping white men."*

THE PLAYBOY INTERVIEW

FIDEL CASTRO: *"I believe that the United States, with its imperialist foreign policy, is accelerating the radicalization process of revolutionary movements not only in Cuba but throughout the world."*

PRINCESS GRACE: *"I don't think birth control is something one can say arbitrarily should or shouldn't be practiced. As adult human beings, we should be able to decide such a personal thing for ourselves."*

BOB DYLAN: *"The word 'message' has a hernia-like sound. And message songs, as everybody knows, are a drag. Only college newspaper editors and single girls under 14 could possibly have time for them."*

Spiritual leaders, entertainers, activists and politicians all sat down for important PLAYBOY interviews during the mid-Sixties. Alex Haley's conversation with the controversial Black Muslim spokesman led to their collaboration on the revolutionary treatise *The Autobiography of Malcolm X.*

JOHN LENNON: *"If you say you're nonreligious, people assume you're antireligious. We're not sure what we are, but we're more agnostic than atheistic."*

PAUL MCCARTNEY: *"We'd be idiots to say it isn't a constant inspiration to be making a lot of money. It is to anyone. Why do business tycoons stay tycoons?"*

GEORGE HARRISON: *"Ringo and I are gettin' married to each other. But that's a thing you better keep a secret. People would probably think we're queers."*

RINGO STARR: *"We used to get in the car, and I'd look over at John and say, 'Christ, you're a bloody phenomenon!' and laugh—'cause it was only him."*

The *Playboy Interview* of the Beatles was the only one ever conducted by Jean Shepherd—better known as the magazine's four-time humor award winner—who happened to be an acquaintance of the band's manager, Brian Epstein. The result appeared in the February 1965 issue.

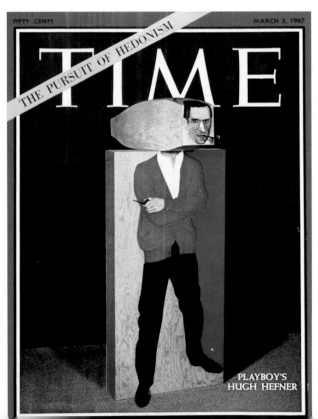

Late in 1966 Playboy's publishing, Club and related enterprises moved into new headquarters in the former Palmolive Building. The 37-story skyscraper on Chicago's Michigan Avenue (above) was rechristened—in nine-foot-high block letters—the Playboy Building. The sight of the Lindbergh Beacon atop the building sweeping across Chicago's skyline had inspired Hefner's fantasies; now he owned it. Hefner's own offices were in the Playboy Mansion, where he spent more and more of his time (opposite, he reviews photo transparencies on his circular, motor-driven, rotating, vibrating bed). By now, Hefner was world famous and instantly recognizable on the March 3, 1967 *Time* magazine cover.

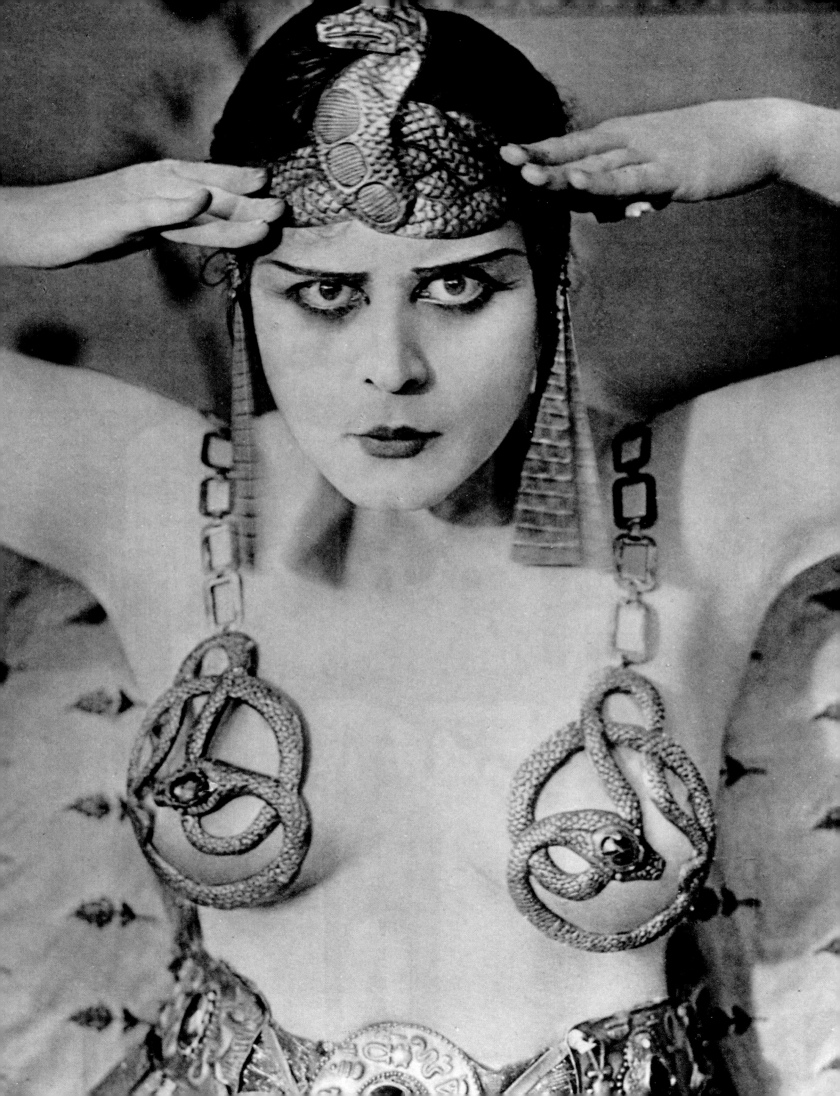

In 1965 PLAYBOY introduced one of its most ambitious projects to date, *The History of Sex in Cinema.* Authored by noted critics Arthur Knight and Hollis Alpert, the series ran for 19 installments and has continued via yearly updates ever since. The shot of *The Kiss,* with May Irwin and John C. Rice (left)—a sensation in the nickelodeons of 1896—led off the series.

Screen goddesses recalled in the *Sex in Cinema* series included Theda Bara (opposite), Mae West (above) and Jean Harlow (right, in previously unseen shots submitted by a reader and published in April 1966).

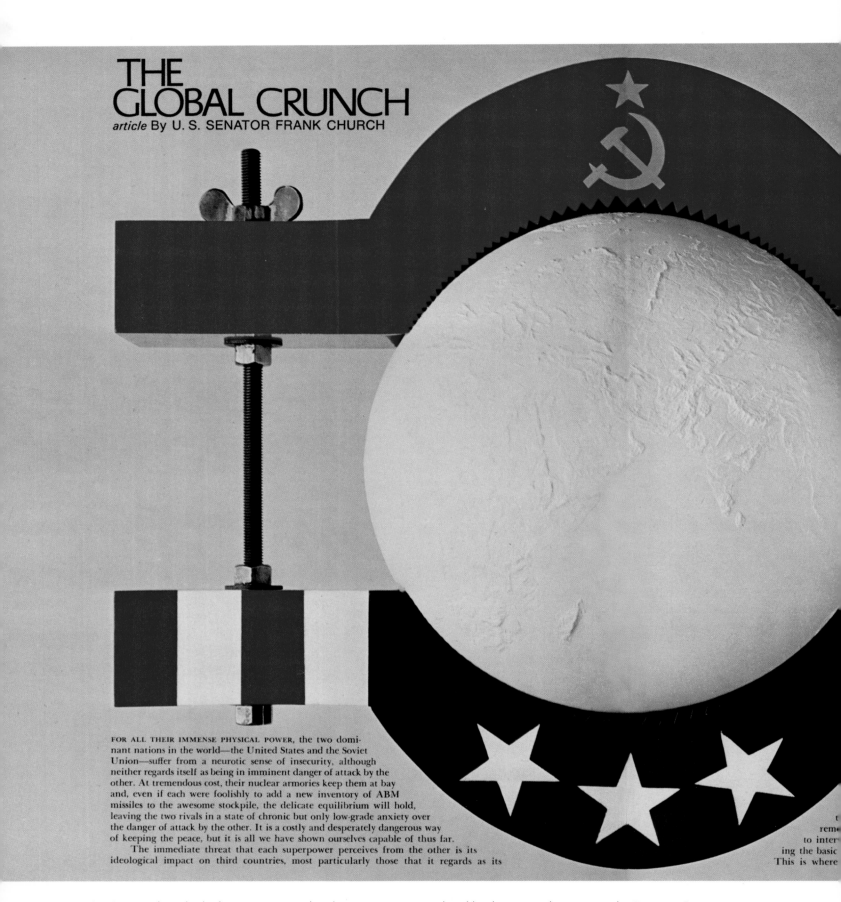

THE GLOBAL CRUNCH

article By U. S. SENATOR FRANK CHURCH

FOR ALL THEIR IMMENSE PHYSICAL POWER, the two domi-
nant nations in the world—the United States and the Soviet
Union—suffer from a neurotic sense of insecurity, although
neither regards itself as being in imminent danger of attack by the
other. At tremendous cost, their nuclear armories keep them at bay
and, even if each were foolishly to add a new inventory of ABM
missiles to the awesome stockpile, the delicate equilibrium will hold,
leaving the two rivals in a state of chronic but only low-grade anxiety over
the danger of attack by the other. It is a costly and desperately dangerous way
of keeping the peace, but it is all we have shown ourselves capable of thus far.

The immediate threat that each superpower perceives from the other is its
ideological impact on third countries, most particularly those that it regards as its

Issue-oriented articles by big-name writers, legislators, economists, political leaders, even clergymen and a Supreme Court justice were
hallmarks of PLAYBOY in the mid to late Sixties. The Cold War and Vietnam monopolized political discourse. Senator Frank Church wrote
of the hair-trigger nerves of the world's dueling superpowers, and in 1967 John Kenneth Galbraith proposed, in *Resolving Our Vietnam
Predicament* (opposite), an honorable way out of Vietnam eight years before the last helicopter lifted off the U.S. Embassy roof in Saigon.

a member of the senate committee
n foreign relations makes the case for abandoning
"spheres-of-influence" foreign policy in favor of a
realistic new approach

protective buffers. It is one of the supposed realities of
international politics—a kind of higher law transcending
such legal documents as the United Nations Charter—that
great powers are allowed to have spheres of influence made
up of "friendly" neighbors. In the case of maritime powers such
as the United States, the neighborhood may extend to the fringes
distant continents; but, whether or not the buffer is contiguous,
principle is the same: In order to guard itself against even the most
r hypothetical threat to its security, a great power is held entitled
in the affairs of its small neighbors, even to the extent of mak-
sions as to how they will organize and run their own societies.
ology comes in. Neither the Soviet (continued on page 86)

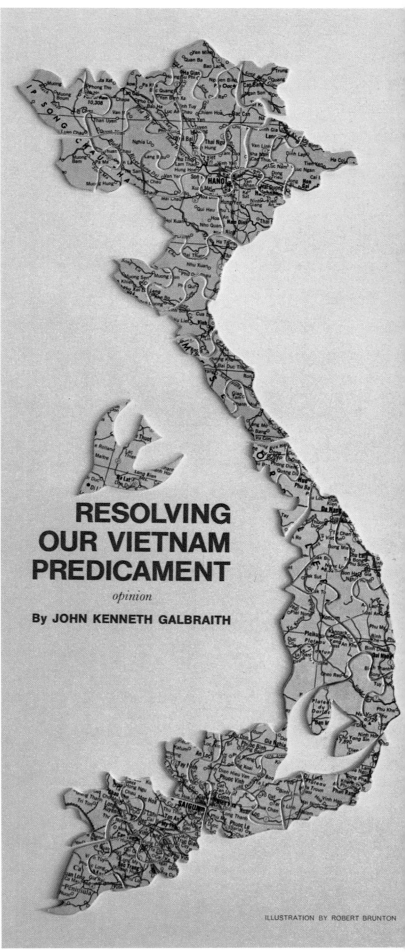

RESOLVING
OUR VIETNAM
PREDICAMENT

opinion

By JOHN KENNETH GALBRAITH

ILLUSTRATION BY ROBERT BRUNTON

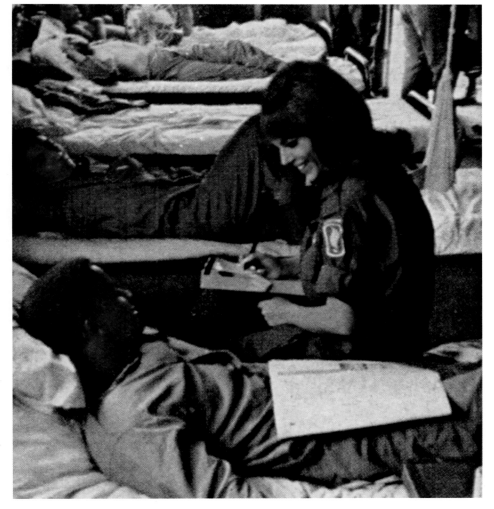

Writing in the *Washington Post* in 1967, Ward Just observed: "If World War Two was the war of *Stars and Stripes* and Betty Grable, the war in Vietnam is PLAYBOY's war and the centerfold Playmate is everybody's girlfriend, mistress or wife." In 1965 Hefner received a letter from an Army second lieutenant in Bien Hoa requesting that a Playmate deliver an issue of PLAYBOY to the members of his company, who'd chipped in to raise the $150 then advertised as the price of a lifetime subscription. PLAYBOY responded by sending 1965's Playmate of the Year, Jo Collins, to the front—and reporting on her adventures in the May 1966 issue. Reminiscing 20 years later, after attending a reunion of the 173rd Airborne Brigade in Washington, D.C., Jo told a magazine staffer that the trip "was the most wonderful, exciting experience of my life. But it was frightening." And often sad. "At one of the field hospitals," she recalled, "there was a man who had just been brought in off the helicopter. He'd been blown up. They asked me to see him, and I went in. He said, `I'm so glad you're here, sweetheart,' and with that he died. I will never forget that—never."

Shots taken during the filming of Marilyn Monroe's unfinished last movie, *Something's Got to Give*, were published as part of a January 1964 tribute, *MM Remembered*. Other star pictorials featured Woody Allen in the PLAYBOY sendup *Shindai* with model Bettina Brenna (opposite top left), Catherine Deneuve (opposite top right) and Peter Sellers (in the spoof *Sellers Mimes the Movie Lovers*, opposite). In a pose from that April 1964 pictorial, Sellers became the first male on a PLAYBOY cover.

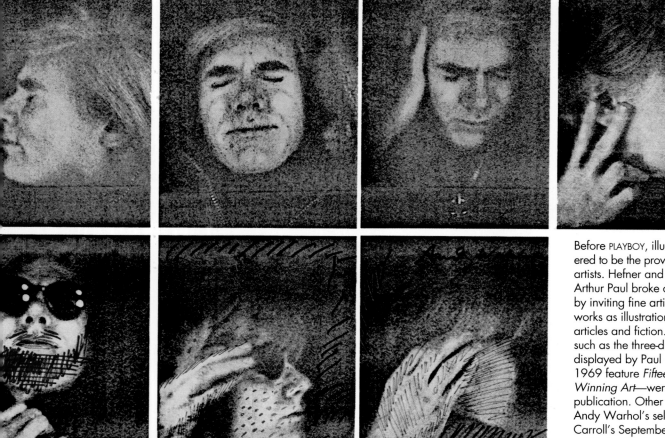

Before PLAYBOY, illustration was considered to be the province of the commercial artists. Hefner and Founding Art Director Arthur Paul broke down that distinction by inviting fine artists to contribute their works as illustrations for the magazine's articles and fiction. Even sculptures—such as the three-dimensional pieces displayed by Paul (top) in the January 1969 feature *Fifteen Years of Award-Winning Art*—were photographed for publication. Other illustrations included Andy Warhol's self-portraits from Paul Carroll's September 1969 piece *What's a Warhol?* (left and above) and Don Punchatz' depiction of an unraveling Sigmund Freud (opposite) from *Crisis in Psychoanalysis* by Morton Hunt.

TEEVEE JEEBIES

satire **By SHEL SILVERSTEIN**

"Of course, I was much younger then ...."

"A lot of cowboys grow attached to their horses, but let's face it—you're *involved!*"

"Look, it shouldn't be so difficult to remember: the back of your collar goes *down* and the back of your hat goes *up!*"

"Which one of you gentlemen called for room service?"

"You little devil—I thought you meant *Lipton's* tea!"

"Every morning—like clockwork—one grade A egg!"

The prolific Shel Silverstein created *Teevee Jeebies,* in which he tacked unlikely captions onto movie stills from TV's late, late shows.

"Now remember, I'm only 12 years old."

"Here come those damn pigeons again!"

"Yes, Mrs. Bernweather of Gary, Indiana, *this is your life* . . . ."

"Look at it his way—it's therapy."

"Oh—you're a telephone operator, for a minute I thought you'd been stabbed in the chest by a buffalo!"

"Now, Mr. Johnson, do you like girls?... Mr. Johnson? ... Mr. Johnson?!"

The series ran to 26 episodes—including this January 1960 example, *More Teevee Jeebies*—before coming to a halt in 1966.

"Wholly Toledo!" exclaimed PLAYBOY's headline writer when he caught sight of Miss December 1968, 39-24-36 Ohio eyeful Cynthia Myers (opposite, left). An early bloomer, Cynthia knew at the age of 15 that she was destined for PLAYBOY's centerfold—and wrote to the magazine to say so. Shortly after her graduation from high school, she flew to Chicago for her Playmate shooting. Argyles were all the rage when Gwen Wong (opposite, right) became PLAYBOY's Miss April 1967. Proving that old centerfold concepts never die, photographer Steven Meisel and pop star Madonna produced a near-identical pose in their October 1992 layout for *Vanity Fair* magazine. The wreck of the Italian liner Andrea Doria was fresh in the mind of Victoria Vetri's agent when the young actress posed for the magazine's September 1967 centerfold. He proposed a *nom de* PLAYBOY for his client, who was introduced to readers as Angela Dorian (top). She kept that ID as Playmate of the Year for 1968, but reassumed her real name for roles in *Rosemary's Baby* and other films. DeDe Lind (left), Miss August 1967, received more letters—"mostly from GIs and college boys"— than any other Playmate in history (the total topped 1600). Connie Kreski (above), Miss January 1968 and Playmate of the Year for 1969, was a student nurse in Detroit when PLAYBOY discovered her. That was before Anthony Newley cast her in the role of Mercy in his *Can Hieronymus Merkin Ever Forget Mercy Humppe and Find True Happiness?*, a 1969 film also starring Joan Collins, his wife at the time.

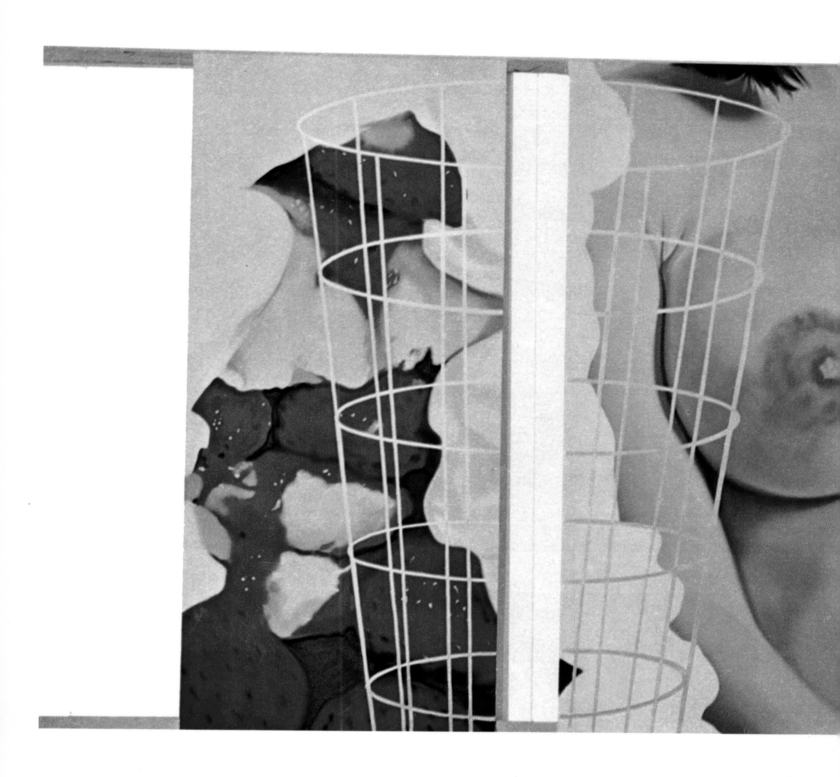

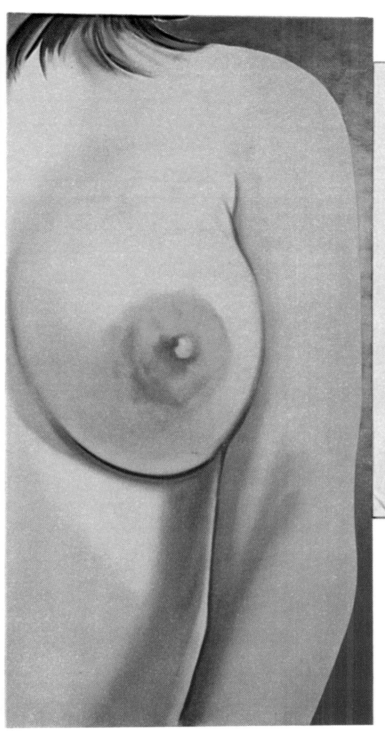

For *The Playmate as Fine Art* (January 1967), PLAYBOY asked 11 famed artists to interpret the magazine's centerfolds in varying media. Top: James Rosenquist's juxtaposition of a girl, wastebasket, pickle and strawberry shortcake, which filled two canvases measuring seven by sixteen feet; at right, Larry Rivers' five-foot-tall plexiglass and metal construction.

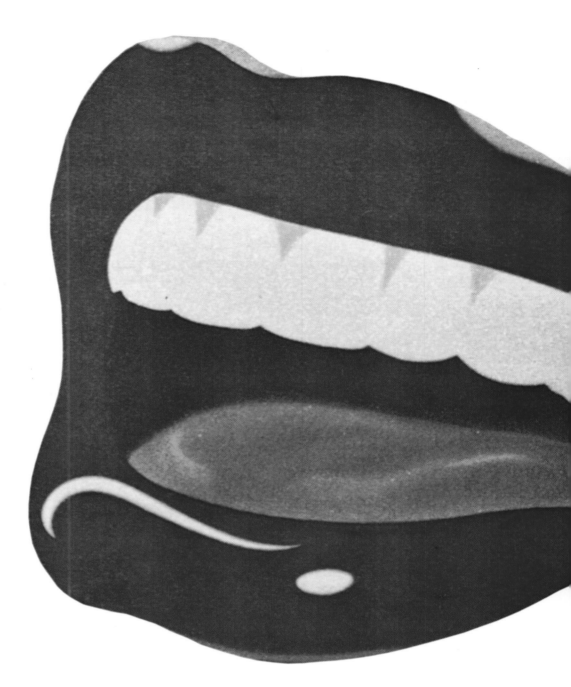

More interpretations of *The Playmate as Fine Art*: Tom Wesselman's reduction of the centerfold to lips, "the one body part that has a high degree of both sexual and expressive connotations"; Andy Warhol's silk screen, which reveals its double Playmate torso only under ultraviolet light (below); George Segal's plaster cast of *Pregnant Woman* (below right); two views of Frank Gallo's epoxy-resin sculpture (far right); Ben Johnson's oil on canvas (extreme right); and the languorous water color from Salvador Dalí's classic period, a conscious imitation of a Velázquez Venus (bottom, far right).

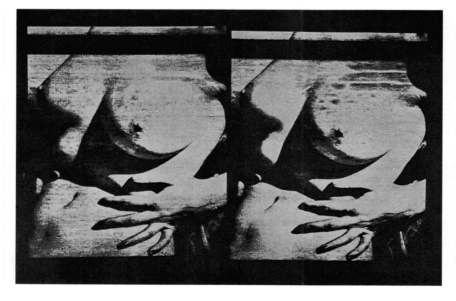

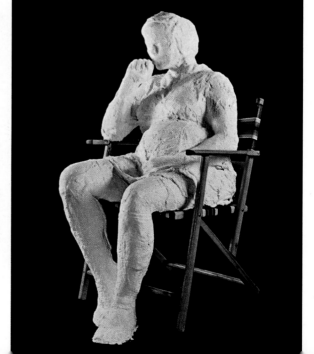

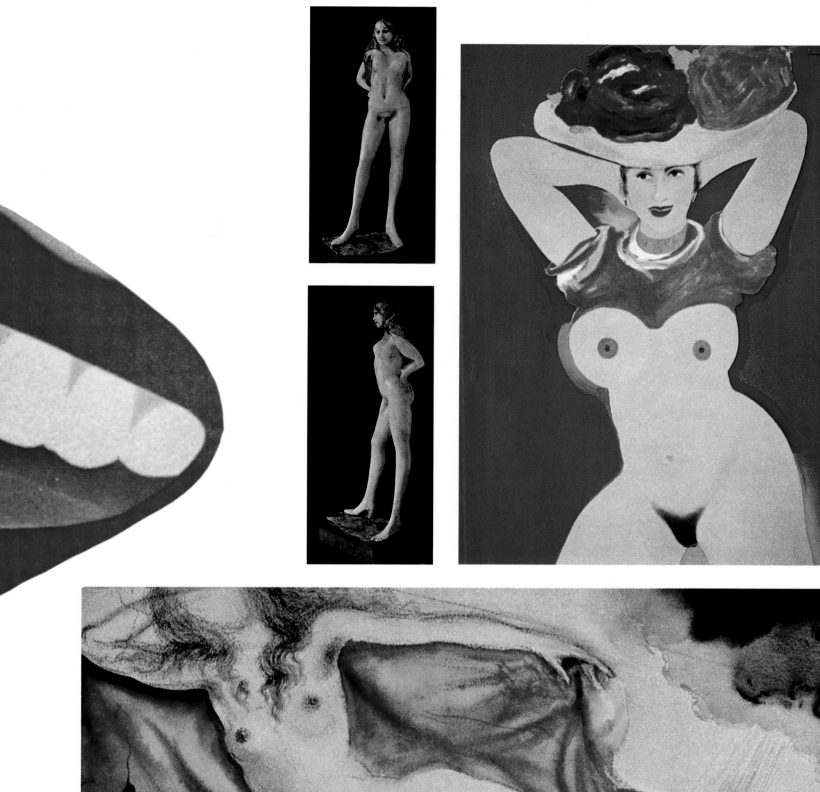

Nehru suits, bell-bottoms, wide ties, medallions and Edwardian jackets seemed like a good idea at the time. PLAYBOY's fashion forecast in the late Sixties had an answer for every fashion question and a pictorial for every fashion taste. "A galaxy of avant-garde food, drink, costumes and decor for hosting a way-out wingding" was promised in *Zap-In*, a 1969 Modern Living extravaganza (opposite) that offered a how-to guide for throwing an out-of-this-world New Year's Eve costume ball. Tips included sending out invitations in a plastic spaceship, suggesting to guests they style their garb after far-out science-fiction flicks and decorate with battery-powered zap guns, black lights, swinging mobiles and helium-filled weather balloons.

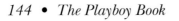

"I always like to shower afterward anyway,
don't you, Miss Wingate?"

"You never sock it to me anymore."

"'Dear Playboy Advisor . . . .'"

*"Either of you gentlemen
care for something to nibble on?"*

"OK, team—here's the opening kickoff . . .!"

During the nearly two decades of his association with PLAYBOY, Alberto Vargas produced exclusive monthly pinups for the magazine. Reid Austin, a former art director at PLAYBOY, was instrumental in getting the relationship off the ground. "I'd always been a fan," recalls Austin, "and in 1960 I discovered some unused slides from our 1957 Vargas pictorial, blew them up to about 20 inches high and stuck them up on the cork wall of my office, directly in Hefner's view whenever he walked by. One day he stuck his head in the door and said 'maybe.' Within three months we had Vargas in PLAYBOY. It was a way to get more sex into the magazine without adding another photo feature, and besides that, I think Vargas spoke to Hef's feelings of nostalgia for the old days at *Esquire*." Vargas would sketch his concepts on tissue and submit them, usually in batches of 12, to Austin and Hefner for alterations and approval. Once all were satisfied and a Vargas girl had been chosen, editorial staffers, spurred by a monthly $50 prize, vied to create the wittiest accompanying caption for the pinup.

"Mirror, mirror, in my hand,
This coat was priced at fourteen grand.
What *I* paid could be shown clearer,
If I but had a full-length mirror."

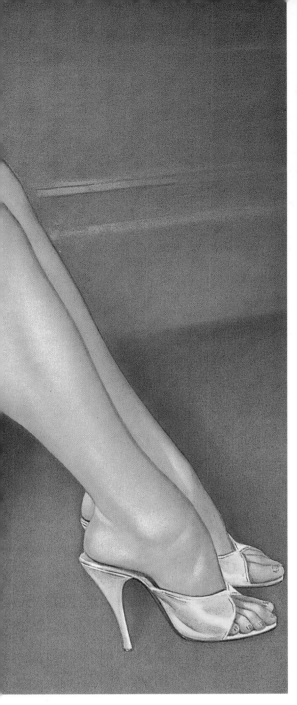

Such Sixties phenomena as psychedelia and body-painting inspired PLAYBOY covers of the decade's closing years. A Sacramento-born coed named Barbara Klein posed for July 1969's cover (opposite); readers were soon to know her better as Barbi Benton.

ENTERTAINMENT FOR MEN

JULY 1969 • ONE DOLLAR

PLAYBOY

PLAYBOY INTERVIEWS ROD STEIGER, GOES ON A FUN-BUGGY BASH, FOCUSES ON A FLOCK OF SEXY AMERICAN BIRDS, EXAMINES THE SENSUAL "LETTING GO" MOVEMENT, PLUGS INTO THE WORLD OF ROBOTS AND OFFERS FACT AND FICTION BY JUSTICE WILLIAM O. DOUGLAS, EVAN HUNTER, J. PAUL GETTY, HEINRICH BÖLL, ROGER PRICE AND DONALD E. WESTLAKE

SEX, ECSTASY AND THE PSYC

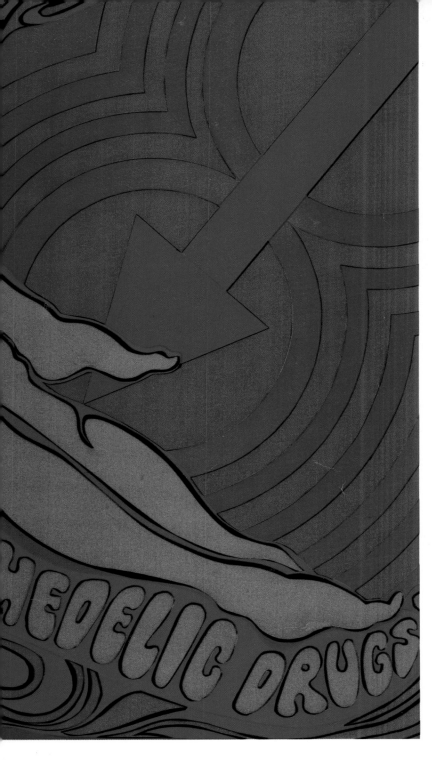

As drug experimentation proliferated in the late Sixties, PLAYBOY cut through the hype and became a respected source of information—pro and con—on the substances of choice. In *Sex, Ecstasy and the Psychedelic Drugs*, author R.E.L. Masters appraised "the delights and hazards of chemically enhanced or induced eroticism." The illustration is by PLAYBOY staffer Chet Suski. In *Pot: A Rational Approach*, Dr. Joel Fort, a leading authority on psychopharmacology, called for a lifting of legal prohibitions and penalties related to marijuana use. In *The Death of Politics* (March 1969), former Goldwater advisor Karl Hess advocated "a real laissez-faire society," in which "the local entrepreneur could go openly into business—selling marijuana, whiskey, numbers slips, books, food or medical advice from the trunk of his car."

Themed pictorials reflected the exuberance of an active decade. Enduring features from the late Sixties: *Brush-On Fashions*, a 1968 concoction that celebrated op art (left) and prefigured *Vanity Fair*'s 1992 cover treatment of Demi Moore in a body-painted business suit (below left); *Oh! Calcutta!* (opposite, top), a report on the notorious nude musical created by PLAYBOY Contributing Editor Kenneth Tynan; and *Sweet Paula* (right), an August 1969 paean to the sensuous dancing of *Sweet Charity*'s Paula Kelly—noteworthy for the fact that it marked the first appearance of pubic hair in the magazine.

LIONEL HAMPTON
vibes

GINGER BAKER
drums

BOOKER T.
organ

HERB ALPERT
first trumpet

AL HIRT
second trumpet

DON
SEVER
thir

JIMI HENDRIX
guitar

J. J. JOHNSON
first trombone

SI ZENTNER
second trombone

KAI WI
third tro

PLAYBOY ALLSTARS
197

PETE FOUNTAIN
clarinet

CANNONBALL
ADDERLEY
first alto sax

PAUL DESMOND
second alto sax

STAN G
first ten

RAVI
SHANKAR
sitar

DAVE BRUBECK
piano

TOM JONES
male vocalist

JANIS JOPLIN
female vocalist

HENRY MANCINI
leader

P
McCA
electr
songwrite

Frank Sinatra

Louis Armstrong

Dave Brubeck

Dating from 1956, the venerable *Playboy Jazz Poll* was almost as old as the magazine, and in 1969, was transformed into the *Playboy Jazz & Pop Poll*. The results of that competition were very telling about the times and about PLAYBOY itself: The magazine had retained its early readers from the Fifties and had become one of the few institutions to span the much-vaunted generation gap as it picked up young new readers during the Sixties. Readers' tastes ranged from Cannonball Adderley and Boots Randolph to Jimi Hendrix and the Beatles. Musicians chosen by readers to become members of the Hall of Fame were immortalized in busts created by Jack Gregory.

ILLUSTRATION BY BILL UTTERBACK

MILES DAVIS
fourth trumpet

BOB
BROOKMEYER
fourth ~~~~~hone

BOOTS
RANDOLPH
second tenor sax

GERRY
MULLIGAN
baritone sax

BLOOD, SWEAT & TEARS
instrumental combo

BEATLES
vocal group

JOHN LENNON
songwriter/composer

NEY
~ass,
omposer

John Coltrane

Benny Goodman

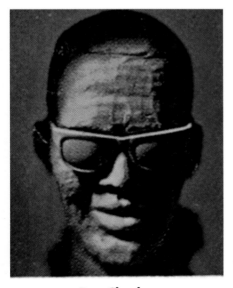

Ray Charles

Duke Ellington

Ella Fitzgerald

Count Basie

A TESTAMENT OF HOPE

in his final published statement, the fallen civil rights leader points the way out of america's racial turmoil into the promised land of true equality

By DR. MARTIN LUTHER KING, JR.

WHENEVER I AM ASKED my opinion of the current state of the civil rights movement, I am forced to pause; it is not easy to describe a crisis so profound that it has caused the most powerful nation in the world to stagger in confusion and bewilderment. Today's problems are so acute because the tragic evasions and defaults of several centuries have accumulated to disaster proportions. The luxury of a leisurely approach to urgent solutions—the ease of gradualism—was forfeited by ignoring the issues for too long. The nation waited until the black man was explosive with fury before stirring itself even to partial concern. Confronted now with the interrelated problems of war, inflation, urban decay, white backlash and a climate of violence, it is now *forced* to address itself to race relations and poverty, and it is tragically unprepared. What might once have been a series of separate problems now merge into a social crisis of almost stupefying complexity.

I am not sad that black Americans are rebelling; this was not only inevitable but eminently desirable. Without this magnificent ferment among Negroes, the old evasions and procrastinations would have continued indefinitely. Black men have slammed the door shut on a past of deadening passivity. Except for the Reconstruction years, they have never in their long history on American soil struggled with such creativity and courage for their freedom. These are our bright years of emergence; though they are painful ones, they cannot be avoided.

Yet despite the widening of our stride, history is racing forward so rapidly that the Negro's inherited and imposed disadvantages slow him down to an infuriating crawl. Lack of education, the dislocations of recent urbanization and the hardening of white resistance loom as such tormenting roadblocks that the goal sometimes appears not as a fixed point in the future but as a receding point never to be reached. Still, when doubts emerge, we can remember that only yesterday Negroes were not only grossly exploited but negated as human beings. They were invisible in their misery. But the sullen and silent slave of 110 years ago, an object of scorn at worst or of pity at best, is today's angry man. He is vibrantly on the move; he is forcing change, rather than waiting for it in pathetic futility. In less than two decades, he has roared out of slumber to change so many of his life's conditions that he may yet find the means to accelerate his march forward and overtake the racing locomotive of history.

These words may have an unexpectedly optimistic ring at a time when pessimism is the prevailing mood. People are often surprised to learn that I am an optimist. They know how often I have been jailed, how frequently the days and nights have been filled with frustration and sorrow, how bitter and dangerous are my adversaries. They expect these experiences to harden me into a grim and desperate man. They fail, however, to perceive the sense of affirmation generated by the challenge of embracing struggle and surmounting obstacles. They have no comprehension of the strength that comes from faith in God and man. It is possible for me to falter, but I am profoundly secure in my knowledge that God loves us; He has not worked out a design for our failure. Man has the capacity to do right as well as wrong, and his history is a path upward, not downward. The past is strewn with the ruins of the empires of tyranny, and each is a monument not merely to man's blunders but to his capacity to overcome them. While it is a bitter fact that in America in 1968, I am denied equality solely because I am black, yet I am not a chattel slave. Millions of people have fought thousands of battles to enlarge my freedom; restricted as it still is, progress has been made. This is why I remain an optimist, though I am also a realist, about the barriers before us. Why is the issue of equality still so far from solution *(continued on page 194)*

A Testament of Hope, which appeared in the January 1969 issue, was the last published work by the Reverend Dr. Martin Luther King. In this thoughtful statement, the fallen civil rights leader pointed the way out of America's racial turmoil and into the promised land of true equality. A quarter of a century before passage of the Brady law, former Senator Joseph Tydings pleaded for gun control. In *Americans and the Gun* (March 1969), Tydings bemoaned the fact that guns were involved in 130,000 crimes per year.

R.F.K.—HARBINGER OF HOPE

his political philosophy and his deep humanity are recalled by a distinguished colleague and a family friend

THE STATESMAN
BY ARTHUR SCHLESINGER, JR.

IT IS HARD to write about a man murdered on the threshold of his highest possibility—hard because one recoils from the horror of the deed, hard because all one has left is speculation. Abraham Lincoln and John Kennedy at least had their time in the White House before they were shot down. Robert Kennedy was denied the full testing of his gifts. No one can say now what sort of President he might have been. But one can say something, I believe, about the nature of his impact on American politics and the character of his legacy.

When he was killed, Robert Kennedy was seeking the Presidential nomination of the Democratic Party. This fact automatically defines the traditions with which he began. He was, first of all, a Kennedy; and that is a tradition by itself. It meant that he was committed to courage, public service, self-discipline, ambition, candor, asking questions, getting things done, finishing first, children, banter, dogs, physical fitness and other life-enhancing goals.

It also meant that this total and ardent commitment to life was enveloped by a somber apprehension of human mortality. His oldest brother was killed in the War, his next oldest by an assassin; his sister and three of his wife's family died in airplane accidents; his younger brother nearly died in an airplane accident. Every Kennedy had to make his personal treaty with tragedy. Robert Kennedy read Aeschylus and Camus and evolved a sort of Christian stoicism and existentialism that gave him both a fatalism about life and an understanding that man's destiny was to struggle against his fate. No one would have been less surprised by the way his own life came to an end.

He also inherited a tradition as a Democrat. In this century, the Democratic Party has been the popular party in America, the party of human rights and social justice. His father had been a conservative Democrat who first supported and then deplored Franklin Roosevelt. The

THE MAN
BY BUDD SCHULBERG

I FIRST MET Bob Kennedy eight years ago, through an unlikely intermediary—the late, irrepressible Hollywood producer Jerry Wald. Wald called me at my home in Mexico City to ask me if I would be interested in writing the screenplay of Kennedy's then-recent best seller, *The Enemy Within*. He told me that the Attorney General had chosen me from a list of five likely screenwriters Jerry had sent him. I said that was interesting. I was curious to know why.

"Bobby"—Jerry began, being the kind of bubbly character who would, on first meeting, have called De Gaulle "Charley" and Einstein "Al"—"Bobby says he loved *On the Waterfront* and he's read quite a few of your pieces in magazines and he feels you haven't lost your zing for social causes." So I'd like you to fly up right away—I'll meet you in Washington tomorrow and then, if Bobby likes you personally, we can fly right back to Hollywood and work out the terms; so call me back and let me know what time you're coming in—I'll meet you at the airport or send the limo for you—what hotel do you like—Hay Adams? The Carlton?—I'll reserve a suite for you and——"

"Jerry—wait a minute! I'm glad he likes *Waterfront* and the other stuff, but I need time to think. I have to reread the book in terms of how I feel it could work as a picture——"

"You can be doing that on the plane," Jerry broke in.

"Hold it, Jerry—I need time. And then—this thing about personally liking me goes both ways. You say he has to have screenplay approval——"

"Budd, it's his book, and he is the Attorney General and——"

"Jerry, I need the kind of creative freedom I've had with Kazan, like a playwright in the theater. It could be that the Attorney General is too——"

I didn't use the word "arrogant," but of course it was on my mind. All those news

---

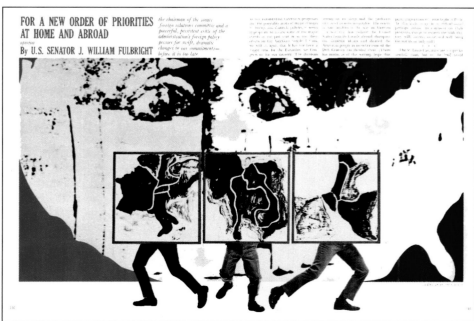

FOR A NEW ORDER OF PRIORITIES AT HOME AND ABROAD
By U.S. SENATOR J. WILLIAM FULBRIGHT

the chairman of the senate foreign relations committee and a powerful, persistent critic of the administration's foreign policy presses for swift, dramatic changes in our commitments—before it is too late

The January 1969 issue also memorialized 1968's other noteworthy assassination victim, Senator Robert F. Kennedy, with important pieces by Arthur Schlesinger Jr. and Budd Schulberg. The portrait of Kennedy, like that of King on the opposite page, is by Shelly Canton. In 1968 Senator J. William Fulbright, who served for 15 years as chairman of the Senate Foreign Relations Committee, used the magazine as a forum to ask *For A New Order of Priorities at Home and Abroad*, in which he warned that U.S. foreign policy was "turning Vietnam into a charnel house."

By the fall of 1968 Hefner was ready to alter his lifestyle. He embarked on a contemporary counterpart to *Playboy's Penthouse*, the new television venture *Playboy After Dark*—on the set of which he met a new love, Barbi Benton (top)—and made a guest appearance on the hit show *Laugh-In* (above left). His Playboy Clubs—which already numbered 16 urban locations and had enrolled more than 700,000 keyholders around the world—had expanded to include lavish properties in Jamaica (above and near right) and Lake Geneva, Wisconsin. Construction was planned for a third resort at Great Gorge, New Jersey (opposite). To facilitate visits to this growing empire, and to expand his personal horizons as well, Hefner ordered a stretch DC-9 jet, the Big Bunny, aboard which he planned to fly into a new decade.

THE SEVENTIES

The Sixties had so much momentum going that they overflowed into the Seventies. As 1970 dawned, the country was at war with itself over Vietnam, and PLAYBOY reflected both the tension in the country and the need to escape from it. The magazine came out swinging with some of the hardest-hitting journalism being published anywhere. David Halberstam's *The Americanization of Vietnam* and *The Vietnamization of America* laid bare the devastating consequences of America's continuing presence in that hapless country and the cost of that struggle to our own society. The testimony of John Kerry—now a Senator from Massachusetts, then a leader of Vietnam Veterans Against the War—was published in the *Playboy Forum* as "The Voice of the Winter Soldier." Heated pro- and anti-war debates in the *Forum*, letters to the editor, even cartoons, all took notice of the war's growing toll. The nation was so polarized that archconservative pundit William F. Buckley Jr. admitted that writing for PLAYBOY—despite his political differences with the magazine—was his only way of speaking directly to his son.

By the time the bitter conflict was finally reduced to a single chopper lifting off a rooftop in Saigon, America was caught up in another national drama: Watergate. Once again, PLAYBOY was in the thick of it. Early on, the magazine ran a spoof, *The Watergate Tapes*, which offered the absurd notion that President Nixon might have bugged his own office. A year later PLAYBOY took off the gloves and pre-published Woodward and Bernstein's blockbuster best-seller *All the President's Men*, giving the magazine's readers a ringside seat for the biggest political story of the decade.

But the political issue many readers may remember best from the Seventies is the *Playboy Interview* that ran in November 1976, the month of the national elections. At the end of his final taping session, presidential candidate Jimmy Carter confessed that he had "looked on a lot of women with lust." He went on to say that God forgave him for it—and the electorate did, too, by voting him in. That issue of PLAYBOY became a collector's item overnight, disappearing within days from every newsstand in the world.

With the sexual revolution, a spate of imitators riding in PLAYBOY's wake began a rush toward raunch, waging what the press termed the great Pubic Wars. Au naturel became natural. Frontal nudity was finally considered acceptable; January 1971 centerfold Liv Lindeland was the first to reveal a hint of pubic hair. As the Pubic Wars escalated, however, Hefner became something of a conscientious objector, insisting that the magazine remain true to the traditions of pinup art. The Playmate of the Month had become an American icon and he had no intention of allowing her to slip into sleaze. "Stop imitating the imitators" was Hefner's final word on the subject.

The Seventies saw the company turn its creative energies to film, television, records and book publishing. The Playboy Clubs expanded to more than 30 cities and a chain

Before it became a best-seller, before it was a movie with Redford and Hoffman—even before its real target, Richard M. Nixon, waved goodbye from a helicopter on the White House lawn—*All the President's Men* was serialized in PLAYBOY. It was one of the stories that defined the decade. The authors, a previously unheralded, dissimilar pair of *Washington Post* reporters named Bob Woodward and Carl Bernstein, turned in a bravura performance of investigative journalism that traced the coverup of a bungled burglary all the way to the Oval Office.

UCLA coed Barbara Klein, renamed Barbi Benton, reigned through much of the Seventies as Hefner's "personal playmate"—and starred in many PLAYBOY pictorials, though never as a Playmate of the Month. A powerful catalyst in his life, Barbi urged Hefner to purchase the property that would become Playboy Mansion West, then coaxed him into adventures as alien to the legendary indoorsman as world travel, skiing and parasailing. It was the first time, he declared, he'd ever really been in love.

When Playboy Enterprises, Inc. went public in 1971, many investors purchased single shares as collector's items. It was the only stock on the market that bore the image of a nude on each certificate: a reclining Willy Rey, that year's Miss February. "How far is too far?" editors and advertisers asked themselves as a swarm of skin magazines took on PLAYBOY in the anything-goes "Pubic Wars" of the mid-Seventies. The race toward raunch wasn't for PLAYBOY, Hefner decided, and the magazine maintained a sizable circulation edge over its more explicit competitors.

of multimillion-dollar hotels, resorts and casinos in America and abroad. Hefner took the company public in 1971, issuing a stock certificate illustrated with a reclining nude. It promptly became a collector's item.

The magazine's portrayal of women has always been a collaborative effort. When Superman's girlfriend Margot Kidder posed for PLAYBOY photos ("the prettiest ever taken," she said), Hefner let her write her own copy. Raquel Welch, Linda Evans, Victoria Principal, Veruschka, Barbara Bach and a reprise of Brigitte Bardot at 40 were just a few of the stars who brightened PLAYBOY's pages in the Seventies. For its 25th Anniversary the editors launched the first Great Playmate Hunt, and found Candy Loving, a college coed at the University of Oklahoma, for PLAYBOY's 25th Anniversary Playmate. More than 3000 women were tested—Dorothy Stratten among them; she came in second. Hefner (never one to let a good idea go unrepeated) would conduct Playmate Hunts for the magazine's 30th, 35th and 40th anniversaries.

Hefner was a dashing figure—the first magazine publisher to enjoy worldwide celebrity. He traveled in his custom ebony-black DC-9—the Big Bunny—flying from Playboy's headquarters in Chicago to L.A. for the weekly taping of his new television show, *Playboy After Dark*, and jetting off to such exotic locales as Acapulco, London, Paris or Rome. He picked up a six-acre Tudor estate in Holmby Hills, California that became his personal Shangri-La and the most famous private residence in the world. At Playboy Mansion West, surrounded by stars and centerfolds, Hef settled down to savor the fruits of the dream.

It was the most famous private plane in the world, and it took Hefner, his friends and PLAYBOY executives everywhere. The stretched DC-9 Big Bunny was the largest (119 feet long) and costliest ($5.5 million) big-business aircraft in the sky. *Look* magazine labeled it "the world's most extravagant toy" but conceded that it "was an effective aerial advertisement for its proprietor's product." The Big Bunny's unique features included a galley equipped for gourmet cuisine, a living room, disco, state-of-the-art movie and video equipment, a wet bar, sleeping quarters for 16 guests—and Hefner's own suite, which boasted a shower and an elliptical bed covered by a custom spread of Tasmanian opossum skins.

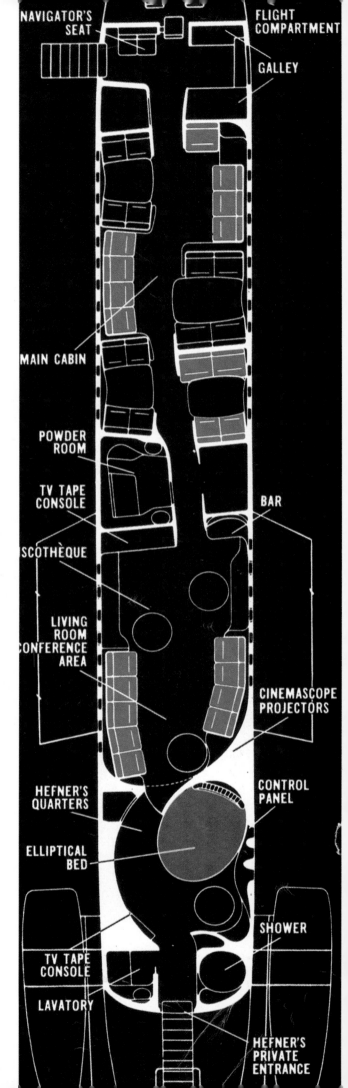

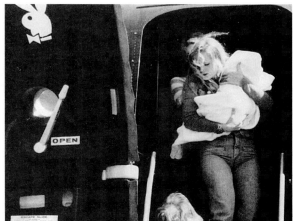

The Big Bunny was staffed by an elite corps of certified flight attendants called Jet Bunnies, who were outfitted in wet-look minidresses. It carried Hefner on an extended overseas trip—to Europe and Africa—in the summer of 1971 (above, with Barbi in Venice's Piazza San Marco). Jet Bunny (and Miss November 1970) Avis Miller serves Hefner and friend Shelly Kasten en route to Nairobi (top right). The Big Bunny sometimes carried unusual passengers: Answering a plea from Amanda Blake (*Gunsmoke*'s Miss Kitty), Hefner once lent the craft to advance a cross-country simian romance when no commercial airline would agree to fly a 283-pound male gorilla from Baltimore to console a recently widowed female at the Phoenix Zoo. In the Bunny Babylift of 1975 (right center), the jet transported 141 Vietnamese orphans from San Francisco to Denver and New York.

Five years before the fall of Saigon, Pulitzer Prize-winning reporter David Halberstam's wrenching *The Americanization of Vietnam* (painted by Ed Paschke, above) described the devastation that American policy visited on that country. Alvin Toffler expanded *Future Shock*, his treatise on the frightening pace of change in society, into a best-seller after its 1970 publication in the magazine (illustrated with constructions by Ron Bradford, right).

Seventy of PLAYBOY's most prestigious contributors (some of them shown at left) met with the magazine's editors during the Playboy International Writers' Convocation in October 1971. They flew to Chicago from the corners of the globe: Arthur C. Clarke from Sri Lanka, Alberto Moravia from Rome, V.S. Pritchett from London, Michael Crichton, Gay Talese, Alex Haley and dozens more from all over the U.S.—to participate in panel discussions, cocktail parties, a Playboy Mansion gala and the premiere of Playboy's new movie, Roman Polanski's *Macbeth*.

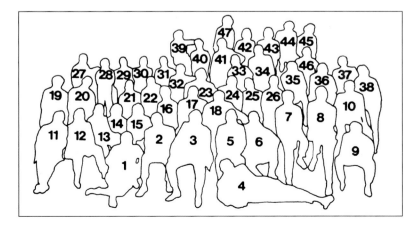

1. Gay Talese
2. A.C. Spectorsky
3. Hugh M. Hefner
4. Arthur C. Clarke
5. Art Buchwald
6. Shel Silverstein
7. Marvin Kitman
8. John Cheever
9. Arthur Schlesinger Jr.
10. Kenneth Tynan
11. Saul Braun
12. Richard Warren Lewis
13. Ken W. Purdy
14. John Kenneth Galbraith
15. Dan Greenburg
16. Herbert Gold

17. Sean O'Faolain
18. Nicholas Von Hoffman
19. Hal Bennett
20. George Axelrod
21. Mary Calderone
22. Joel Fort
23. Jean Shepherd
24. Calvin Trillin
25. Morton Hunt
26. Larry L. King
27. Larry DuBois
28. Garry Wills
29. William Simon
30. Carl B. Stokes
31. Stanley Booth
32. Warner Law

33. John Clellon Holmes
34. Jules Feiffer
35. V. S. Pritchett
36. David Halberstam
37. Michael Arlen
38. LeRoy Neiman
39. Harvey Kurtzman
40. Bruce Jay Friedman
41. Hollis Alpert
42. Arthur Knight
43. Brock Yates
44. Stephen Yafa
45. Robert Sheckley
46. Alan Watts
47. Michael Crichton
48. Donn Pearce

Texan Karen Christy (far left), Miss December 1971, also won a place in Hefner's heart. (She later married Baltimore Colts linebacker Ed Simonini.) Claudia Jennings (left) was a receptionist at the Playboy Building when she was chosen for the November 1969 centerfold. After becoming Playmate of the Year in 1970, she won the lead in an off-Broadway play and a rave review from *The New Yorker*. She was enjoying a highly successful movie career with 13 films (earning her the affectionate title "Queen of the Bs") when she died in a 1979 automobile accident. Malta's Mary and Madeleine Collinson (above) became, in October 1970, PLAYBOY's first centerfold twins. Before long, they too were in the movies, in *Twins of Evil* and *The Love Machine*.

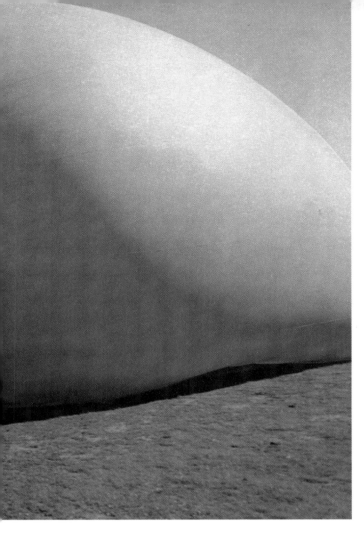

Continuing to devote coverage to films and film stars, PLAYBOY presented several movie-based features in the early Seventies. A pair of doting husbands, actor-director John Derek and writer Joe Hyams, photographed the glamourous actresses to whom they were then married, Linda Evans (top right) and Elke Sommer (right), for the magazine. Of Elke, her husband quipped: "She's the perfect wife—inexpensive to dress." Woody Allen (dodging the breast, above) wrote the text for PLAYBOY's feature *Everything You Always Wanted to Know About Sex...You'll Find in My New Movie—Plus a Couple of Things You Never Bargained For*. Valerie Perrine (far left) was introduced at the time of her *Slaughterhouse Five* film debut in 1972. The Russ Meyer epic *Beyond the Valley of the Dolls* (that's a body-painted Haji, veteran of Meyer films, at near left) showcased a number of bosomy beauties, including a pair of PLAYBOY Playmates. Two decades after its release, critics Gene Siskel and Roger Ebert were still debating the merits of Ebert's *BVD* screenplay.

The long-running *Playboy Pad* series illustrated all kinds of living space, from desert hideaway to an art-gallery home in Miami. *The Bubble House: A Rising Market* (top three photos and those at left and right) touted the Pneumodome, an inflatable dome 25 feet in diameter that came packed in a 60" by 42" by 12" box and cost $1950, including blower. In terms of reader response, the all-time most popular such feature was 1970's *Playboy's Portable Playhouse*, about a vacation home that could be picked up by helicopter and set in place on the site of your choice (below).

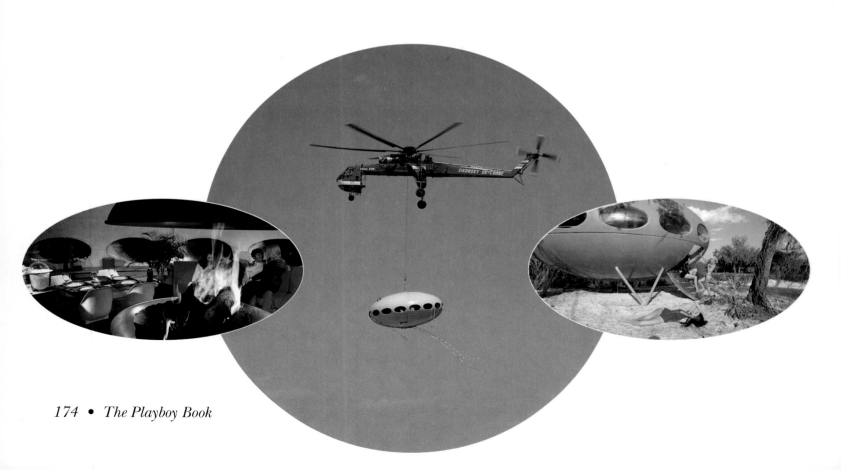

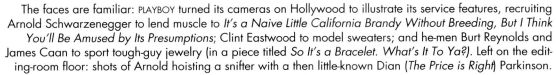

The faces are familiar: PLAYBOY turned its cameras on Hollywood to illustrate its service features, recruiting Arnold Schwarzenegger to lend muscle to *It's a Naive Little California Brandy Without Breeding, But I Think You'll Be Amused by Its Presumptions*; Clint Eastwood to model sweaters; and he-men Burt Reynolds and James Caan to sport tough-guy jewelry (in a piece titled *So It's a Bracelet. What's It To Ya?*). Left on the editing-room floor: shots of Arnold hoisting a snifter with a then little-known Dian (*The Price is Right*) Parkinson.

Kinuko Y. Craft's evocation of Christina Rossetti's *Goblin Market* (above) brought out the essence of a Victorian nursery tale filled with repressed eroticism. Artist Warren Linn depicted music's oddest couple, the Los Angeles Philharmonic's Zubin Mehta and rocker Frank Zappa, who had reassembled his Mothers of Invention for a joint performance with Mehta's classical musicians. F.P. Tullius told readers all about it in April 1971's *Zubin and the Mothers*. Herb Davidson's haunting portrait and John Bowers' profile *All She Needs Is Love* merged to capture the essence of Janis Joplin just weeks before her death from a heroin overdose in the fall of 1970 (opposite).

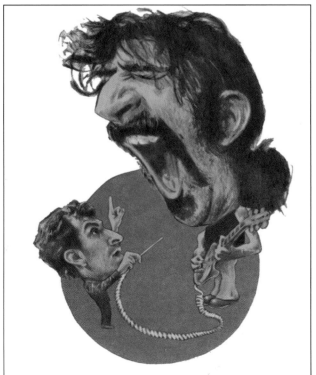

In 1972, when PLAYBOY sent writer Dan Greenburg off to California in search of *My First Orgy*, his quest was almost as complicated as the creation of Richard Fegley's accompanying photograph. It was 100 degrees in the shade when Fegley shot the above picture in a Las Vegas garage, adding, he says, "one person at a time." Assistant Art Director Gordon Mortensen then designed a four-page spread with a die-cut opening (opposite, top) through which the torso of an edgy Greenburg, stripping on the fourth page (opposite, bottom), was visible.

article

MY FIRST ORGY
BY DAN GREENBURG

*the craven coward in me
said no, but the journalist
in me said yes, yes, yes!*

A FEW MONTHS AGO, I was having dinner with my PLAYBOY editor in a Chinese restaurant in Chicago, and midway between my Beef and Snow Peas Thousand Fragrance and my Hot and Sour Sherbet, he matter-of-factly slipped me the information that the guys at the mag had come up with what they thought was a rather amusing assignment for me: Basically, how would I feel about going to a sex orgy and writing what it felt like?

"What do you mean," I said, "just go and observe and sort of take notes, or what?"

"Well, we were thinking really more along the lines of your actually taking *part* in one," he said.

My chopsticks suddenly became too heavy to hold and I lowered them carefully to the table. I should tell you at this point that I am so shy with women that it took me till the age of 23 to lose my virginity, till 30 to get married, and today, at 36, I am still unable to go to an ordinary cocktail party and chitchat with folks like any regular grown-up person. The idea of sending old Greenburg to take part in an orgy was, frankly, tantamount to sending someone with advanced vertigo to do a tap dance on the wing of an airborne 747.

True, I had recently done an article on New York fire fighters and in my research had managed to overcome a deep phobia of fire by spending five months riding on fire trucks and racing into burning buildings with firemen—yet somehow that seemed tame by comparison with what I was now being asked to do. After all, the worst that could have happened to me in a burning building was that a flaming ceiling might have collapsed on me and crushed me to death. At an orgy, there was the distinct possibility that I might be seriously laughed at.

"How about if I just go to an orgy and take notes?" I said.

My editor shrugged. "Don't you think that'd be sort of a cop-out, journalistically?" he said.

"I suppose you're right," I said. "Look, give me a few days to think it over."

• • •

"They want you to do *what*?" said my wife.

"Go to an orgy and kind of take part," I said.

"How about if you just go and take notes?" she said.

"Don't you think that'd be sort of a cop-out, journalistically?" I said.

"No," she said, "I don't."

"Oh," I said.

• • •

Several days later, having mulled over all facets of the situation, having pondered the feats of Sir Edmund Hillary, Sir Francis Chichester, Ernie Pyle, Robert Capa, Thor Heyerdahl and others, having decided that, my experiences with fire fighters notwithstanding, I had led a comparatively bland life and that only through the continual meeting of challenges and overcoming of fears was I going to attain any growth as a writer and, mainly, having learned from my agent the exact sum I was being offered for this

DESIGNED BY GORDON MORTENSEN
PHOTOGRAPHED BY RICHARD FEGLEY

Martin Hoffman created nine portraits of *Woman Eternal*—among them the two at left—for PLAYBOY's December 1972 issue. Some of the canvases still hang in PLAYBOY's Chicago offices. Franco Rubartelli photographed Countess Vera Gottlieb von Lehndorff—known in the world of high-fashion modeling (and to fans of the movie *Blow-Up*)—as Veruschka, lightly camouflaged in the 1971 pictorial *Stalking the Wild Veruschka*.

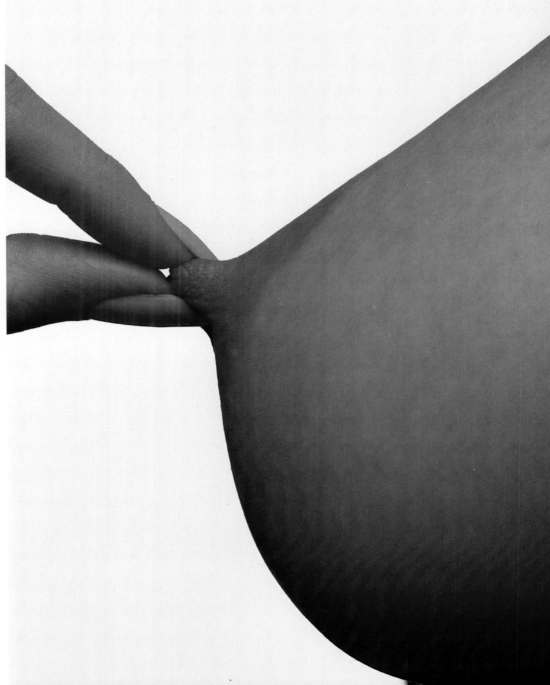

Nine noted photographers shared their *Personal Visions of the Erotic* with readers of PLAYBOY's December 1971 issue. With his pose of the twosome at top right, Douglas Kirkland said he "tried to give a sense of being in an erotic atmosphere and a feeling of actual participation." He did participate: the man's arm is his. Pete Turner, explaining the rationale of his picture of a woman pulling on another woman's nipple, noted "Eroticism is a personal thing. It's whatever turns you on as an individual."

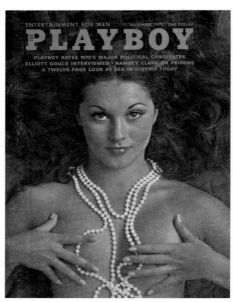

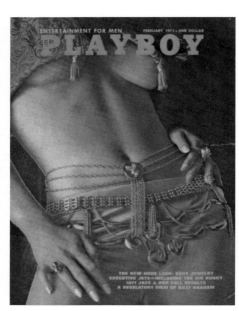

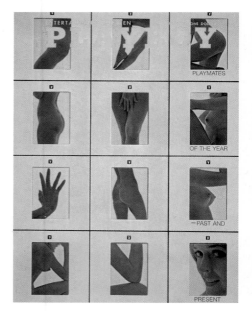

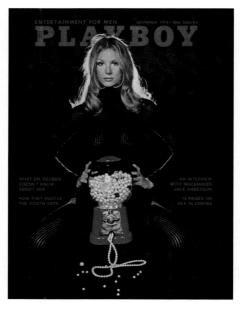

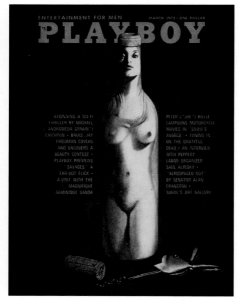

The Rabbit has appeared on every cover since the second, showing up everywhere from bubble baths to corkscrews to strings of pearls. Art directors and photographers vied to create new twists, like the gumballs on the November 1972 issue (bottom center).

ENTERTAINMENT FOR MEN   OCTOBER 1971 •   DOLLAR

PLAYBOY

BUTKUS: MR. MEAN

THE PORNO GIRLS

YOUR JAZZ AND
POP POLL BALLOT

FOUR POEMS BY
YEVTUSHENKO

FALL AND WINTER
FASHION FORECAST

Norwegian-born Liv Lindeland made history of a sort in her January 1971 centerfold photograph when a ray of sunshine highlighted a tuft of pubic hair—a first for a Playmate. In June 1972, Liv became Playmate of the Year, winning a cornucopia of gifts ranging from a $10,000 Lincoln Mercury De Tomaso Pantera (in Playmate Pink, as were her Easy Rider all-terrain vehicle and Schwinn ten-speed bike) to a case of pink brut champagne.

Marilyn Cole had just been promoted from Bunny duties to a new job, as public relations officer for the London Playboy Club, when she appeared as PLAYBOY's January 1972 centerfold. A native of Portsmouth, England, she used to worry about appearing in a bathing suit on the beaches of her seaside hometown: "I was afraid my legs were too thin." She found posing for photographers boring as well. Fortunately for her career, Marilyn got over all that, appearing many times in the magazine (including, in 1973, as Playmate of the Year). Now the wife of former Playboy executive Victor Lownes, she is mistress of a showplace home in a fashionable district of London.

Movies got racier in the Seventies, and PLAYBOY was right there to chronicle the uncoverage. Russ Meyer's nudie films were a sensation, and in March 1973 he photographed another of his wives, actress Edy Williams (opposite), for PLAYBOY. The Italian film *Stay As You Are* paired Marcello Mastroianni with a budding new talent, Nastassja Kinski (above), introduced in the August 1979 issue. Dancer Rudolf Nureyev leapt into the role of Hollywood's most legendary lover (and into the arms of Michelle Phillips, above right) for Ken Russell's *Nureyev's Valentino*. But the most controversial film of its era—and one of the few major movies ever released with an X rating—was *Last Tango in Paris*, starring Maria Schneider and Marlon Brando (right). PLAYBOY's February 1973 issue showcased both movie and Maria.

"All I sell is cheeseburgers, but I sell a _lot_ of cheeseburgers."

"Is this all I am to you, Arnold—a medium for social protest?"

" Hélène isn't here anymore. She met Mr. Right."

"Would it help any if I snarled?"

Critics were unprepared for the caliber and scope of the films released by Playboy Productions—starting with a 1971 version of Shakespeare's *Macbeth*, directed by Roman Polanski and starring Francesca Annis and Jon Finch (above); it was voted Best Picture of the Year by the National Board of Review. A behind-the-scenes story appeared in the magazine (above left). Monty Python (below) was introduced to moviegoers in 1972's *And Now For Something Completely Different*, produced under the Playboy banner by Victor Lownes, head of the company's British operations. Anthropologist Desmond Morris's book *The Naked Ape*, which summarized 10 million years of evolution, was brought to the screen by Playboy in 1973, starring Johnny Crawford (left center) and Victoria Principal (below left).

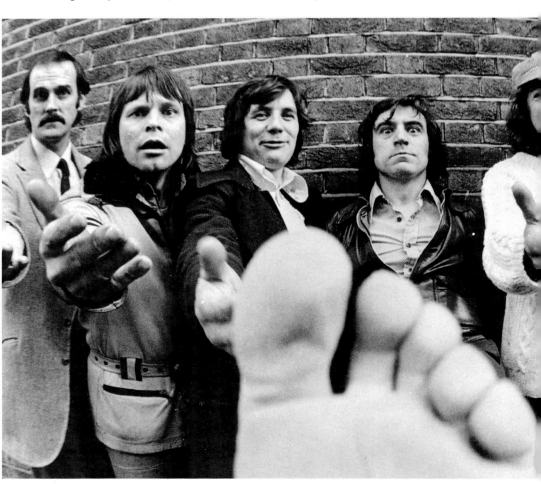

At the same time, Playboy was producing highly rated ABC-TV specials including an annual *Bunny of the Year Pageant,* such as the 1973 telecast in which Lake Geneva's Coni Hugee won the title (above). Featured guests included such stars as George Burns and Tina Turner. Of PLAYBOY's TV movies, perhaps the most celebrated was the 1981 TV film *A Whale for the Killing* (below, right), starring Peter Strauss, which reflected a concern for the decimation of the whales.

Other magazines editorialized about romantic, upscale travel destinations; PLAYBOY actually created them. By 1972, Club keyholders and their guests could be pampered in their choice of three Playboy Club-Hotels—in Ocho Rios, Jamaica (above); Lake Geneva, Wisconsin (opposite); and Great Gorge, in the scenic, mountainous ski country of northwest New Jersey (below, left and right). The stateside resorts offered winter and summer sports as well as luxurious accommodations, name entertainment and gourmet cuisine. The Jamaica spa specialized in fun in the sun: Visitors who clambered up nearby Dunn's River Falls (near left) were rewarded with "Fall Guy" and "Fallen Woman" certificates. All three resorts boasted elaborate convention facilities—including kitchens for lavish banquets.

RAQUEL WELCH: *"There's no one who's liberated to the point the American woman is and yet handles it worse. She holds her freedom like a club and beats the guy with it until he's got stars coming out of his head."*

WILLIAM F. BUCKLEY JR.: *"I have discovered a new sensual treat, which the readers of* PLAYBOY *should be the first to know about. It is to have the President of the United States take notes while you are speaking to him."*

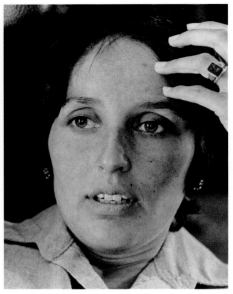

JOAN BAEZ: *"If people are serious about revolution, they have to wage a revolution for all oppressed people—and that includes policemen, who must be some of the most oppressed people in this society."*

THE PLAYBOY

JACK NICHOLSON: *"The censors say that they're protecting the family unit in America, when the reality of the censorship is if you suck a tit, you're an X, but if you cut it off with a sword, you're a GP."*

GERMAINE GREER: *"Every man should be fucked up the arse as a prelude to fucking women, so he'll know what it's like to be the receiver. Otherwise, he'll think he's doling out joy unlimited to every woman he fucks."*

BOB HOPE: *"If we had declared war in Vietnam, it would have ended in a year, because the military would have taken over. We'd have gone all out and—bang, bang, bang—it would have been over."*

Playboy Interviews of the Seventies encouraged their subjects to speak out on an astonishing variety of views. In no other magazine could one find such an assortment: conversations with sex goddess Raquel Welch, pundit William F. Buckley Jr. (who once said PLAYBOY was his best avenue of communication with his son), singer/activist Joan Baez, actor Jack Nicholson, feminist Germaine Greer and entertainer Bob Hope.

MAE WEST: *"I don't remember how many lovers I've had, there were so many. I was never interested in the score, though—only the game. Like my line, 'It's not the men in my life that counts but the life in my men.'"*

JOHN WAYNE: *"We can't all of a sudden get down on our knees and turn everything over to the leadership of the blacks. I believe in white supremacy until blacks are educated to a point of responsibility."*

ALBERT SPEER: *"So many people expect me to offer justifications for what I did. I cannot. There is no apology or excuse I can ever make. The blood is on my hands. I've not tried to wash it off—only to see it."*

INTERVIEW

HUGH HEFNER: *"I enjoy the public's fantasies about the way I live almost as much as the way I <u>really</u> live. And I can't deny being amused at the mixed reactions I arouse, often in the same people."*

CLINT EASTWOOD: *"I'm not a person who advocates violence in real life, and if I thought I'd made a film in which the violence inspired people to commit more violence, I wouldn't make those films."*

GROUCHO MARX: *"I remember once when I visited the offices of 'The New York Times,' they showed me my obituary. It wasn't very good. I offered to punch it up for them, but they turned me down."*

PLAYBOY's corps of interviewers—some of them staff members, others free-lancers—queried subjects as diverse as irrepressible sex symbol Mae West and Albert Speer, who'd been Adolf Hitler's right-hand man. Writer Charlotte Chandler expanded on her *Playboy Interview* of Groucho Marx to compose his biography, entitled *Hello, I Must Be Going.* Mr. Playboy himself was interrogated for PLAYBOY's 20th Anniversary Issue.

PART I: THE AMERICAN DREAM

article By RICHARD HAMMER   *from modest beginnings and clumsy first efforts—the roots of empire*

"DEAD RABBITS" GANG STALKS STREETS OF GOTHAM
"DEAD RABBITS" GANG RAMPAGED THROUGH THE LOWER EAST SIDE OF NEW YORK
RABBIT IMPALED ON A STAKE. THE GANG'S FAME SPREAD AFTER THE CIVIL WAR

...ontrolled energy— ...c, violent, sometimes ...ss and at war with it- ...ts nobler aspirations ...osophies. ...one of a society is in- ...t set by those at the top. ...he period between the ...f the Civil War and the

beginning of World War One was the age of the robber barons, an age when the only goal seemed the accumulation of vast wealth and power. In that untrammeled quest, conscience played no part. Members of Presidential Cabinets —and there were rumors even

about Presiden... and of Cong... on every level... precincts to th... ernment, bec... inside inform... vors, using se... them for thei... became the...

A DIRECTORY OF NOTED CHICAGO BUSINESSMEN

Colosimo lacked corporate ambition and was kicked upstairs.

Torrio sensibly moved to New York for the sake of his health.

Capone, nailed on taxes, found the pen mightier than the sword.

O'Banion regretted his remark "To hell with them Sicilians."

A classic drawing by Paul Cadmus inspired Kinuko Y. Craft's depiction (left) of the Atlantic City meeting where crime became truly organized. Artist Seymour Fleishman followed Reginald Marsh's lead in his rendering of Al Capone's baseball-bat-wielding disciplinary session with his underlings (above). Peter Palombi patterned his cover art (below) after a work by Rudolph Belarski.

Moran arrived late at his own Saint Valentine's Day party.

Weiss's North Side leadership was terminated by tommy guns.

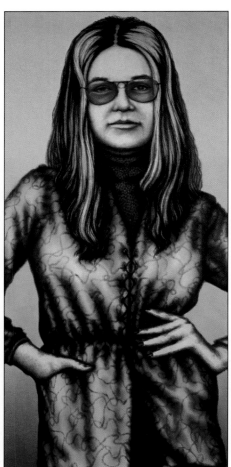

article
BY LARRY L. KING

THE BEST LITTLE WHOREHOUSE IN TEXAS

when a true son of texas discovers they've closed down "the chicken farm," he takes his business to the free-lancers. man's got to do what a man's got to do

IT WAS AS NICE a little whorehouse as you ever saw. It sat in a green Texas glade, white-shuttered and tidy, surrounded by leafy oak trees and a few slim renegade pines and the kind of pure clean air the menthol-cigarette people advertise.

If you had country values in you, and happened to stumble upon it, likely you would nod approval and think, *Yes, yes, these folks keep their barn painted and their fences up and probably they'd do to ride the river with.* There was a small vegetable garden and a water-melon patch, neither lacking care. A good stand of corn, mottled now by bruise-colored blotches and dried to parchment by hot husky-whispering summer winds, had no one to hear its rustling secrets.

Way back yonder, during the Hoover Depression, they raised chickens out there. Money was hard to come by; every jack rabbit had three families chasing it with the stewpot in mind. Back then, in rural Texas, people said things like, "You can hear everthang in these woods but meat afryin' and coins aclankin'." No matter where a boy itched and no matter how high his fevers, it wasn't easy to come up with three dollars, even in exchange for a girl's sweetest gift. And so the girls began accepting poultry in trade. That's how the place got its name, and if you grew up most anywhere in Texas, you knew at an early age what the Chicken Farm sold other than pullets. (Generations since mine have called it the Chicken *Ranch*. I won't argue the point.)

You might have originally thought it a honeymoon cottage. Except that as you came closer on the winding dirt road that skittered into the woods off the Austin-to-Houston highway on the southeastern outskirts of

130

PAINTING BY BRAD HOLLAND

Women's libbers just don't get it, postulated Frederick Exley in *Saint Gloria and the Troll*, a recounting of his snake-bitten interview with doctrinaire Gloria Steinem (and his more engaging encounters with three other femmes). The accompanying paintings are by Ed Paschke.

Larry L. King struck it rich with *The Best Little Whorehouse in Texas*, a humorous PLAYBOY piece about the closing of a Lone Star State institution called the Chicken Ranch. To King's astonishment, *Whorehouse* became first a Broadway musical and then a major motion picture starring Burt Reynolds and Dolly Parton. Brad Holland provided the painting.

When Hefner moved into Playboy Mansion West, he turned it into a palace which his editors grandly characterized as "Playboy's paradise by the Pacific, a contemporary Shangri-La for work and play." The 30-room mansion, modeled after a 15th century English manor, is smaller than its Chicago predecessor but boasts more spacious surroundings—six lushly landscaped acres in the exclusive Holmby Hills area of Los Angeles. On the grounds are guest houses, swimming pools, a grotto, tennis courts and an entire cottage devoted to elaborate toys, from pinball machines to an illuminated organ. There's plenty of room for a private zoo, tropical birds, brilliantly colored fish and all sorts of animals, including Lambert the llama (below). Once he'd settled in, Hefner seldom left the place. A January 1975 pictorial showed readers why PMW exerted such a powerful mystique.

From the start, parties at PMW attracted celebrities, including Ringo Starr and Harry Nilsson (above) and Groucho Marx, with Playmate Marilyn Cole (below).

High-concept pictorials were the rage when a master surrealist and a veteran PLAYBOY photographer, Pompeo Posar, teamed to produce *The Erotic World of Salvador Dalí* (left). Lensman Paul Gremmler filmed the shot at bottom left for *Hindsight,* a celebration of derrieres. Veruschka returned in *Painted Lady* (below), for which it's reported she applied the pigment—proving herself to be contortionist as well as countess. To create *Instant Warhol,* his debut as a PLAYBOY photographer, Andy aimed his trusty Polaroid at some of his own stars (at top opposite, Dominique Darel and Max Delys).

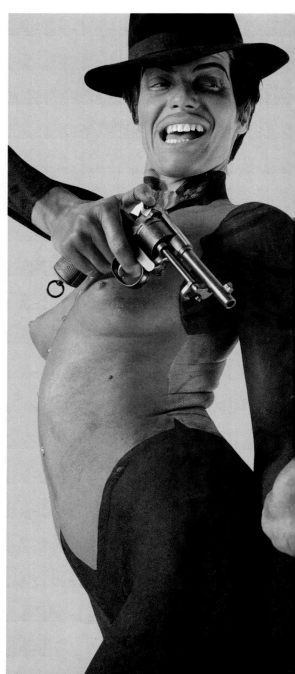

BORN ON THE FOURTH OF JULY
memoir By RON KOVIC

an ex—marine sergeant brings you as close to the searing horror that was vietnam as you're likely to get

THE BLOOD is still rolling off my flak jacket from the hole in my shoulder and there are bullets cracking into the sand all around me. I keep trying to move my legs, but I cannot feel them.

"Oh, get me out of here, get me out of here, please, someone help me! Oh, help me, please help me. Oh, God, oh, Jesus!"

I try to breathe, but it is difficult. I have to get out of this place, make it out of here somehow.

Someone shouts from my left now, screaming for me to get up. Again and again he screams, but I am trapped in the sand.

"Is there a corpsman?" I cry. "Can you get a corpsman?"

There is a loud crack and I hear him begin to sob. "They've shot my fucking finger off! Let's go, Sarge! Let's get outta here!"

"I can't move," I gasp. "I can't move my legs! I can't feel anything!"

I watch him go running back to the tree line.

"Sarge, are you all right?" Someone else is calling to me now and I try to turn around. Again there is the sudden crack of a bullet and a boy's voice crying. "Oh, Jesus! Oh, Jesus Christ!" I hear his body fall in back of me.

I think he must be dead, but I feel nothing for him, I just want to live. I feel nothing.

And now I hear another man coming up from behind, trying to save

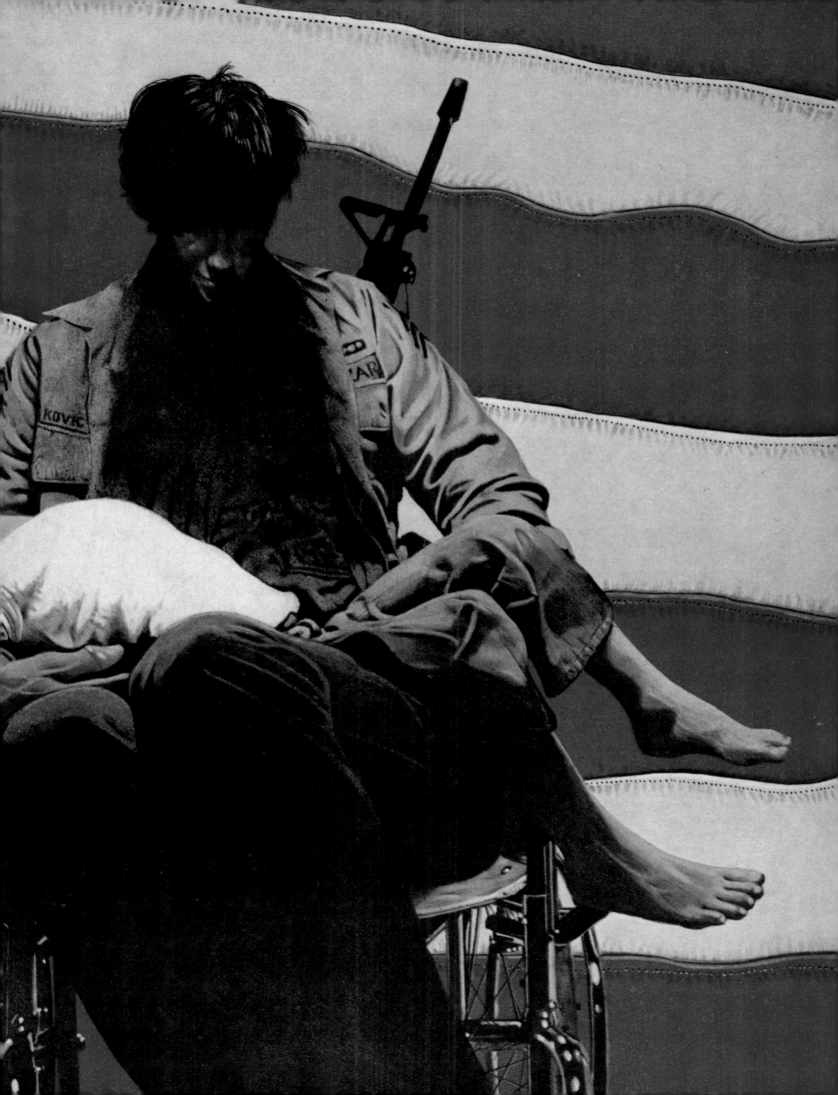

he was given the name esteban, for that alone seemed to fit this godlike figure swept in by the tide

fiction **By GABRIEL GARCIA MARQUEZ**

THE FIRST CHILDREN who saw the dark and slinky bulge approaching through the sea let themselves think it was an enemy ship. Then they saw it had no flags nor masts and they thought it was a whale. But when it washed up on the beach, they removed the clumps of seaweed, the jellyfish tentacles and the remains of fish and flotsam and only then did they see that it was a drowned man. And so they made a toy of him. They had been playing with him all afternoon, burying him in the sand and digging him up again, when someone chanced to see them and spread the alarm in the village. The men who carried him to the nearest house noticed that he weighed more than any dead man *(continued on page 122)*

The Handsomest Drowned Man In the World

ILLUSTRATION BY PATRICK D'ANGELO

Of PLAYBOY, Thomas Weyr wrote in 1978: "No intelligent reader can do without it and pretend to any serious understanding about the United States." It achieved that distinction by publishing work such as Ron Kovic's searing memoir *Born on the Fourth of July* (preceding spread; illustration is by Greg Wray), which became a critically acclaimed film starring Tom Cruise. PLAYBOY also provided the nation's best showcase for creative writing. Three prestigious authors published during the Seventies were Nobel Prize winner Gabriel García Márquez, who wrote *The Handsomest Drowned Man in the World*; Paul Theroux, an ex–foreign service officer turned novelist whose *Adulterer's Luck*, illustrated by Kathy Calderwood (below), is set in Malaysia; and Joyce Carol Oates, whose first contribution, *Saul Bird Says: Relate! Communicate! Liberate!* (illustrated by Don Punchatz, right), won her an award for PLAYBOY's best short story of 1970.

THE **PLAYBOY** DIME MYSTERY

10¢

THE CASE
OF THE
COCKAMAMIE
SISTERS

drawings by
ROBERT ANDREW PARKER

text by
JOHN BLUMENTHAL

★★★ THE FIGHT ★★★
by
NORMAN MAILER
Part II

ALL NIGHT LONG

finally, ali and foreman stepped into the ring and made all the waiting worth it

IT WAS A GRIM dressing room. Perhaps it looked like a comfort station in a Moscow subway. A big room, all white, with round pillars tiled in white, and white wallpaper with a design of white tile. It also looked like an operating room or a small gas chamber. It was certainly a morgue. In this room, all groans were damped. White tile was everywhere. What a place to get ready!

The men gathered there had no more cheer than the decor. Dundee, Pacheco, Plimpton, Mailer, Walter Youngblood, Pat Patterson, Howard Bingham, Ali's brother Rachman, his manager, Herbert Muhammad, his business manager, Gene Kilroy, Bundini, a small fat Turk named Hassan and Roy Williams, his sparring partner, were in the room and no one had anything to say. "What's going on here?" said Ali as he entered. "Why is everybody so scared? What's the matter with you?" He began to peel off his clothes and, wearing no more than a jockstrap, was soon prancing around the room, shadowboxing with the air.

Roy Williams, dressed to go into the ring for his semi-final fight with Henry Clark, was sitting on the rubbing table. Through a miscalculation of others', he had arrived at the stadium with the convoy, too late for a ten-round semi-final. They were planning to hold it now after the main

★ ★ ★ ★ ★ ★ ★ ★ ★ ★ ★ ★ ★ ★

"Ali caught Foreman by the neck like a big brother chastising an enormous and stupid kid brother . . . and stuck out one long white-coated tongue."

Assistant Editor John Blumenthal and artist Robert Andrew Parker teamed up to create a potboiler spoof, *The Playboy Dime Mystery*, all about Myrna Leroy and her missing sister Gesundheit. In *The Puppet and the Puppetmasters* (illustrated by Eraldo Carugati, above), Larry DuBois and Laurence Gonzales followed the threads connecting Howard Hughes, Richard Nixon and the CIA; the piece won a Sigma Delta Chi Distinguished Service Award for journalism. Norman Mailer's two-part *The Fight* chronicled the meeting in Zaïre of heavyweight boxers Muhammad Ali and George Foreman.

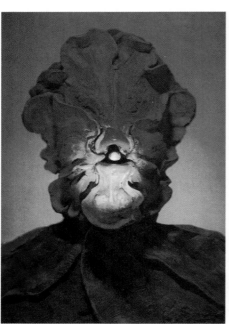

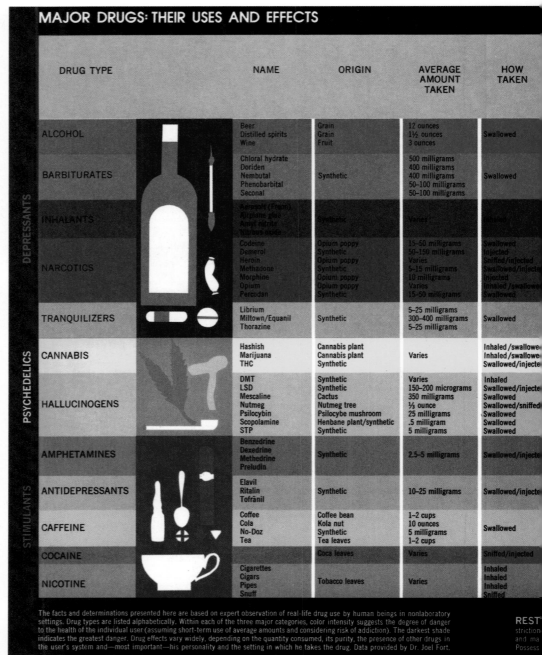

MAJOR DRUGS: THEIR USES AND EFFECTS

	DRUG TYPE	NAME	ORIGIN	AVERAGE AMOUNT TAKEN	HOW TAKEN
DEPRESSANTS	ALCOHOL	Beer Distilled spirits Wine	Grain Grain Fruit	12 ounces 1½ ounces 3 ounces	Swallowed
	BARBITURATES	Chloral hydrate Doriden Nembutal Phenobarbital Seconal	Synthetic	500 milligrams 400 milligrams 400 milligrams 50–100 milligrams 50–100 milligrams	Swallowed
	INHALANTS	Aerosols (Pam) Airplane glue Amyl nitrite Nitrous oxide	Synthetic	Varies	Inhaled
	NARCOTICS	Codeine Demerol Heroin Methadone Morphine Opium Percodan	Opium poppy Synthetic Opium poppy Synthetic Opium poppy Opium poppy Synthetic	15–50 milligrams 50–150 milligrams Varies 5–15 milligrams 10 milligrams Varies 15–50 milligrams	Swallowed Injected Sniffed/injected Swallowed/injected Injected Inhaled/swallowed Swallowed
	TRANQUILIZERS	Librium Miltown/Equanil Thorazine	Synthetic	5–25 milligrams 300–400 milligrams 5–25 milligrams	Swallowed
PSYCHEDELICS	CANNABIS	Hashish Marijuana THC	Cannabis plant Cannabis plant Synthetic	Varies	Inhaled/swallowed Inhaled/swallowed Swallowed/injected
	HALLUCINOGENS	DMT LSD Mescaline Nutmeg Psilocybin Scopolamine STP	Synthetic Synthetic Cactus Nutmeg tree Psilocybe mushroom Henbane plant/synthetic Synthetic	Varies 150–200 micrograms 350 milligrams ½ ounce 25 milligrams .5 milligram 5 milligrams	Inhaled Swallowed/injected Swallowed Swallowed/sniffed Swallowed Swallowed Swallowed
STIMULANTS	AMPHETAMINES	Benzedrine Dexedrine Methedrine Preludin	Synthetic	2.5–5 milligrams	Swallowed/injected
	ANTIDEPRESSANTS	Elavil Ritalin Tofränil	Synthetic	10–25 milligrams	Swallowed/injected
	CAFFEINE	Coffee Cola No-Doz Tea	Coffee bean Kola nut Synthetic Tea leaves	1–2 cups 10 ounces 5 milligrams 1–2 cups	Swallowed
	COCAINE		Coca leaves	Varies	Sniffed/injected
	NICOTINE	Cigarettes Cigars Pipes Snuff	Tobacco leaves	Varies	Inhaled Inhaled Inhaled Sniffed

The facts and determinations presented here are based on expert observation of real-life drug use by human beings in nonlaboratory settings. Drug types are listed alphabetically. Within each of the three major categories, color intensity suggests the degree of danger to the health of the individual user (assuming short-term use of average amounts and considering risk of addiction). The darkest shade indicates the greatest danger. Drug effects vary widely, depending on the quantity consumed, its purity, the presence of other drugs in the user's system and—most important—his personality and the setting in which he takes the drug. Data provided by Dr. Joel Fort.

PLAYBOY never advocated drug use, but it did try to free discussion of the subject from its *Reefer Madness* heritage. The magazine's objective approach is reflected in the spooky sculptures by Martin Wanserski (left) that accompanied a series of articles about drugs in the September 1972 issue. The drug coverage included a chart summarizing the medical knowledge of the day. Since then, experts have revised their findings about the effects of caffeine, nicotine and cocaine. Two hard-hitting PLAYBOY pieces from early 1976, *An American Gestapo* and *Who Can Arrest You?*, indicted the ruthless tactics employed by such government agencies as the Drug Enforcement Administration.

	SHORT-TERM EFFECTS OF AVERAGE AMOUNT		SHORT-TERM EFFECTS OF LARGE AMOUNT	RISK OF DEPENDENCE			LONG-TERM EFFECTS (continued excessive use)	MEDICAL USES
	DESCRIPTION	DURATION		HABITUATION (psychological)	ADDICTION (physical)	TOLERANCE (increasing amounts needed for same effect)		
	Relaxation, breakdown of inhibitions, euphoria, depression, decreased alertness	2–4 hours	Stupor, nausea, unconsciousness, hangover, death	High	Moderate	Yes	Obesity, impotence, psychosis, ulcers, malnutrition, liver and brain damage, delirium tremens, death	None
	Relaxation, euphoria, decreased alertness, drowsiness, impaired coordination, sleep	4–8 hours	Slurred speech, stupor, hangover, death	High	High	Yes	Excessive sleepiness, confusion, irritability, severe withdrawal sickness	For insomnia, tension and epileptic seizures
	Relaxation, euphoria, impaired coordination	1–3 hours	Stupor, death	High	None	Possibly	Hallucinations; liver, kidney, bone-marrow and brain damage; death	None / None / Dilation of blood vessels / Light anesthetic
	Relaxation, relief of pain and anxiety, decreased alertness, euphoria, hallucinations	4 hours	Stupor, death	High	High	Yes	Lethargy, constipation, weight loss, temporary sterility and impotence, withdrawal sickness	For cough / Painkiller / None in U.S. / Withdrawal from heroin / Painkiller / For diarrhea / Painkiller
	Relief of anxiety and tension, suppression of hallucinations and aggression, sleep	12–24 hours	Drowsiness, blurred vision, dizziness, slurred speech, allergic reaction, stupor	Moderate	Moderate / Moderate / None	No	Destruction of blood cells, jaundice, coma, death	For tension, anxiety, psychosis; alcoholism
	Relaxation, breakdown of inhibitions, alteration of perceptions, euphoria, increased appetite	2–4 hours	Panic, stupor	Moderate	None	No	Fatigue, psychosis	For tension, depression, headache, poor appetite
	Perceptual changes—especially visual, increased energy, hallucinations, panic	½ hour / 10–12 hours / 12–14 hours / Varies / 6–8 hours / Varies / 12–14 hours	Anxiety, hallucinations, psychosis, exhaustion, tremors, vomiting, panic	Low	None	Yes	Increased delusions and panic, psychosis	(LSD and psilocybin have been tested for treatment of alcoholism, drug addiction, mental illness and migraine)
	Increased alertness, excitation, euphoria, decreased appetite	4–8 hours	Restlessness, rapid speech, irritability, insomnia, stomach disorders, convulsions	High	None	Yes	Insomnia, excitability, skin disorders, malnutrition, delusions, hallucinations, psychosis	For obesity, depression, excessive fatigue, narcolepsy, children's behavior disorders
	Relief of anxiety and depression, temporary impotence	12–24 hours	Nausea, hypertension, weight loss, insomnia	Low	None	No / Yes / No	Stupor, coma, convulsions, congestive heart failure, damage to liver and white blood cells, death	For anxiety or over-sedation, children's behavior disorders
	Increased alertness	2–4 hours	Restlessness, insomnia, upset stomach	High	None	Yes	Restlessness, irritability, insomnia, stomach disorders	For oversedation and headache
	Feeling of self-confidence and power, intense exhilaration	4 hours	Irritability, depression, psychosis	High	None	Yes	Damage to nasal septum and blood vessels, psychosis	Local anesthetic
	Relaxation, constriction of blood vessels	¼–2 hours	Headache, loss of appetite, nausea	High	None	Yes	Impaired breathing, heart and lung disease, cancer, death	None (used as insecticide)

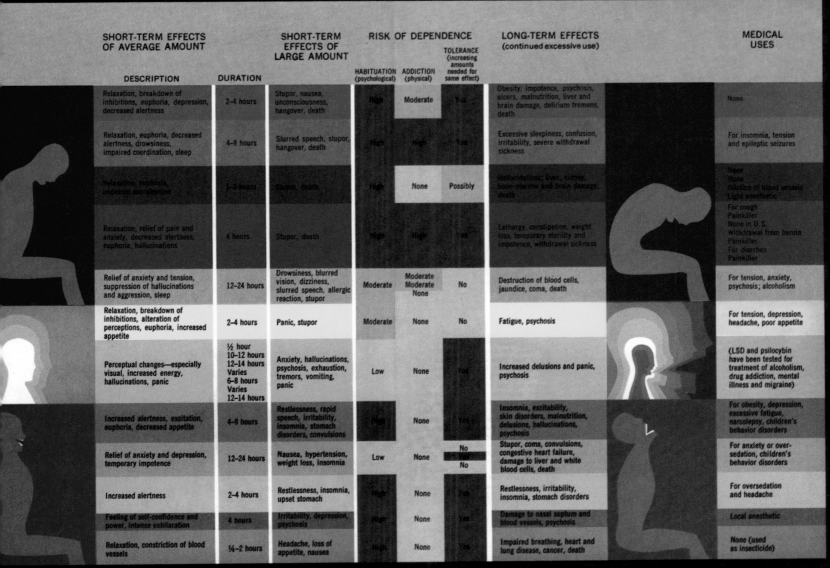

ONS AND PENALTIES: Alcohol, caffeine and nicotine are not legally considered drugs, though some re-...ale of alcohol is banned in scattered localities; Federal laws restrict advertisement of cigarettes and distilled spirits ... of alcoholic beverages; state and local restrictions govern the sale of alcohol and nicotine products to minors. ...ale of inhalants are generally unrestricted, though amyl nitrite and nitrous oxide require prescriptions. Possession of barbiturates, tranquilizers, amphetamines, antidepressants and some narcotics is legal only if prescribed. Among narcotics, there is no lawful use of opium or heroin, though opium powder is a component of certain prescription drugs. All hallucinogens except nutmeg are similarly illegal, as are cocaine and all Cannabis drugs. Maximum Federal penalties for possession of illegal drugs: first offense—one year in prison and $5000 fine; subsequent offenses—two years and $10,000; much harsher penalties apply to sale. However, most drug convictions are made under state laws, which vary widely and arbitrarily and are often stricter than the Federal laws.

article
By FRANK BROWNING

AN AMERICAN GESTAPO

WHO CAN ARREST YOU? ...in america, almost anybody

artist
By LAURENCE GONZALES

PLAYBOY'S PRO FOOTBALL PREVIEW

AN EARLY LINE ON TEAMS AND PLAYERS IN BOTH CONFERENCES OF THE N.F.L.

BY ANSON MOUNT

Building on his sports-forecasting expertise, Anson Mount branched out to predict winners in pro football and college basketball. His All-Star selections for the *1977 Pro Football Preview* team included two players who made NFL history: Walter Payton and O.J. Simpson. Reagan Wilson's illustration depicts the crucial moment of Super Bowl XI in 1977, a first-quarter Viking fumble.

For its 20th Anniversary Issue in January 1974, PLAYBOY posed Nancy Cameron for the magazine's only front-and-back centerfold. Marilyn Lange (opposite, near right) was a cocktail waitress in Honolulu when she became Miss May 1974. By this time, the magazine's writers had abandoned the fiction that all of its Playmates were unattached and thus potentially available; Marilyn's story openly described her relationship with a live-in boyfriend. That didn't stop her from being named 1975's Playmate of the Year. Azizi Johari (opposite top right), Miss June 1975, made several movies and was a regular contributor to the *Dear Playmates* page, a popular feature of the Eighties. *Barbi's Back!* read the headline of a 1973 pictorial on Barbi Benton (opposite); the title referred to her reappearance in the magazine, but the story was prepared during a period of tension in her relationship with Hefner. Upset over his liaison with Karen Christy, she had briefly moved out of Playboy Mansion West.

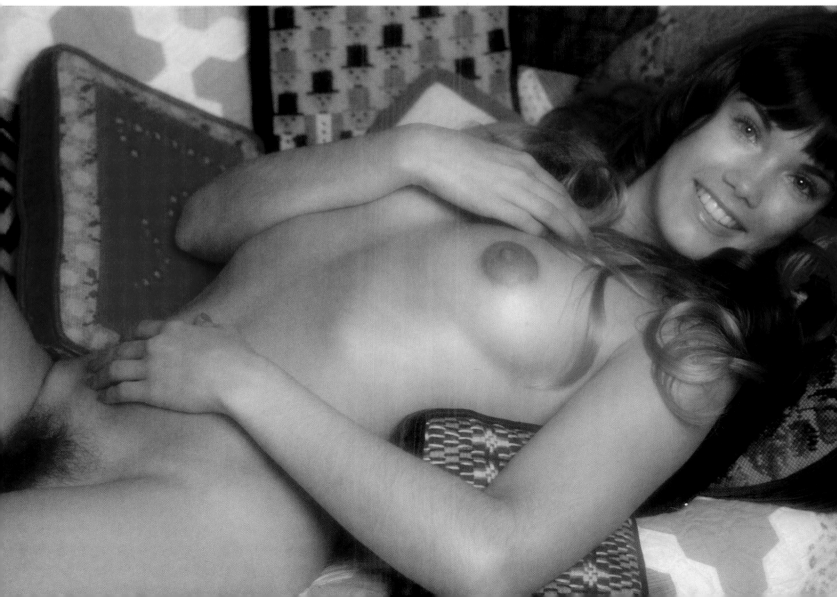

The Pennington sisters, Ann (opposite, far left) and Janice (opposite, top), appeared as centerfolds five years apart—Janice in May 1971 and Ann in March 1976. Janice has been working on *The Price Is Right* virtually ever since. Miss February 1973, Cyndi Wood, graced PLAYBOY's 20th Anniversary cover (above), became 1974's Playmate of the Year and portrayed a Playmate in *Apocalypse Now*. Photographer Richard Fegley, vacationing in Nevada, found Nancie Li Brandi (below), Miss December 1975, dealing blackjack. One of PLAYBOY's most photographed Playmates, 1976 PMOY Lillian Müller (right) appeared on five covers and in more than a dozen pictorials, beginning with her August 1975 centerfold.

"We can't make him take it down.
She's his grandmother."

"No, not this time … but I think the machine did."

"I turn you on. I turn everybody on!"

"In my day, nice girls didn't do that."

ROOTS
The Mixing
Of the Blood

From the book by
ALEX HALEY

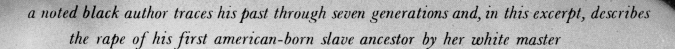

For 12 years, Alex Haley researched and wrote the story of the seven generations of his family that he would call "Roots." It began when Haley, a writer who conducted the first "Playboy Interview" and many others, was on a PLAYBOY assignment in England and first saw the Rosetta stone, the key to deciphering Egyptian hieroglyphics. He became curious about some African phrases he remembered hearing from his relatives as a boy in Tennessee and, in particular, the name Kunta Kinte, whom he believed was his African ancestor.

Poring over old records, consulting experts in linguistics, anthropology and genealogy, Haley tracked down every lead until his research finally led him to a village in Gambia. There, in a moment of high drama, the tribal historian, known as a griot, was retelling the story of the village through past generations and came to a day in 1767 when a 17-year-old boy was abducted by white men in the woods near the village and never heard from again. His name was Kunta Kinte.

Beginning with life in the village of Juffure, "Roots" describes Kunta Kinte's early years, his kidnaping, his transportation in the filthy, hellish hold of a slave ship across the Atlantic and his sale to John Waller, a Virginia planter. Rebellious and fiercely independent, Kunta tried to escape so often that his pursuers chopped off part of his foot as punishment. He eventually married Bell, the plantation cook, who gave birth to a girl named Kizzy. Bell taught their daughter how to get along with whites and was delighted when, for instance, Kizzy became fast friends with the Waller niece, Missy Anne, who taught her to read and write. But Kunta remained stubbornly committed to passing along at least some of his African heritage, telling her about Juffure and relating old village customs—such as his method of keeping track of time by dropping pebbles into a gourd. By the early 1800s, the first of Kunta's descendants to be born in America had grown to be a pretty girl and was living a relatively sheltered life as a house slave.

"DO I GOT a gran'ma?" asked Kizzy.

"You got two—my mammy and yo' mammy's mammy."

"How come dey ain't wid us?"

"Dey don' know where we is," said Kunta. "Does you know where we is?" he asked her a moment later.

"We's in de buggy," Kizzy said.

"I means where does we live?"

"At Massa Waller's."

"An' where dat is?"

"Dat way," she said, pointing down the road. Uninterested in their subject, she

WILCOX

Longtime PLAYBOY contributor Alex Haley rocketed to fame with the publication of *Roots*, his seminal story of the search for his ancestors. Murray Fisher, Haley's editor at PLAYBOY, spent a dozen years as the book's midwife, helping Haley structure *Roots* from what the author describes in his acknowledgement as "a seemingly impassable maze of researched materials." So it was fitting that an excerpt from *Roots* was published in PLAYBOY (preceding spread) in October 1976, more than a year before it was turned into television's first truly epic miniseries. The following July, Asa Baber advised readers that to succeed on *The Commodities Market: You've Really Got to Be an Animal*; Charles Bragg's illustration (above) proves the point.

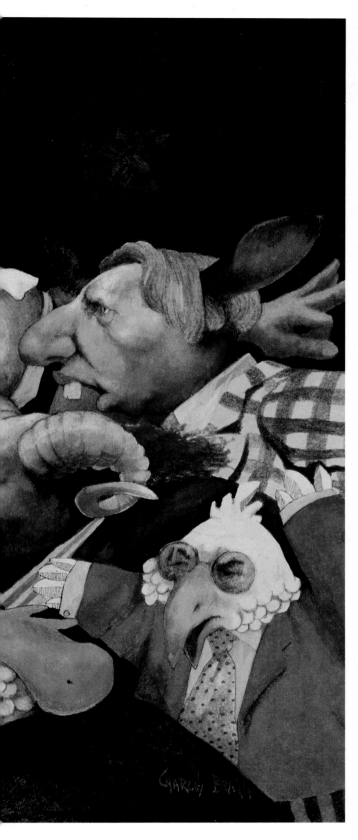

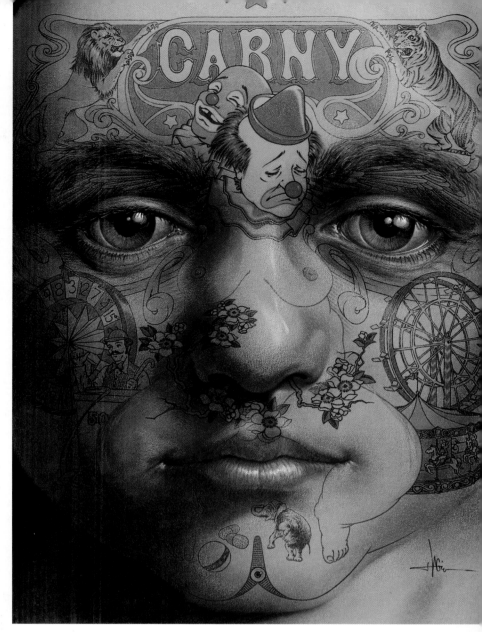

Carny, for which professional wildman Harry Crews ran away (on PLAYBOY's dime) and joined one of the last of the old-time carnivals, appeared in September 1976 (with Kunio Hagio's illustration, top right). Roger Brown illustrated *Used in Evidence* (right), a 1979 yarn by Frederick (*The Day of the Jackal*) Forsyth.

Screen stars shed clothes and inhibitions for well-remembered layouts of the late Seventies. At 19, Melanie Griffith (left) posed with her husband, Don Johnson (below left). Barbara Bach (above) did a 1977 pictorial based on the Bond movie *The Spy Who Loved Me*. Barbara Carrera's role in the 1977 film of H.G. Wells's science-fiction classic *The Island of Dr. Moreau* inspired photographer Chris von Wangenheim, with the result below. On the cover of the 414-page December 1979 issue—with inserts, PLAYBOY's biggest ever—the magazine hailed Raquel Welch (opposite) as "the decade's most desired woman." In the accompanying text, Buck Henry compared Raquel to Helen of Troy.

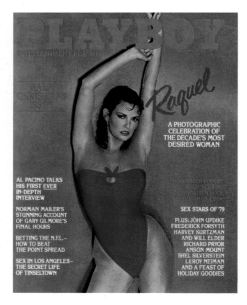

A host of celebrities graced PLAYBOY covers in the Seventies: Barbra Streisand, Dolly Parton, Farrah Fawcett, Raquel Welch, along with Burt Reynolds, the first man on a cover since Peter Sellers' 1964 appearance. Looking to hide the Rabbit in May 1976's takeoff of Georges Seurat's pointillist masterpiece, *Grande Jatte* (top left), designer Tom Staebler followed the dots and found the Rabbit's likeness foreshadowed by the artist's own hand.

ENTERTAINMENT FOR MEN

NOVEMBER 1976 • $1.50

PLAYBOY

NOW, THE <u>REAL</u>
**JIMMY
CARTER**
ON POLITICS,
RELIGION,
THE PRESS
AND SEX
IN AN
INCREDIBLE
PLAYBOY
INTERVIEW

**MUCH MORE
SEX IN
CINEMA**

YOU AND THE
STOCK MARKET:
WHERE THE
BIG MONEY IS

TURN ON TO OUR
C.B. PLAYMATE:
COVER GIRL
PATTI McGUIRE

PLAYBOY seldom published poetry, but it made an exception for Shel Silverstein's rollicking *The Devil & Billy Markham* (illustrated by Brad Holland, left). One verse from the January 1979 ballad describes the guests at Billy Markham's wedding: "And J. Edgar Hoover's in drag." Non-PLAYBOY readers had to wait 14 years to learn, in a tell-all bio, about the FBI director's taste in evening wear. Norman Mailer's riveting *The Executioner's Song*, the story of the life and death of Gary Gilmore, was serialized in late 1979. Marshall Arisman's compelling illustrations accompanied the magazine's three installments.

JOHN DEAN: *"I think the decision not to prosecute Nixon will influence his role in history. There's also the question of whether or not there will be further revelations involving him. I believe there will be. Big ones."*

NORMAN LEAR: *"This country is far more hip and sophisticated than the networks think, but TV has psyched out such large segments of our society that many people have come to believe that they are witless, corn-fed rubes."*

JIMMY CARTER: *"I'm human and I'm tempted. I've looked on a lot of women with lust. I've committed adultery in my heart many times. This is something that God recognizes I will do, and God forgives me for it."*

THE PLAYBOY

BARBRA STREISAND: *"A person who's bitchy would seem to be mean for no reason. I am not a mean person. I don't like meanness in anyone. Maybe I'm rude without being aware of it—that's possible."*

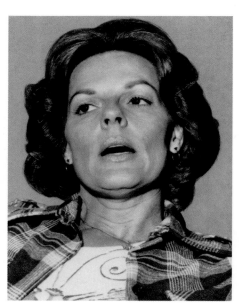

ANITA BRYANT: *"When I was a child, you didn't even mention the word homosexual, much less find out what the act was about. You couldn't imagine what they did. It was too filthy to think about."*

SYLVESTER STALLONE: *"After 'Rocky,' I went through a period of too much too soon, and the pressures got to me. I was extremely foolish in that I directed my frustrations at the people I love the most—my family."*

Just before he went to jail for his part in the Watergate coverup, John Dean spoke to PLAYBOY about his involvement and that of his former boss, Richard Nixon. Anita Bryant, who preceded Burt Reynolds and Rush Limbaugh as Florida's orange-juice pitch person, inveighed against gays. But the most famous *Playboy Interview* ever featured a presidential candidate who confessed to lust.

ALEX HALEY: *"My old cousin Georgia told me something that galvanized me—and sustained me ever since: 'Boy, yo' sweet grandma and all of 'em—dey up dere, watchin'. So you go do what you got to do'."*

ERICA JONG: *"Many women have the gut feeling that their genitals are ugly. One reason women are gratified by oral-genital relations is that it's a way of a man's saying, 'I like your cunt. I can eat it.'"*

JOHN BELUSHI: *"No, nobody on the show takes drugs. In fact, two or three vice-presidents at NBC are not here because of Aykroyd's undercover work."*

INTERVIEW

DOLLY PARTON: *"I think there is due a person like Elvis, a female, which there has never been. A person with magnetism and charisma to draw people to her. Your next question: Do I think it is me?"*

MARLON BRANDO: *"I have a burning resentment that when people meet you, they're meeting some asshole movie actor, instead of a person concerned with other things. This idiot part of life has to go in the forefront."*

BURT REYNOLDS: *"I wanted the 'Cosmopolitan' thing laid out like a Playmate story. Behind the centerfold, I wanted to be shown pushing a shopping cart and saying, 'My favorite colors are blue and pink and yellow.'"*

The tables were turned when Alex Haley, who'd conducted the first *Playboy Interview* and went on to do nine others, was interviewed in 1977, shortly after completing *Roots*. Novelist Erica Jong, author of *Fear of Flying*, pulled no punches on the subject of women's sexuality.

Saturday Nite Jive

BY BILL JOHNSON

HERE'S ONE: "SWF, 31, ATHLETIC BODY, INTO ROLLER SKATING AND DANCE, SEEKS SWM, 30+."

WOO

TOO ATHLETIC.

HERE'S ANOTHER: "LIBERATED LADY SEEKS MALE COMPANION WHO BELIEVES IN WOMEN'S RIGHTS."

NO

TOO ASSERTIVE.

HOW ABOUT "SELF-AWARE WOMAN DESIRES SELF-CONFIDENT MAN FOR SELF-GRATIFICATION."

NO

TOO SELFISH.

KNOW WHAT YOUR PROBLEM IS? YOU'RE TOO CHOOSY. NO ONE COULD LIVE UP TO YOUR STANDARDS.

NOT TRUE!

I'D BE PERFECTLY HAPPY WITH A "SWF, 18+, 36-24-36, GREEN EYES, WHO LIKES ITALIAN FOOD, OLD MOVIES AND WALKING IN THE RAIN."

YOU JUST DESCRIBED THE PLAYMATE OF THE YEAR!

SIGH A MAN CAN DREAM, CAN'T HE?

THE LONER

By Frank Baginski & Reynolds Dodson

OK, MIRROR. TONIGHT I THINK I'LL HAVE BO DEREK, RAQUEL WELCH, CHERYL TIEGS AND FARRAH FAWCETT!

YECHHH! HOW SUPERFICIAL!

WHEN ARE YOU GOING TO LEARN THAT THOSE WOMEN ARE PLASTIC AND THAT A FEMALE SHOULD BE ADMIRED FOR HER NOBILITY AND INTELLECT?!

JUST MY LUCK -- I'VE GOT BETTY FRIEDAN'S OLD CEILING MIRROR!

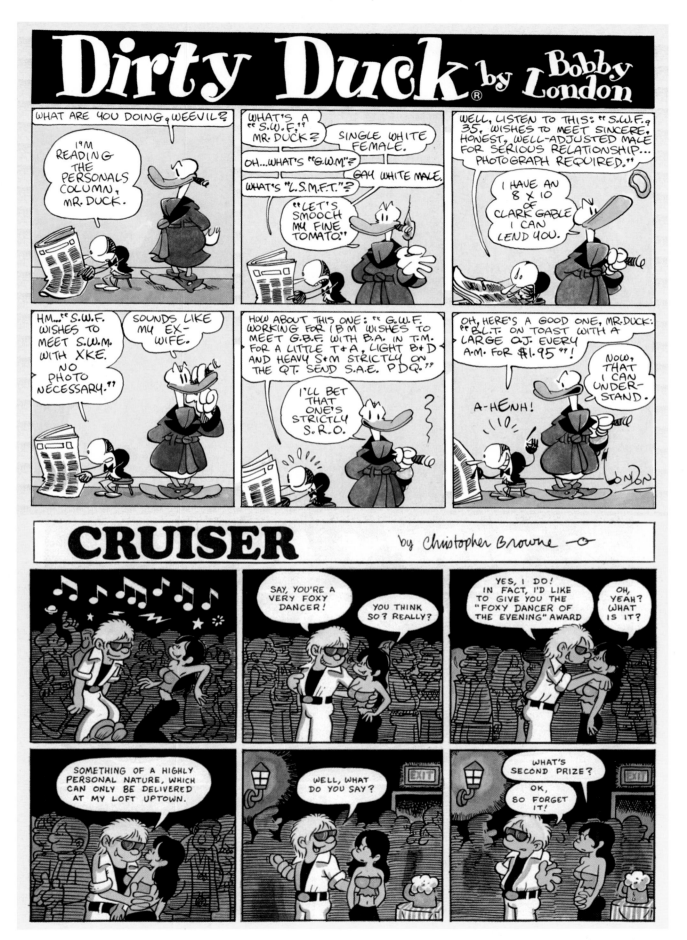

From 1977 to 1985 the *Playboy Funnies* exposed readers to the hip sensibility of sexy comics for adults—of a sophisticated type familiar in Europe but not previously introduced in America. Artists whose work appeared in family-style syndicated strips joined with underground comix cartoonists to produce for PLAYBOY a cross between comic books and Sunday funnies.

One of the magazine's most popular (and widely imitated) features, the Playmate Data Sheet, was conceived by Hefner and introduced in the July 1977 issue, in which readers learned the vital statistics and likes and dislikes of a former Sunday-school teacher, Sondra Theodore (above). Like the signature on the centerfold, added in 1975, it further personalized the Playmate. Miss July was also Hefner's latest main squeeze; the relationship lasted four years. November 1978's centerfold, Monique St. Pierre (left), was born just a few days after the first issue of PLAYBOY hit the newsstands. In 1979 she became the magazine's 20th Playmate of the Year. Patti McGuire (right), Miss November 1976 and 1977's Playmate of the Year, married tennis star Jimmy Connors.

As other magazines moved more toward raunch in their erotic photography, PLAYBOY strove for romantic artistry, as is evidenced in these shots. There was the girl with the incredible hair, 1978 Playmate of the Year Debra Jo Fondren (opposite left). Miss September 1978 Rosanne Katon (top) is now an established stand-up comedienne. Hawaiian Denise Michele (opposite center) was Miss April 1976. Professional model Karen Hafter (opposite bottom) became Miss December 1976. Chicago Bunny and cover girl Candace Collins (above) was Miss December 1979, and Miss January 1979, Candy Loving (right), became the 25th Anniversary Playmate.

FOR CHRIST'S SAKE

renouncing the image of Jesus as a melancholy ascetic, a progressive theologian calls out for his resurrection as a joyous revolutionary

opinion **By HARVEY COX** A yuletide toast! Lift the brimming beaker to that much maligned and badly misunderstood figure in Christmas lore, Ebenezer Scrooge. A heavy too long in hearthside morality tales, Ebenezer deserves an immediate rehabilitation, if only for one reason: His classic two-word description of Christmas is so elegant, so succinct and so true that saying anything more seems almost redundant. "Christmas? Bah, humbug!" As another Santa season closes, my deepest impulse is to echo his eloquent sentiment, adding only a W. C. Fieldsian cane swat at the nearest beaming Tiny Tim.

Christmas *is* humbug in the precise dictionary sense; i.e., "a fraud or imposition, sham, trickery, deception or swindle." Christmas is all these things and more. Oh, I'm not denying there are some good things about it. The whole season exudes a funny magic that gets to almost everyone in some way. But this happens *despite* what we've *(continued on page 122)* 11

ILLUSTRATION BY FRED BERGER

GALLO

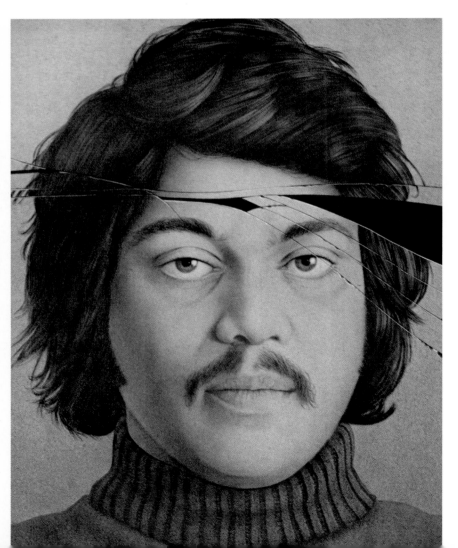

The Reverend Dr. Harvey Cox, a Baptist minister and professor of divinity at Harvard, began as a critic of the magazine but ended up as a valued contributor. His best-known piece, *For Christ's Sake*, was illustrated by Fred Berger's extraordinary portrait of a laughing Jesus. In his article, Cox excoriated ecclesiastical authorities for trying to turn Jesus, who broke taboos, kept company with shady characters and provided wine for a wedding reception, into "a prissy androgyne." Alan Magee won a PLAYBOY award for his 1977 portrait of Freddie Prinze (left), illustrating Peter Greenberg's report on the young actor's brief life and shocking suicide, *Good Night, Sweet Prinze*.

Stories by John Updike have been appearing in PLAYBOY for more than a quarter of a century. Some of them were excerpts from his prize-winning novels; others, such as 1978's *The Faint*, were original short stories. The illustrative sculpture is by another PLAYBOY favorite, artist Frank Gallo.

On joining PLAYBOY, staffers are told never to refer to a centerfold as a former Playmate: "Once a Playmate, always a Playmate" is the rule. *Playmates Forever!*, a December 1979 pictorial, featured centerfolds as beautiful as when they first posed for the magazine: Miss August 1967, DeDe Lind (left), a dozen years later; October 1969 Playmate Jean Bell (above left), who became a Hollywood actress; Heidi Becker (top right), whose June 1961 centerfold dated back 18 years; and 1965 Playmate of the Year Jo Collins (below), PLAYBOY's beloved ambassador to the boys in Vietnam.

PLAYBOY celebrated its first quarter century with a host of special events. At a publisher's dinner in Manhattan (above), *Esquire*'s Clay Felker presents Hefner with a mockup of a five dollar bill, symbolizing the raise denied Hefner when he worked at *Esquire*. Earlier, at a Playboy Mansion West benefit for the National Organization for Women's ERA strike force, Los Angeles NOW coordinator Gloria Allred and Christie Hefner watch as Hefner signs a petition asking Congress to extend the deadline for ratification of the Equal Rights Amendment.

In the fall of 1979, 136 centerfolds gathered at Playboy Mansion West for a *Playmate Reunion*. "Without you," Hefner told his guests with undisguised emotion, "I'd have a literary magazine." Above, Hef hugs three-time Playmate Janet Pilgrim (top right) and Phi Beta Kappa centerfold Vicki McCarty, Miss September 1979. Above, he is surrounded by 11 Playmates of the Year. In the front row, from left, are Cyndi Wood (1974), Monique St. Pierre (1979), Debra Jo Fondren (1978), Liv Lindeland (1972) and Linda Gamble (1961); behind them are Connie Kreski (1969), Claudia Jennings (1970), Lillian Müller (1976), Jo Collins (1965), Allison Parks (1966) and Lisa Baker (1967).

THE EIGHTIES

In the Eighties, PLAYBOY proved Nietzsche's aphorism, "If it doesn't kill you, it'll make you stronger." *It* began with the election of Ronald Reagan at the start of the decade, which immediately spawned an unholy (as well as un-American) alliance between church and state. In return for gaining the conservative vote, it appeared that Reagan handed over the Justice Department to a band of misguided zealots inspired more by born-again rhetoric than by the Constitution.

Right-wing members of the government had made their opposition to PLAYBOY known from the beginning. Hefner had to go to court in the Fifties to get a second-class permit to send his magazine through the mail. (The Post Office thought the Marilyn Monroe nude was obscene.) In 1963 he was arrested in Chicago for publishing pictures of Jayne Mansfield in scenes from her movie *Promises, Promises*. His presence on Nixon's enemies list led to harassment by both the IRS and the SEC in the Seventies, and a specious drug investigation by the DEA cost a loss of reputation and the life of one of his closest associates.

But in the Moral Majority mentality of the Eighties, it got worse—PLAYBOY was besieged by enemies from both the right and the left. The Justice Department allocated $750,000 to Judith Reisman, a former songwriter for *Captain Kangaroo*, to study the question of child pornography in PLAYBOY, *Penthouse* and *Hustler*. She cited Harvey Kurtzman's *Little Annie Fanny* as an example of kiddie porn; the Justice Department eventually rejected her report.

Reagan crony Edwin Meese put up another $500,000 to fund the Attorney General's Commission on Pornography, a cross-country witch-hunt that did no actual research, but associated PLAYBOY with pornography in the press. At one point Commission member Father Bruce Ritter (later accused of sexually molesting minors) explained his position: "I would say that pornography is immoral, and the source of my statement is God, not social science."

The Meese Commission chose fundamentalist minister Donald Wildmon of Tupelo, Mississippi as its expert witness on pornography. Based on Wildmon's testimony, Alan Sears, the director of the Commission, wrote a letter to major drug and convenience stores accusing them of selling pornography. Half of the Southland Corporation's 7-Eleven stores and a number of other drug and convenience stores across the country dropped PLAYBOY directly because of the intimidation. When the Commission hearings were concluded, Sears went to work for the Reverend Mr. Wildmon.

It seemed like old times at PLAYBOY as sexual politics took a sharp right turn in the Eighties—the decade of greed and Reaganism. From the man who wanted government off the people's backs came an era of increasing legal intrusions into citizens' private lives. Reporter Robert Scheer—who'd watched Reagan operate as governor of California—exposed the essence of the politician who preached cost-cutting but ended up nearly tripling the federal deficit: "Believe what I say, not what I do, and let's not haggle over the facts."

Hefner and PLAYBOY fought back. He responded with a stinging editorial, *Sexual McCarthyism*, which likened this form of political coercion to the McCarthyism of the Fifties. James Baldwin wrote a powerful memoir of phony evangelism, *To Crush the Serpent*, which became a finalist for the National Magazine Awards of 1988. The magazine even responded with a playful pictorial on convenience store employees who did approve of PLAYBOY, titled *The Women of 7-Eleven*. The clamor began to subside as fundamentalists Jimmy Swaggart and Jim Bakker fell from grace later in the decade, following Jessica Hahn's revelations concerning corruption in televangelism and Swaggart's dalliance with a prostitute.

Attacking the sexual hysteria of the Eighties in other forms, PLAYBOY became the first voice to provide responsible information on the AIDS epidemic. In an ironic twist, during the decade in which a government agency persecuted PLAYBOY for its content, the magazine received top honors for best fiction—the National Magazine Award of 1985—as it triumphed over entries from *The New Yorker, Harper's* and other prestigious publications. People really were reading the magazine for the articles and fiction, with the likes of John Updike, Joseph Heller, Gabriel García Márquez, Robert Coover, Elmore Leonard, Thomas McGuane and Larry McMurtry appearing in its pages.

In 1982, Hefner's daughter Christie—who had joined the company as a Special Assistant to the Chairman in 1975—was named President of Playboy Enterprises, Inc. Before the end of the decade, she was to become Chairman and Chief Executive Officer, overseeing all Playboy operations. Her father, after living the life of the quintessential bachelor for more than three decades, married Miss January 1988, Kimberley Conrad (right).

The tragedy of Dorothy Stratten captured the hearts of readers, television viewers and moviegoers in the early Eighties. Dorothy, a beautiful young woman from British Columbia who became Miss August 1979, seemed headed for great things when she became Playmate of the Year in 1980. But she had held the title only three months when she was killed by her estranged husband, who was jealous because she was leaving him for film director Peter Bogdanovich. Her story was quickly picked up by TV (*Death of a Centerfold*, starring Jamie Lee Curtis) and by Hollywood (*Star 80*, with Mariel Hemingway as Dorothy), but neither version captured the real Dorothy. Hefner commissioned a documentary telling her true story as well as a touching tribute written by Richard Rhodes (which Hefner himself edited) for PLAYBOY's May 1981 issue. The article drew an unprecedented volume of supportive mail from readers.

The first installment of *Man and Woman*—an ambitious seven-part series in which authors Jo Durden-Smith and Diane deSimone examined the physiological and psychological characteristics that make the sexes think and behave differently—was accompanied by *The Playboy Readers' Sex Survey*, which drew more than 100,000 responses. Associate Editor Barbara Nellis is surrounded by some of the mail.

The *Playboy Interview* continued making headlines with newsmakers such as Fidel Castro, Ferdinand and Imelda Marcos, Daniel Ortega and Yasir Arafat. Perhaps the most unforgettable *Playboy Interview* of the decade— and one of the most moving—was the last published conversation with John Lennon. That issue featuring Lennon and Yoko Ono was on the stands the night he was killed. Speaking of King and Gandhi, Lennon had asked prophetically, "What does it mean when you're such a pacifist, you get shot?"

In the stress of the mid-Eighties, Hefner suffered a stroke. The crisis made the Editor-Publisher reassess his priorities, and he subsequently referred to it as his "stroke of luck." After 35 years as the world's most celebrated bachelor, he announced that he had found a Playmate for life in the 1989 Playmate of the Year Kimberley Conrad. They married in July of that year in a ceremony telecast around the world. *People* magazine reported the news with the cover headline HOLY MATRIMONY! The apt subhead added: "Next week: Hell freezes over."

John Updike, a PLAYBOY contributor since 1969, achieved publishing's triple crown in 1981 with *Rabbit Is Rich*, excerpted in the magazine's September 1981 issue. It won the National Book Critics Circle Award, the American Book Award and the Pulitzer Prize. Joyce Carol Oates, also a PLAYBOY regular, contributed *The Sunken Woman* in December 1981; the accompanying artwork (opposite) is by Mel Odom. In the same issue, novelist James Baldwin investigated a subject that was all too real: the murder and disappearance of 28 black children in Atlanta. The poignant illustration at left is by Vincent Topazio.

*who would have thought sweet cindy
could be such a dirty little thing?*

RABBIT IS RICH

"I HIT THE BALL OK," Rabbit Angstrom says, "but damned if I could score." It is the great weekend of gas drought, June 1979. He is sitting in green bathing trunks at a white outdoor table at the Flying Eagle Tee and Racquet Club with the partners of his round and their wives and, in the case of Buddy Inglefinger, girlfriend. Buddy had once had a wife, too, but she left him for a telephone lineman down near West Chester. You could see how that might happen, because Buddy's girlfriends are sure a sorry lot.

"When did you *ever* score?" Ronnie Harrison asks him so loudly heads in the swimming pool turn around. Rabbit has known Ronnie for 30 years and never liked him, one of those locker-room show-offs always soaping himself for everybody to see and giving the J.V.s redbellies and out on the basketball court barging around all sweat and elbows trying to make up in muscle what he lacked in style. Yet when Harry and Janice joined Flying Eagle, there old Ronnie was, with a respectable job at Schuylkill Mutual and this quiet, proper wife who taught third grade and must be great in bed, because that's all Ronnie ever used to talk about, he was like crazy on the subject, in the locker room. He's gone completely bald on top, which doesn't change him that much, since his hair was always very fine and kind of pink anyway. Rabbit likes playing golf with him because he loves beating him, which isn't too hard: He has one of those herky-jerky punch swings short guys gravitate toward and when he gets excited he tends to roundhouse a big banana right into the woods.

"I heard Harry was a big scorer," Ronnie's wife, Thelma, says softly. She has a narrow forgettable face and still wears that quaint old-fashioned kind of one-piece bathing suit with a little pleated skirt. Often she has a towel across her shoulders or around her ankles, as if to protect her skin from the sun; except for her sunburned nose, she is the same sallow color all over. Her wavy mousy hair is going gray strand by strand. Rabbit can never look at her without wondering what wild things this biddy must do to keep Harrison happy. He senses intelligence in her, but intelligence in women has never much interested him.

"I set the B-league county scoring record in 1951," he says, to defend himself, and to defend *(continued on page 114)*

BY JOHN UPDIKE

111

ILLUSTRATION BY JEFF WACK

Having had a look at early takes from the 1979 film *10*, PLAYBOY's editors wasted no time in proclaiming Bo Derek the hottest prospect on its list of *Sex Stars* that December. Movie fans couldn't get enough of her, and when Bo starred in her own March 1980 pictorial—as "the first sex star of the Eighties"—the issue became one of PLAYBOY's most popular ever, selling an impressive 6,602,488 copies. Bo was photographed by her husband, John Derek, whose wives were something of a fixture in PLAYBOY: He'd previously shot pictorials on spouses Ursula Andress and Linda Evans for the magazine. As the decade progressed, the Dereks made other movies—among them *Tarzan, the Ape Man* and *Bolero*—and collaborated on two more PLAYBOY layouts.

Attorney General Edwin Meese—whose Commission on Pornography spent the mid-Eighties trying to effect a moral purification of American society—sports the T-shirt likeness of the Fifties witch-hunter Joe McCarthy in Steve Brodner's portrait for *Inside the Meese Commission*, a 1986 exposé by Robert Scheer. PLAYBOY joined the American Booksellers Association and other groups in suing Meese and the Commission's executive director, Alan Sears, for sending out a letter with unsubstantiated charges that the magazine had been linked with "violence, crime and child abuse." PLAYBOY won a retraction, but not before one of the corporations to which the letter had been addressed, the parent company of 7-Eleven stores, dropped the magazine from its shelves. Earlier, Peter Ross Range had warned, in *Inside the New Right War Machine*, that conservatives emboldened by Reagan's election were embarking on a moral search-and-destroy mission. The artwork (right) is by John Craig.

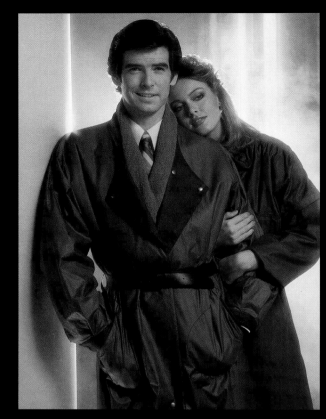

THE MODERN MAN'S GUIDE TO LIFE

listen up as we reveal the essence of civilized manhood in an uncivilized world

article
By DENIS BOYLES, ALAN ROSE and ALAN WELLIKOFF

A YEAR OR TWO AGO, we sent out what amounted to a chain letter asking modern men for advice about modern life. We hoped that by doing so, we could raise a sort of extended barroom conversation, nationwide, and get the best take on life from the three or four modern guys sitting next to the pretzels there under the TV in bars across the country. We could ask, for example, "Hey, what do you think of rats?" and somebody would probably tell us a little more than we really needed to know about rats. And mice. And how to take a gentlemanly piss. And how to win a woman. How to survive losing one.

Most important, while collecting answers, we discovered something about figurative colorization.

Colorization is what they do to old black-and-white movies so they can make some money off their re-release. It's complicated, expensive and very progressive. Trouble is, it screws up somebody's film in the process.

Colorization of one kind or another is everywhere. All the stuff that is supposed to make our lives so much easier only makes them more complicated. The most trivial daily activi-

ties—getting dressed and going to work, for example—have become fraught with political, social and moral implications. To be a man in the late 20th Century is to be a confused oppressor who dresses funny.

The New Man, who looked so promising in the Seventies, has broken down completely. The guy wimps around and cries on cue and is very sensitive and all, but he's useless in the sack and a pain at work and, worst of all, it turns out that girls, who were supposed to be the market for the New Man, hate the sucker.

The Modern Man is, in fact, an old-fashioned kind of guy, a reasonably thoughtful fellow who has listened with varying amounts of patience to all the new ideas so passionately advocated by well-intentioned people (sometimes including himself) over the past two decades and has discovered that while all of them may be new ideas, 90 percent of them are also bad ideas. So what appears here is conventional wisdom. Much of it was conventional 25 years ago; much of it will be conventional for the foreseeable future.

And that's just as well. *(continued overleaf)*

PLAYBOY never forgot its obligation to help guys with life's gracious details. Role models show how to dress: trumpeter Wynton Marsalis, embodying *The New Man* in a 1987 fashion feature; Pierce Brosnan, then starring in television's *Remington Steele*, looking dashing in raincoats, and kick-boxer Chuck Norris acting the part in pajamas. The December 1987 issue introduced an ambitious effort to tie all the loose ends together. Denis Boyles, Alan Rose and Alan Wellikoff's *The Modern Man's Guide to Life*, from a book they'd been preparing for years, was illustrated by Dave Calver. In succeeding issues, Boyles followed up on the concept with articles such as *The Thinking Man's Guide to Living with Women*.

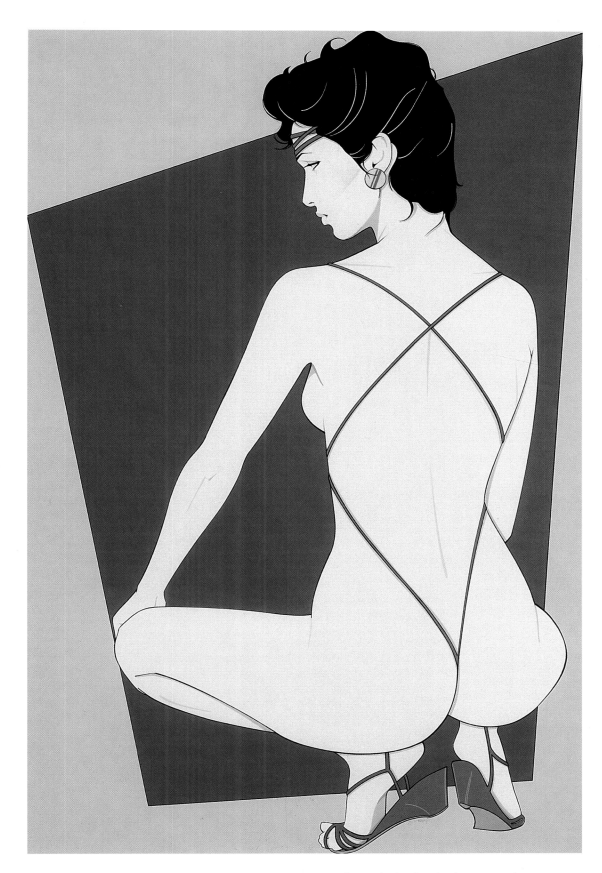

Patrick Nagel began contributing artwork to PLAYBOY in 1974, first with sketches for the pages of *Playboy After Hours* and illustrations for *The Playboy Advisor* and *The Playboy Forum*. Before long, he was creating major accompaniments to works of fiction and nonfiction. He was only 38 when he died in February 1984—ironically, of a heart attack after having participated in a benefit for cardiac research—but he had already developed a cult following. Not since Alberto Vargas had an artist captured the sensuousness of the female figure with such strikingly simple lines.

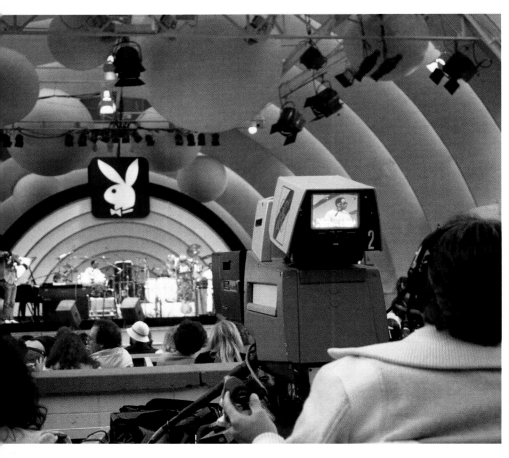

DOES YOUR television lose its flavor in the bedroom overnight? Do you often find yourself switching from channel to channel, hoping (ever in vain) to find late-night entertainment with a little more spice than Johnny Carson dressed up as a bag lady or the rampaging reptile in *Son of the Thing That Ate New Hampshire*? Don't despair. The antidote to your television doldrums is here. Dr. Playboy has just arrived with a potent prescription: the new Playboy Channel, available on more than 180 cable-television systems throughout the country; the Playboy television magazine, available to more than 600,000 over-the-air pay-TV subscribers in ten major cities; and *Playboy Video*, cassettes and discs that bring you up to 90 minutes of the best of the electronic PLAYBOY, plus special features available only to home-video-cassette and disc buyers. If you like PLAYBOY magazine, you'll love The Playboy Channel, which brings to life many

join us as we ride the new wave in adult home entertainment with video cassettes, discs, cable and on-the-air pay tv

of the magazine's most popular features: the Playmates, for instance. We do our best in this magazine to convey the personalities of these lovely ladies through photographs and words, but with the added dimension of movement and sound, our television profiles of Playmates will give you, shall we say, a more well-rounded view.

Take another example: You've seen our pictorial coverage of the annual New Year's Eve pajama party at Playboy Mansion West. But (believe us!) photographs and written words cannot fully convey the sensuous and frolicsome atmosphere that prevails when several hundred of Hollywood's most beautiful people get together in their nighties under the moonlight with good food, good drink and no holds barred. This year, Playboy Channel subscribers (and their ladyfriends) are invited to don their pajamas and join the party—via a Playboy Channel Special—to (text concluded on page 236)

VIDEO PLAYMATES. Sexy centerfolds from the magazine come alive in video versions of Playmate pictorials. Among those to enter your living room via TV are (on monitors, from left) Playmate of the Year Shannon Tweed, Patricia Farinelli, Linda Rhys Vaughn, Karen Witter.

"There's more to PLAYBOY than meets the page," the magazine advised in introducing the Playboy Channel and its pay-per-view and videocassette cousins. The December 1982 feature took readers behind the scenes to tapings of the Playboy Jazz Festival at the Hollywood Bowl, to Playmate video shootings at Playboy Mansion West (that's Kimberly McArthur in the video dish, Lynda Wiesmeier emerging from the pool), to the recording of a Mansion appearance by Manhattan Transfer (at mikes, above left, center) and the filming of a *Ribald Classic* by Casanova (above).

The Eighties • 259

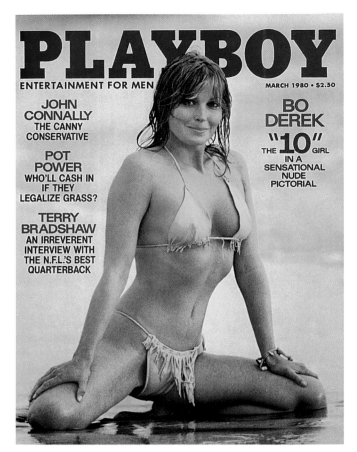

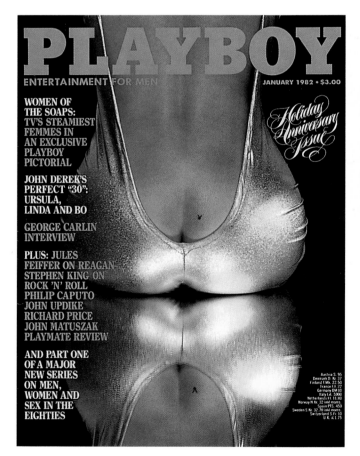

Although sexy actresses—here Bo Derek, Dorothy Stratten, Valerie Perrine and Kim Basinger—graced many Eighties covers, the golden derriere reflected at bottom left came not from Hollywood but from the offices of PLAYBOY's French edition, reversing the usual direction of transatlantic traffic. The U.S. magazine hailed it as "the best Franco-American product since Spaghetti-Os."

PLAYBOY

ENTERTAINMENT FOR MEN

FEBRUARY 1983 • $3.00

COVER GIRL

KIM BASINGER

SHE'S 007'S
NEW WOMAN
AND SHE'S A
LOOKER!
SEE EIGHT
KNOCKOUT
PAGES INSIDE

ROCKY MOUNTAIN
SIGHS...
THE WOMEN
OF ASPEN

PLAYBOY
INTERVIEWS
NOBEL PRIZE
WINNER
GABRIEL GARCÍA
MÁRQUEZ

JOSEPH WAMBAUGH'S
TOUGH NEW COP STORY
MAKES "HILL STREET"
LOOK LIKE "SESAME STREET"

THE HARSH EDUCATION
OF OLYMPIC HOCKEY
HERO JIM CRAIG

E. L. DOCTOROW
COMING SOON—1984
A LOOK AT TODAY'S REALITY
VS. ORWELL'S PROPHECY

THE YEAR IN SEX
HIGHLIGHTS OF A
WILD AND CRAZY YEAR

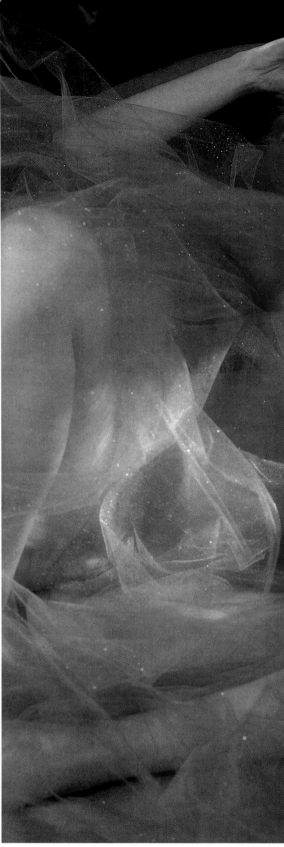

Two of the decade's most popular Playmates of the Year were Canadians: 1980's Dorothy Stratten (left) and 1982's Shannon Tweed (above). Dorothy's promising future in films was cut short by her death. Shannon was originally rejected as a Playmate candidate; she won a second chance at a test shooting on a Canadian game show. Her PMOY appearance brought her to Hollywood's attention, and she has successfully pursued a career in movies and television. She's also the live-in companion of Kiss' Gene Simmons—and mother of his offspring.

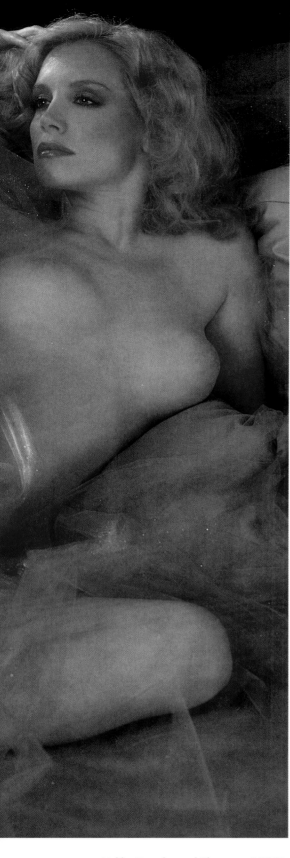

Unlike Dorothy and Shannon, 1983's Marianne Gravatte (right) never had acting aspirations. She has found happiness as a wife and mother of three lively boys (but, as demonstrated in an April 1994 pictorial, she's still in terrific shape).

FAST TIMES AT RIDGEMONT HIGH

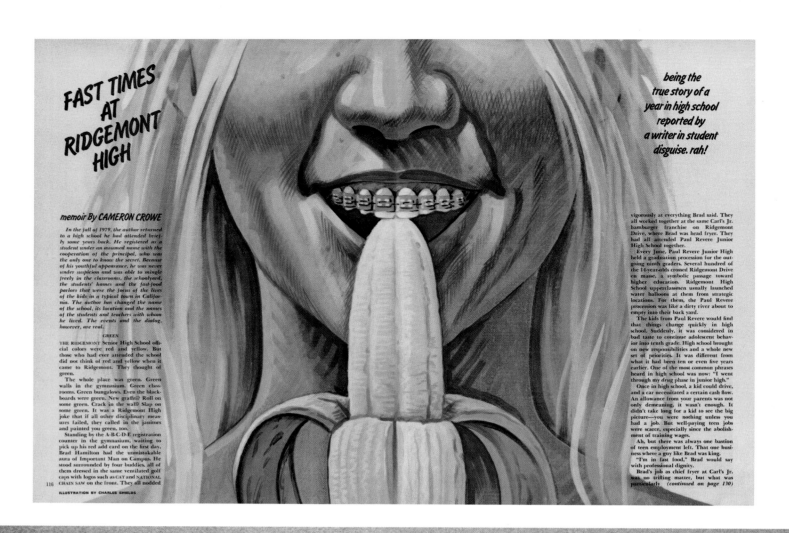

being the true story of a year in high school reported by a writer in student disguise. rah!

memoir By CAMERON CROWE

In the fall of 1979, the author returned to a high school he had attended briefly some years back. He registered as a student under an assumed name with the cooperation of the principal, who was the only one to know the secret. Because of his youthful appearance, he was never under suspicion and was able to mingle freely in the classrooms, the schoolyard, the students' homes and the fast-food parlors that were the focus of the lives of the kids in a typical town in California. The author has changed the name of the school, its location and the names of the students and teachers with whom he lived. The events and the dialog, however, are real.

GREEN

THE RIDGEMONT Senior High School official colors were red and yellow. But those who had ever attended the school did not think of red and yellow when it came to Ridgemont. They thought of green.

The whole place was green. Green walls in the gymnasium. Green classrooms. Green bungalows. Even the blackboards were green. New graffiti? Roll on some green. Crack in the wall? Slap on some green. It was a Ridgemont High joke that if all other disciplinary measures failed, they called in the janitors and painted you green, too.

Standing by the A-B-C-D-E registration counter in the gymnasium, waiting to pick up his red add card on the first day, Brad Hamilton had the unmistakable aura of Important Man on Campus. He stood surrounded by four buddies, all of them dressed in the same ventilated golf caps with logos such as CAT and NATIONAL CHAIN SAW on the front. They all nodded

vigorously at everything Brad said. They all worked together at the same Carl's Jr. hamburger franchise on Ridgemont Drive, where Brad was head fryer. They had all attended Paul Revere Junior High School together.

Every June, Paul Revere Junior High held a graduation procession for the outgoing ninth graders. Several hundred of the 14-year-olds crowd Ridgemont Drive en masse, a symbolic passage toward higher education. Ridgemont High School upperclassmen usually launched water balloons at them from strategic locations. For them, the Paul Revere procession was like a dirty river about to empty into their back yard.

The kids from Paul Revere would find that things change quickly in high school. Suddenly, it was considered in bad taste to continue adolescent behavior into tenth grade. High school brought on new responsibilities and a whole new set of priorities. It was different from what it had been ten or even five years earlier. One of the most common phrases heard in high school was now: "I went through my *drug phase* in junior high."

Once in high school, a kid could drive, and a car necessitated a certain cash flow. An allowance from your parents was not only demeaning, it wasn't enough. It didn't take long for a kid to see the big picture—you were nothing unless you had a job. But well-paying teen jobs were scarce, especially since the abolishment of training wages.

Ah, but there was always one bastion of teen employment left. That one business where a guy like Brad was king.

"I'm in fast food," Brad would say with professional dignity.

Brad's job as chief fryer at Carl's Jr. was no trifling matter, but what was particularly *(continued on page 130)*

116

ILLUSTRATION BY CHARLES SHIELDS

REAL MEN DON'T EAT QUICHE
(And Other Guidelines for the Modern Male)

humor By BRUCE FEIRSTEIN

"REAL MEN don't eat quiche," said Flex Crush, ordering a breakfast of steak, prime rib, six eggs and a loaf of toast.

We were sitting in the professional-drivers' section of an all-night truckers' stop somewhere west of Tulsa on I-44. Flex, a 225-pound nuclear-waste driver, was pensive:

"American men are all mixed up today," he began, pausing to dab a cleaning rag at the 12-gauge shotgun broken open over his knees. "There was a time when this was a nation of Ernest Hemingways. *Real Men.* The kind of guys who could defoliate an entire forest to make a breakfast fire—and then wipe out an endangered species while hunting for lunch. But not anymore. We've become a nation of wimps. Pansies. Alan Alda types who cook and 'relate' to their wives. Phil Donahue clones who are 'sensitive' and 'vulnerable' and 'understanding' of their children. And where's it gotten us? I'll tell you where. The Japanese make better cars. The Israelis, better soldiers. The Irish, better violence. And the rest of the world is using our embassies for target practice."

The entire restaurant was mesmerized. It was so quiet you could hear the day's fresh-caught fish thawing in the freezer.

"Now, I ask you," Flex continued. "Did John Wayne have relationships? Was Clark Gable ever worried about giving his women enough space? Was Bogart ever lonely because he couldn't carry on a meaningful dialog with some dame? *Of course not.* But that's the whole point. I'm convinced things were better in the old days. Men were Men. Women were sex objects. And the rest of the world understood: One false move and we'd nuke 'em."

At that point, Flex excused himself from the table to dispense his own brand of justice to several loutish dress designers who were making a ruckus at the far end of the bar. But while his desire to return to the days of "Me Tarzan, you Jane" may be somewhat impractical, Flex does raise some important questions:

How—in a world in which you're expected to be sensitive, sympathetic and split half the household chores—do you remain a Real Man? Is it possible to have relationships and shared experiences without turning into an Alan Alda? Are we doomed to abandon the principles of Strength, Dignity and Sylvester Stallone forever? Is there a way to accept the concept of the female orgasm and still command the respect of your foreign-auto mechanic?

It made us think. And in order to help the PLAYBOY reader through these emotionally troubled times, we herewith offer a guide to treading the social tightrope that has come to be the special hell

in this feminist-infested, designer-dominated, more-sensitive-than-thou world, the time has come to draw the line

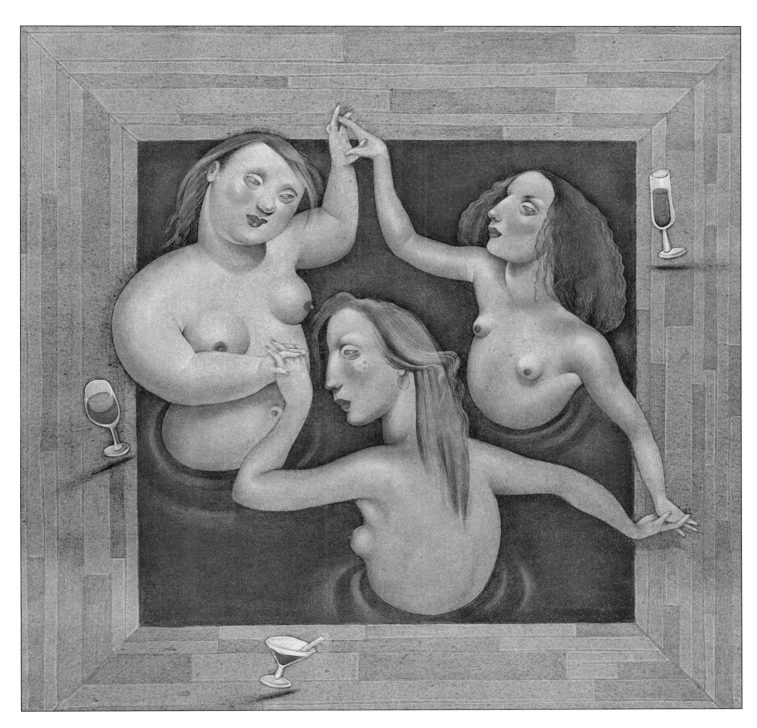

Cameron Crowe was only 16 when PLAYBOY assigned him to review the Who in 1974; five years later, still looking youthful, he went underground as a "student" at his old alma mater and wrote *Fast Times at Ridgemont High* (changing names and places). The piece, which appeared in PLAYBOY's September 1981 issue, became a 1982 movie noteworthy for the performances of Sean Penn and Jennifer Jason Leigh. It was an assignment for PLAYBOY's May 1982 issue that got writer Bruce Feirstein started on *Real Men Don't Eat Quiche*, which he expanded into a best-selling book.

Three years after its PLAYBOY publication, John Updike's *The Witches of Eastwick* came to movie theaters with Susan Sarandon, Michelle Pfeiffer and Cher—who bear little resemblance to the ladies in Anita Kunz' illustration above—in the title roles. Robert Silverberg, one of the giants of the science-fiction genre, has contributed more than a dozen stories to PLAYBOY, among them *Tourist Trade*, in which more than the earth moves for an art dealer in Morocco when he indulges in intergalactic sex. The illustration (overleaf) is by Pater Sato.

STEVE MARTIN: *"Celebrities have an obligation to have a cause to live for. I chose gay rights. I joined it and worked for it, but then I quit. Why? Because that organization is infiltrated with <u>homosexuals</u>!"*

BETTE DAVIS: *"Me? <u>Low-key</u>? Never! I did not buy that argument. Never, never! I think acting <u>should</u> be bigger than life. The scripts should be bigger than life. It should <u>all</u> be bigger than life!"*

TED TURNER: *"You know what? You're finding that I've really made it. Much as you hate to admit it, you're really impressed, aren't you? You bet your sweet ass you are. I've made it now and I've made it in television."*

THE PLAYBOY INTERVIEW

BILL COSBY: *"I was physical with my son just once, very physical. I just didn't see any other way of getting him to make a change, so along with being physical, I begged him to understand that I truly, truly loved him."*

LECH WALESA: *"We cannot overthrow the [Communist] Party, for that would be a disaster for all of us. Do you think that without the party I wouldn't push myself for president? We'd all shoot each other down!"*

PATRICIA HEARST: *"My reaction afterward was, 'No, no, they didn't do that to me!' It was almost better to think I had willingly, happily joined them than to think they had been able to play with my mind."*

Bette Davis' *Playboy Interview* revelation that she'd once posed for a nude sculpture touched off a nationwide search for the statue. It was eventually found in a private collection, having been removed from a Boston park in 1933 for being too risqué.

YOKO ONO: *"People around John saw me as a terrible threat. I mean, I heard there were plans to <u>kill</u> me. Not the Beatles, but the people around them."*

JOHN LENNON: *"Yoko was playing Beethoven's 'Moonlight Sonata' on the piano. Suddenly, I said, 'Can you play that backward?' Then I wrote 'Because.'"*

PAUL McCARTNEY: *"I don't work at being ordinary. It's quite rational. It's not contrived at all. It is actually my answer to the question, What <u>is</u> the best way to be? I think ordinary."*

LINDA McCARTNEY: *"Nobody knows what or who I am. <u>I</u> don't even know what or who I am. If I hadn't married Paul, I'd have meandered through life. I quite like meandering."*

Yoko Ono and John Lennon spoke about life with and without the Beatles in a January 1981 *Playboy Interview* that was on the newsstands when he was fatally shot outside his New York City apartment house. Paul McCartney and his wife, Linda, had their say in December 1984.

Morganna, the Kissing Bandit (above), had been bussing baseball players for 13 years before PLAYBOY readers got a look at her personal stats in 1983. Two housewives in their 30s, Marilyn Parver (below left) and Marilyn Griffin (below right)—Mrs. Georgia 1981 and Mrs. Oklahoma 1980, respectively—posed for *Meet the Mrs.* At 31, Rita Jenrette (opposite, top) described the time she and the scandal-prone congressman she married made love on the Capitol steps. Vikki La Motta was an astonishing 51 when she appeared in PLAYBOY (opposite, bottom), looking much better than she did in snapshots of her at 15, when she first caught the eye of boxer Jake La Motta.

"I just didn't think it applied to the cleaning staff as well, that's all."

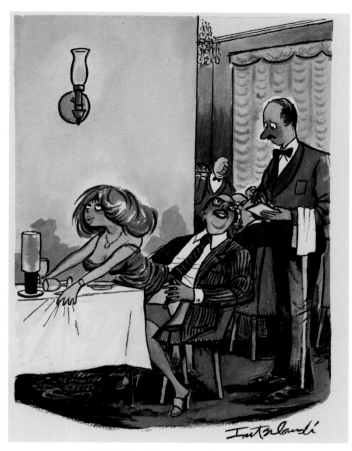

"Ah! Finally noticed us, eh?"

" I know the Grand High Warlock does his best, but there'll never be another Busby Berkeley."

"Skip the flowers, girlie, where's the lay the travel agency promised me?"

fiction

By JAMES MICHENER

*it was the final apollo mission. three men
were on their way to the far side of the moon*

SPACE

THE THREE ASTRONAUTS went to bed early on the night of April 22, 1973. On April 23, they were wakened for breakfast at 0400, and Deke Slayton, with five other NASA officials, was surprised when Major Randy Claggett lifted his glass of orange juice and toasted: "To William Shakespeare, whose birthday we celebrate with a mighty bang." Claggett, the ex-football hero, profane, tough and make-believe illiterate, was always full of surprises.

Slayton helped the three dress and accompanied them to Complex 39, where a score of searchlights played on the waiting rocket and nearly 1,000,000 spectators gathered in the predawn to watch the flight.

Despite NASA's unhappiness with the inaccurate description "expedition to the dark side of the moon," that had become the popular designation, and more than 3000 newsmen and -women waited in and around the grandstand erected on the far side of the protective lagoons, five miles distant. Automatic cameras, emplaced in bunkers around the complex, would ensure excellent shots of the historic moment.

By elevator, the astronauts rode 340 feet into the air, walked across a bridge to the White Room and, with hardly a pause, proceeded directly to the command module Altair. Without ceremony, Flight Commander Claggett eased himself into the left-hand seat, and while he adjusted his bulky suit, Dr. Paul Linley awaited his turn, assuring Slayton, who had picked him for this flight, that he would surely bring back rock samples that would answer some of the questions about the moon's structure and, perhaps, its origin. Linley, a civilian geologist from the University of New Mexico, would be the first scientist—and the first black man—to walk on the moon. He slipped into the right-hand seat, after which Command Module Pilot John Pope eased himself into the one in the middle.

When the men were finally in place, strapped flat on their backs to the seats especially molded to their forms, the critical moment of the countdown

SPACE

arrived. At 00-00-00, there was a blinding flash of fire and the ground trembled as 28,000 gallons of water per second gushed forth to quench the flames and another 17,000 gallons protected the skin of the machine. From that deluge, the rocket began to rise.

Inside the capsule, the three astronauts barely felt the lift-off. Linley, who had not flown before, said, "Instruments say we're off," and Pope, busy with check sheets, tapped the geologist on the arm and nodded.

At that moment, when it was assured that Apollo 18 would be successfully airborne, control passed from Cape Canaveral, whose engineers had done their job, to Houston, where Mission Control had hundreds of experts prepared to feed information and instructions into the system:

HOUSTON: All systems go.

APOLLO: We're getting ready for jettison.

In less than three minutes, the huge stage one had discharged its obligation, lifting the entire burden of 6,300,000 pounds eight miles straight up. So Claggett watched as automatic switches—he had more than 600 above and about him—blew stage one away, allowing it to fall harmlessly into the Atlantic some miles offshore. With satisfaction, Pope noted that all events so far had adhered to his schedule.

The first moments of flight were extremely gentle, no more than a g and a half developing, but when Claggett ignited the five powerful engines of stage two, the rocket seemed to leap upward from an altitude of a mere eight miles to a majestic 112 and to a velocity of more than 15,000 miles an hour. The flight was on its way.

Then Claggett jettisoned stage two, with its five massive engines, and Apollo 18 was powered by only the single strong engine in stage three, the one that would be burned once to insert the vehicle into orbit around Earth and once more to thrust Apollo into its course to the moon, after which it, too, would be discarded. But, of course, the

James Michener contributed a pre-publication excerpt from his novel *Space*, the story of a fatal expedition to the dark side of the moon, to the October 1982 issue; Kerig Pope's die-cut illustration of the moon (opposite) opens, when the page is turned, onto a skull. John Gardner's last short story, *Julius Caesar and the Werewolf*, was one of three works that, taken together, won PLAYBOY the National Magazine Award for fiction in 1985. (The other two were Gabriel García Márquez' *The Trail of Your Blood on the Snow* and Andre Dubus III's *Forky*.) The portrait of Caesar, above, is by Bruce Wolfe.

Terri Welles (left), Miss December 1980, won the Playmate of the Year title for 1981; Barbara Edwards (below), September 1983's centerfold, took the honors in 1984. Karen Velez (above), Miss December 1984, won the title of Playmate of the Year for 1985—and the heart of Six Million Dollar Man Lee Majors. Kathy Shower (opposite) was, at 33, the oldest woman ever to become Playmate of the Year; that was in 1986, the first year of the Playmate Phone-in, in which readers could support their choices for the title by calling a 900 number. Since then, Kathy has appeared in a dozen or more action-adventure films.

MORE THAN THE SUM OF HIS PARTS

after the accident they pieced him back together—but something happened in the process

fiction

By JOE HALDEMAN

21 AUGUST 2058

THEY SAY I am to keep a detailed record of my feelings, my perceptions, as I grow accustomed to the new parts. To that end, they gave me an apparatus that blind people use for writing, like a tablet with guide wires. It is somewhat awkward. But a recorder would be useless, since I will not have a mouth for some time and I can't type blind with only one hand.

Woke up free from pain. Interesting. Surprising to find that it has been only five days since the accident. For the record, I am, or was, Dr. Wilson Cheetham, senior engineer (quality control) for U.S. Steel's Skyfac station, a high-orbit facility that produces foam steel and vapor-deposition materials for use in the cislunar community. But if you are reading this, you must know all that.

Five days ago, I was inspecting the aluminum-deposition facility and had a bad accident. There was a glitch in my jet-seat controls, and I suddenly flew straight into the wide beam of charged aluminum vapor. Very hot. They turned it off in a second, but there was still plenty of time for the beam to breach the suit and thoroughly roast three quarters of my body.

Apparently there was a rescue bubble right there. I was unconscious, of course. They tell me that my heart stopped with the shock, but they managed to save me. My left leg and arm are gone, as is my face. I have no lower jaw, nose or external ears. I can hear after a fashion, though, and will have eyes in a week or so. They claim they will craft for me testicles and a penis.

I must be pumped full of mood drugs. I feel too calm. If I were myself, whatever fraction of myself is left, perhaps I would resist the insult of being turned into a sexless half-machine.

Ah, well. This *(continued on page 92)*

ILLUSTRATION BY ANITA KUNZ

In *More Than the Sum of His Parts*, writer Joe Haldeman crafted a modern morality play in which well-intentioned scientists perform "cyborg augmentation" on a critically injured engineer, only to create a 21st century Frankenstein's monster—a sort of RoboCop gone wrong (invigorated here by Anita Kunz' powerful illustration).

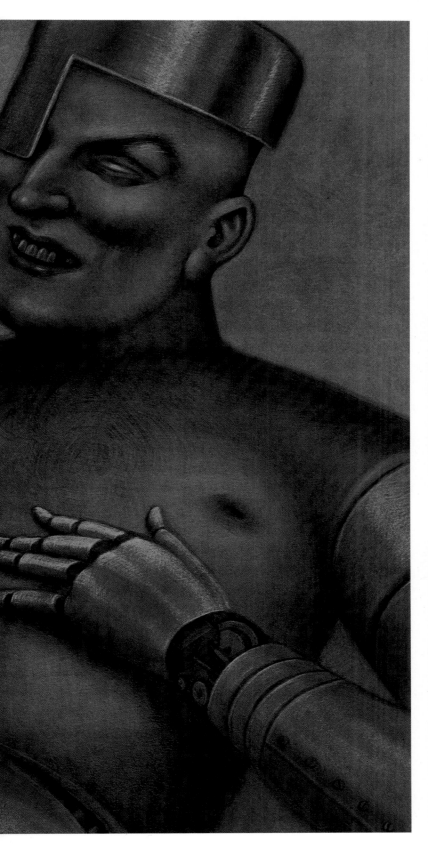

Two noted novelists, Kurt Vonnegut Jr. and Irwin Shaw—both long-time PLAYBOY contributors—wrote for the 30th Anniversary Issue in January 1984. Vonnegut, believed by the ACLU to be America's most censored author, defended the First Amendment in *The Idea Killers*, illustrated (top, right) by his daughter, Edith Vonnegut. Shaw reflected on his 70 years of life to sum up *What I've Learned About Being a Man*. It was Shaw's final piece for PLAYBOY; he died that May. The portrait (right) is by Robert Andrew Parker.

Movie fans were rewarded by layouts on Brazil's Sonia Braga (opposite, top left), introduced in PLAYBOY the year before the release of her first English-language movie, *Kiss of the Spider Woman;* Mariel Hemingway (working out for her role in *Personal Best,* opposite, top right); Kim Basinger (opposite, bottom), who has credited her 1983 PLAYBOY exposure—a pictorial with testimonials from many who'd crossed her path on her way up—with giving her career a welcome boost; Maud Adams (above), who appeared with and without tattoos in her October 1981 appearance to promote her film *Tattoo;* feisty action-film queen Sybil Danning (left), who bodily ousted her press agent–boyfriend from the premises during her interview with a PLAYBOY editor; and in 1984, Terry Moore (below), who opened up on the subject of her life as the secret bride of Howard Hughes while proving she was as much a knockout in her 50s as during the Fifties (below right).

PLAYBOY called upon Andy Warhol to collaborate with writer Truman Capote in memorializing playwright Tennessee Williams in *Remembering Tennessee* (January 1984). More stylized is Robert Risko's portrait of Reggie Jackson from June 1984 (below). Jeff Gold recalled Bogart and Bergman for Robert Coover's *You Must Remember This*, an erotic 1985 reworking of the movie *Casablanca*. Coover, who won the William Faulkner Award for best first novel of 1966, got his start as a writer in PLAYBOY's promotion department.

mr. october looks at his yankee years the way he looks at hanging curves—he measures them patiently, then takes a vicious rip

MY LIFE IN PINSTRIPES

memoir By REGGIE JACKSON with MIKE LUPICA

IT WAS APRIL 27, 1982, and to tell you the truth, I didn't feel much like Mr. October. After five years with the New York Yankees, after all the home runs and the fighting with George and the fighting with Billy, after the whole crazy story with me right in the middle of it all the time, I was coming back to Yankee Stadium and number 44 was on the back of a California Angels uniform. The problem was, I needed a home run, and I didn't know if I could hit one. After all the nights when I had come to the stadium carrying my black bat like it was a .44 Magnum, it felt like a cap pistol now. All in all, I figured it was a

hell of a situation for Reginald Martinez Jackson to be in.

There was always one thing I was supposed to be able to do: rise to the occasion. Rise to it and rise above it. And I've always done that, maybe better than anyone, at least during my generation in the big leagues. I'll admit that I've always had trouble in meaningless situations. But if you put the meat in the seats and made the game count, then I wanted to play.

People knocked me down, and I got up and hit home runs. That's who I always thought Reggie was.

But now it was April of 1982. I had

somewhere over the rainbow coalition, true power lies, and reverend jackson has his eyes on the prize

WHAT MAKES JESSE RUN?

article **By AMIRI BARAKA**

IF ATLANTA is the capital of the African American Nation in the black-belt South, then Chicago is the capital of black America. Hot is always preferred to cold in the African aesthetic. Yet Chicago is so famous for its bone-shattering, paralyzing cold that it is cited as the site of the African god Oba, whose history transformed him into an icy, death-cold wind, the hawk. And from most accounts, Chicago is his present home.

I mention all this to explain, in part, who Jesse Jackson is and why he is so important. He is, as much as Frederick Douglass was in the 19th Century, the chief spokesman of the African American people. In this sense, whatever Americans make of Jesse, black people are his bone and muscle. He can rise only as high as they are moved.

The only America black people would have any reason to support absolutely would be one in which Jesse Jackson could be elected President. It is clearly his "inelectability" that most obviously identifies the principal defects in U.S. society. The extent to which Jackson, at best, must be shown as some kind of Onyx Quixote is the extent of U.S. social primitivism, the exact measure of the legacy of chattel slavery. But how did Jesse Jackson get to a place in his head where he seriously wanted to be President?

Jackson is rooted in the black-belt South. Born in South Carolina, he went to North Carolina A&T on a football scholarship. He was moved by the dynamic Dr. Martin Luther King, Jr., and the movement for black democratic rights led by the Southern Christian Leadership Conference in the Fifties and Sixties. A combination of the black urban Southern church and the Southern

74

ILLUSTRATION BY DAVID WILCOX

The magazine brought its irrepressible perspective on politics to bear with *The Men Who Would Be President,* Robert Scheer's dissection of 1988 candidates Michael Dukakis and (opposite) George Bush, until then a perennial bridesmaid (portrayed graphically by Herb Davidson); *What Makes Jesse Run?*, an analysis of the Reverend Mr. Jackson by poet-playwright Amiri Baraka; and the 1986 indictment *Reagan and the Revival of Racism*, in which Hodding Carter III noted that Ronald Reagan's America "smells a lot like the old Mississippi."

ILLUSTRATION BY GREG SPALENKA

South Africa at Home
REAGAN AND THE REVIVAL OF RACISM

essay **By HODDING CARTER III**

IN THE EARLY FALL of 1985, the television images from South Africa stirred politicians along the Potomac—including a reluctant President—to unprecedented, if limited, action. They stirred something quite different in me—a sense of vaguely cynical *déjà vu,* of irony only thinly masking deep pessimism about the course of recent American history.

The *déjà vu* is obvious. To a white Mississippian who lived and worked in that state during the days of massive resistance to integration, televised pictures of sprawling black demonstrators and charging white cops are old stuff. Only the locale has changed.

But the cynicism springs from something more recent and far more disturbing. We Americans still seem capable of moral outrage about man's inhumanity to man or racism embodied in official policy. But now, unlike 20 years ago, our outrage grows stronger the farther away the repression. What bores or even angers us is the insistence of the nation's minorities that we are still a long way from the mountaintop

five years of this president has set black america back twenty years

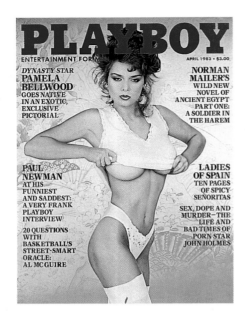

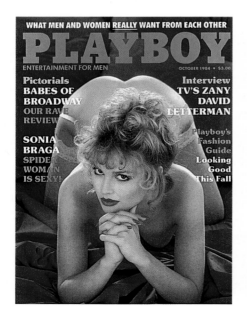

Celebs and Playmates alternated on covers from 1983 to 1985. Madonna was featured on the last PLAYBOY magazine to be stapled together (the October 1985 issue introduced flat-backed perfect binding). Bottom row center, Goldie Hawn imitates Donna Michelle's classic pose.

PLAYBOY

ENTERTAINMENT FOR MEN

SEPTEMBER 1985 • $3.50

OUR
LAST
STAPLED
ISSUE
IT'S A
KEEPER

MADONNA NUDE
UNLIKE A VIRGIN...
FOR THE VERY FIRST TIME

PLUS:
DAN JENKINS
BILLY CRYSTAL
ANSON MOUNT
JOHN HUSTON
ANDREW TOBIAS

Austria S.110, Finland F.Mk 33.50, France F.F. 40, Germany DM 14.00, Norway NOK 45.00 inkl
MVA, Spain PTS. 825, Sweden S.Kr. 49.00 inkl moms, Switzerland S.Fr. 12.50, U.K. £2.50

By the Eighties, models were overtaking movie stars as sex symbols of choice. PLAYBOY gave the trend a boost with Vanna White's 1982 photos from her pre-*Wheel of Fortune* days as a lingerie model (opposite, top left). Erstwhile Charlie's Angel Tanya Roberts (opposite, bottom) hyped her movie *Beastmaster* in a 1982 layout. Iman (near left), a native of Somalia, visited Kenya in the company of photographer Peter Beard for a 1986 pictorial. She's now Mrs. David Bowie. The model-turned-singer-turned-actress at top left used to be known as Denise Matthews. Credits for *Tanya's Island* list her as D.D. Winters; PLAYBOY predicted big things from that role for her in its *Sex Stars of 1979*. Then Prince met her and dubbed her Vanity. By any name, she was hot stuff in 1985 and 1988 PLAYBOY pictorials. Classic photos of Madonna—taken in 1979, when she was working as a nude model to support herself while getting a band together—surfaced in 1985 and helped make PLAYBOY's September issue a best-seller. And Herb Ritts' 1987 photos of yet another ex-model, Brigitte Nielsen (overleaf), turned torn fishnet into a fashion statement. This was Gitte's third PLAYBOY feature; while in New York to shoot her first, in 1985, she dropped off a note and a photo of herself at the hotel where Sylvester Stallone was staying. A speedy courtship and stormy marriage followed.

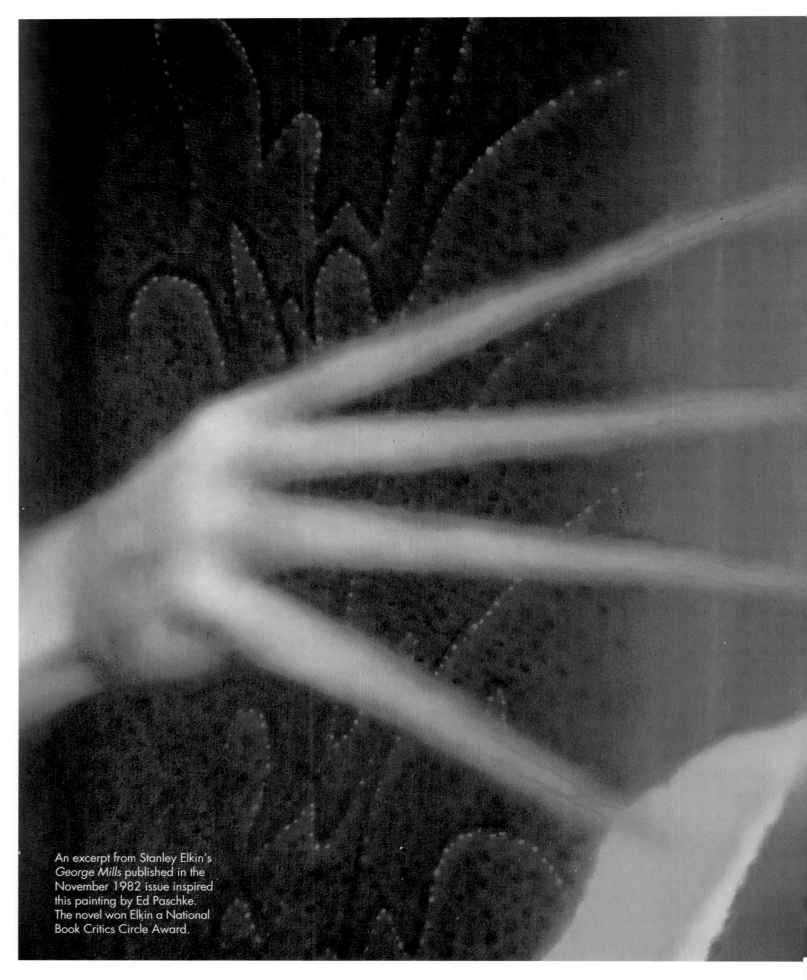

An excerpt from Stanley Elkin's
George Mills published in the
November 1982 issue inspired
this painting by Ed Paschke.
The novel won Elkin a National
Book Critics Circle Award.

The Eighties were notorious for their workaholics, but PLAYBOY's pages still celebrated fun. For dining and dancing, Jay Leno partnered with Kathy Shower to present step-by-step lessons in the newly revived art of the tango (the accompanying text was by Argentine novelist Jorge Luis Borges). *Ten-Point Spread* (opposite, near left) offered guidelines for a Super Bowl party. Pasta also enjoyed a renaissance, as demonstrated by Richard Izui's photography and Herbert Bailey Livesey's words in the April 1986 issue. At bottom, opposite, chef Paul Prudhomme, the man credited with starting America's Cajun food craze, shows off an abundance of regional ingredients for *Critics' Choice: The 25 Best Restaurants in America* (March 1987).

GOLDIE HAWN: *"If a man decides to have a quickie, he can then go to the nearest washbasin and scrub it clean and make it all new again. Girls can't necessarily do that. They walk around knowing things are going on in there."*

DR. RUTH: *"Johnny Carson said he wonders where Fred Westheimer goes when his wife has a headache. In all earnest, talking and teaching about sex is conducive to a better sex life. It has loosened me up and helped my skiing."*

SALLY FIELD: *"I walked up to accept the Oscar thinking, Shit, I've got 30 seconds, and 'Places in the Heart' was such an emotional experience. So I said to myself, 'Don't sell yourself away. Get to what you really feel and fuck 'em.'"*

THE PLAYBOY

KAREEM ABDUL-JABBAR: *"The area under the hoop is serious, serious territory, and because centers play closest to the basket, they have the most serious job. There's very little levity under the basket. That's where most people end up bleeding."*

WHOOPI GOLDBERG: *"I was born a hippie and will be till I die. When I say hippie, I mean humanist. Environmentalist. Someone who wants world peace. Zen politics. Sunshine, rainbows, God. But that was not cool in my neighborhood."*

FERDINAND MARCOS: *"I believe you have to make an accounting to God after death. For instance, He'd probably ask, 'Weren't you a participant in killing Benigno Aquino?' I'd tell Him, 'You know better than that, Lord, because I was sick.'"*

Comedienne Goldie Hawn, sex expert Dr. Ruth Westheimer, actress Sally Field, the Philippines' strongman Ferdinand Marcos, funnywoman Whoopi Goldberg and basketball legend Kareem Abdul-Jabbar spoke out on everything from skirmishes between the sexes to Oscar-night jitters, struggles for political power and battles beneath the hoop. But only Sally sported a Bunny Costume on the cover.

GORE VIDAL: *"If I had been Gary Hart, I'd have told the reporters, 'You guys are sick. All you can think about is sex. Don't you realize there are other relationships? Miss Rice is one of the greatest economists in the U.S.' And walked away."*

ARNOLD SCHWARZENEGGER: *"I experienced a lot of prejudice. The people in Hollywood had many reasons why I could not make it: my accent, my body, my long name. You have to establish yourself in such a way that no one else can compete with you."*

BILLY CRYSTAL: *"One day, I took a clicker counter with me to see how many people would say 'You look mahvelous' to me. I got up to about 170. Ted Kennedy said it to me. Then Kissinger. You know, I'm sick to death of it now."*

INTERVIEW

YASIR ARAFAT: *"In this present uprising, the Israelis are using gas made in the U.S.A., 1988. Why? We have the right to ask! Why does the U.S. support Israel in this way, turning our people into an experiment for new weapons?"*

TOM HANKS: *"If there's any age I analyzed, even before preparing for 'Big,' it was those junior high years, when you can't figure anything out. You're cranky all the time; the chemicals in your body are out of whack."*

CANDICE BERGEN: *"My father made me suspicious of beauty. He said all the beautiful women he knew ended up committing suicide or being failures as human beings. He said I should always cultivate everything in spite of it."*

Morgan Strong had been trying to interview Palestine Liberation Organization leader Yasir Arafat since June 1982, when their planned meeting was postponed by Israel's surprise invasion of Lebanon. Tapes of their long-delayed talks, held in 1987, were temporarily confiscated by an Iraqi security guard at a stopover in Baghdad, but the conversation finally appeared in PLAYBOY's September 1988 issue.

at the peak of his wealth and power, howard hughes ruled his kingdom by correspondence—and tried to take over the u.s. government the same way

CITIZEN HUGHES

PART I

article By MICHAEL DROSNIN

In the early-morning hours of June 5, 1974, unknown burglars staged a daring break-in at 7000 Romaine Street in Hollywood—the nerve center of a vast secret empire, the supposedly impregnable headquarters of Howard Hughes.

The burglars were after not only his money but also his secrets. At the height of his wealth and power, the phantom billionaire commanded his empire by correspondence, scrawling his orders in thousands of handwritten memos, hearing back from his operatives in reports dictated to his aides. And the Romaine Street vaults safeguarded all those hidden files.

Before dawn, the burglars had escaped with nearly 10,000 of the most secret papers of the world's most secretive man, memos Hughes himself called "the very most confidential, almost sacred information as to my very innermost activities."

The CIA, the Mafia, the White House and the Hughes organization itself were all suspect, but despite a top-secret FBI investigation and a $1,000,000 CIA buy-back bid, the break-in was never solved and none of the stolen papers were ever found.

The papers were still missing and the mystery still remained when reporter Michael Drosnin began his own investigation years later—an investigation that eventually led him to the burglars and to the stolen

Howard Hughes was the subject of endless fascination for PLAYBOY editors, who published more than a half-dozen articles about the eccentric recluse. Michael Drosnin spent seven years researching his book *Citizen Hughes,* excerpted by PLAYBOY in November and December 1984; Don Ivan Punchatz' illustration emphasizes the billionaire's famous overgrown fingernails. In *Cocaine: A Special Report,* Laurence Gonzales sounded the alarm that coke is more dangerous than heroin. Keith Haring created some of his trademark figures (opposite) for Laurence Shames' *Yikes! Business Superstars!,* a 1986 swipe at the prevailing myth that corporate CEOs are the new folk heroes.

COCAINE
A SPECIAL REPORT

the world knows that this glamorous drug has turned mean—but only a handful of people know why

article

By LAURENCE GONZALES

IN 1982, a man—call him Tom—was hospitalized for aplastic anemia, a bone-marrow disease. Tom underwent surgery twice. He was 22 years old and psychologically normal, according to his physicians. One effect of his illness was sores in his mouth. As part of his treatment, for pain, he was given the topical anesthetic cocaine—about a third of a gram every four hours for 16 days. It got into his blood stream the same way cocaine gets into the blood stream of people who snort it: through the membranes that line the nose and mouth. A report in the *New England Journal of Medicine* explained what happened as a result:

Day 16 the patient's pulse rose . . . to 140 [beats] per minute, and he had nausea, vomiting, headaches, insomnia, chills and fever, in spite of other normal vital signs. During the next 18 hours, he reported seeing ants on his clothes, in his food, on nursing personnel and throughout his room; his euphoric mood was punctuated by irritability and pressured speech. He saw "shadows" of his mother and related a hallucination in which he witnessed a cardiac arrest in an adjacent room. He became increasingly garrulous and active, pacing his room, cleaning his drawers, upholstering a chair [sic] and retaping his intravenous needle. During the next six hours, he exhibited jerking muscular movement, twitching of his head and extremities and a fine tremor. A tentative diagnosis of toxic cocaine psychosis was made.

There are a number of important implications of Tom's experience. For one

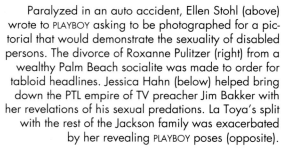

Paralyzed in an auto accident, Ellen Stohl (above) wrote to PLAYBOY asking to be photographed for a pictorial that would demonstrate the sexuality of disabled persons. The divorce of Roxanne Pulitzer (right) from a wealthy Palm Beach socialite was made to order for tabloid headlines. Jessica Hahn (below) helped bring down the PTL empire of TV preacher Jim Bakker with her revelations of his sexual predations. La Toya's split with the rest of the Jackson family was exacerbated by her revealing PLAYBOY poses (opposite).

Cover girl Cindy Crawford became a fan of the magazine in August 1987, when she spotted fellow model Paulina Porizkova on the cover and bought a copy. Then she saw photographer Herb Ritts' layout on Brigitte Nielsen in the December issue—and decided to go for it herself. Ritts' black-and-white photographs of Cindy appeared in the July 1988 issue. Interviewed for *20 Questions* in 1993, Cindy recalled: "When I did PLAYBOY, I got letters from women who didn't consider it feminist to do nude photographs. I thought the whole point of being a feminist was that you got to make your own choices."

"It's a beautiful honeymoon, dear,
but I still miss my vibrator."

" I'm not screwing my secretary, darling. This is my
new boss, and she's screwing _me_!"

"There's a lot of good will here tonight."

"Thank you for that Olympic moment!"

PLAYBOY READERS' CHOICES

R&B

C&W

POP/ROCK

JAZZ

POP/ROCK

1. Keyboards: **Billy Joel**
   Composer / Songwriter: **Billy Joel**
2. Bass: **Paul McCartney**
3. Female Vocalist: **Stevie Nicks**
4. Male Vocalist: **Michael Jackson**

5. Group: **The Police**
6. Drums: **Phil Collins**
7. Guitar: **Carlos Santana**

R&B

1. Group: **Earth, Wind & Fire**
2. Male Vocalist: **Michael Jackson**

3. Female Vocalist: **Donna Summer**
4. Composer / Songwriter: **Lionel Richie, Jr.**

JAZZ

1. Guitar: **George Benson**
2. Keyboards: **Herbie Hancock**

3. Percussion: **Buddy Ri**
4. Male Vocalist: **Al Jarr**
5. Female Vocalist: **Ella**
6. Group: **Manhattan Tra**
7. Woodwinds: **Grover W**

Playboy Music '84 found readers choosing another eclectic group of rockers and musicians, illustrated by the last of a long-running series of caricatures of winners by Bill Utterback.

8. Bass: **Stanley Clarke**
9. Brass: **Chuck Mangione**
10. Vibes: **Lionel Hampton**
11. Composer/Songwriter: **Quincy Jones**

C&W

1. Group: **Alabama**

2. String Instrumentalist: **Roy Clark**
3. Female Vocalist: **Dolly Parton**
4. Male Vocalist: **Kenny Rogers**
5. Composer/Songwriter: **Willie Nelson**

(For complete Poll results, see page 193.)   97

erald
r
ington, Jr.

Readers named Cyndi Lauper (painted by Robert Risko, top) Best Female Vocalist of 1985. The 1986 music package included the Billy Idol makeover, in which editors teased the singer for suddenly turning sensitive (the portrait at center right is by fashion illustrator Antonio Lopez). In 1989 Eddie Van Halen saw his bust added to Playboy's Hall of Fame.

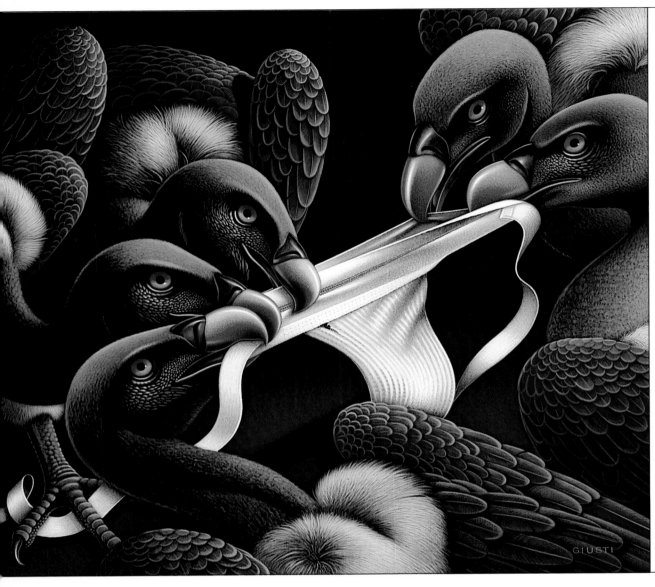

MEAT AND MONEY AT FOOTBALL CAMP

WELCOME

TO THE N.F.L.'S PREMIERE

SCOUTING EVENT,

WHERE THE G.M.S, AGENTS

AND COACHES ARE

LOOKING FOR

A FEW GOOD MEN

THE early-morning flight from Pittsburgh to Indianapolis is mostly business people, studying *The Wall Street Journal.* They settle in, order coffee from the flight attendants and attack the endless gray columns of type and the seas of tiny numbers. A few of them even take notes.

But there are perhaps half a dozen passengers who do not fit the mold. For one thing, they do not wear business suits. They're dressed in sweaters, jeans and cowboy boots.

But it isn't just their clothing that sets these guys off and tells you they are different. These men are big, and not merely *large.* They are big and powerful, radiating strength and a kind of appealing brutality. They are much too big for the airplane seats, and when two of them sit next to each other, the effect is almost comic. They could be grownups sitting in furniture designed for children.

None of the big men reads the *Journal.* None of them reads anything. Some sleep and some look out the windows and some just sit, not bored but utterly (continued on page 104)

article
BY GEOFFREY NORMAN

G

REG NORMAN IS consumed by the hungers. Whatever he wants, he wants it badly. Whatever he does, he does it full force.

If it is a friendly round of golf with his cronies—just a good ol' bunch of salesmen, duffers and hacks—Norman is still grinding away with his powerhouse specialty act that screams past your head like a flaming parrot. When you total up the damage, you see that he has thrown a 62 at you.

If he asks you to follow him out to the house for a beer, you will find yourself involved in a hell-for-leather Mad Max chase scene down some backwoods Florida two-lane, muscling cars out of the way like a moonshiner shaking off revenuers.

If he collected any car in the world, naturally it would be the Ferrari. He has three and recently put a deposit down on a fourth—the new F40, good for 200 mph. Wherever he's going, he's going with the wind howling, the streamers flying and the pedal mashed to the floor.

Modern golf is not overburdened with such swashbucklers. Norman, the Great White Shark, is one of the few professional golfers who actually appear to be full-blooded athletes. He has impressively wide shoulders, narrow waist, muscular poise. Long, angular face framed by his platinum-white surf-Nazi hair. Even amid the monotonous bronzed perfection of American golf, the sight of Norman, rifling his unconscionably long and straight drives and taking divots that should slow the earth's rotation, has inspired deep contemplation and held breath.

He has worked his way into the public

SHARK ATTACK

personality
By CHRIS HODENFIELD

australia's great white, greg norman, plays golf spikes up

Sports became more important to the PLAYBOY of the Eighties. In *Meat and Money at Football Camp,* Geoffrey Norman reported on the goings-on among NFL scouts and prospective players (the illustration is by Robert Giusti). Chris Hodenfield's *Shark Attack* profiled golfer Greg Norman (the accompanying painting is by Wilson McLean). In *Tyson the Terrible,* Pete Dexter wrote that something in Mike reminded him of the creature from *Alien:* "There is something like that inside Tyson, and he isn't the one who gets eaten." Brad Holland provided the illustration (opposite).

HOLLAND

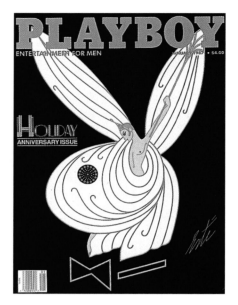

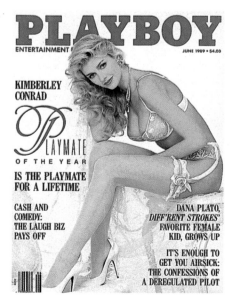

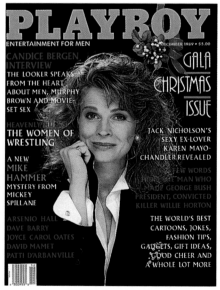

Specially commissioned works by Andy Warhol (opposite), Robert Hoppe (middle row, center) and the octogenarian Erté (top row, right) adorned January issues from 1986 to 1988. But the decade's most unexpected cover was the one from June 1989 proclaiming Hefner's intended as Playmate for a Lifetime (bottom row, center).

Miss July 1989, Erika Eleniak (opposite), was one of the lifeguards in the popular syndicated television series *Baywatch* before being picked to co-star in the feature films *Under Siege, The Beverly Hillbillies* and *Chasers*. Former nurse Susie Owens (opposite, top), discovered by PLAYBOY for its 1983 *Women in White* layout, became Miss March 1988 and later reinvented herself as the comic-book heroine Flaxen. February 1986 Playmate Julie McCullough won legions of fans in TV's *Growing Pains* series. Donna Edmondson, the "Virgin Playmate" (above), confessed in her November 1986 centerfold story that she was sexually inexperienced. Readers loved it; she became 1987's Playmate of the Year.

The decade neared its close with some nagging questions still unanswered: Shouldn't prejudice be a dead issue at the nation's colleges? It's not, answered Trey Ellis and David J. Dent in *Campus Racism*, illustrated by Gary Kelley (opposite). Just what was there about convict Willie Horton that allowed George Bush to use his criminal record to gain a free ride to the presidency? Interviewed by Dr. Jeffrey M. Elliot for *A Few Words from...Willie Horton* (December 1989, left), Horton claimed that "the real con man is George Bush." And wasn't Iran's release of American hostages on the day of Ronald Reagan's first inauguration a little too pat—especially in the wake of Iran-contra revelations? The issue was provocatively examined in October 1988 by Abbie Hoffman and Jonathan Silvers. Their *An Election Held Hostage* was illustrated by Nick Backes (below).

While other publications devoted their space to pop and rock, PLAYBOY never forgot its loyal jazz audience. In 1979 the Playboy Jazz Festival was resurrected in L.A.'s Hollywood Bowl, where it has featured the greatest stars of the genre—and played to standing-room-only crowds—every year since. The extravaganza is preceded by a series of free musical programs staged in and around Los Angeles. In 1994 Bill Cosby will make his 14th appearance as the festival's master of ceremonies.

The Great Playmate Hunt conducted for PLAYBOY's 35th anniversary netted 11 centerfolds for forthcoming issues; Hefner poses with some of the candidates at Playboy Mansion West (below). But his mind became focused on one Playmate—Miss January 1988, Kimberley Conrad, who became Mrs. Hugh Marston Hefner on July 1, 1989, after a yearlong courtship. The wedding was attended by an intimate group of 100 of the couple's closest friends and family at Playboy Mansion West in front of the very wishing well where Hefner had proposed to Kimberley on bended knee. A TV crew taped the ceremony, and it was viewed by millions across the globe. A Smilby cartoon mirrored the world's surprise.

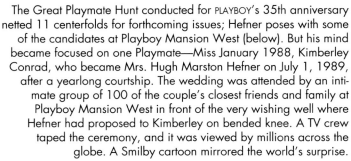

"Hugh Hefner? . . . Married? . . ."

THE NINETIES

our decades had passed since Hefner wrote his first appeal to would-be readers, offering a blueprint for the kind of magazine that would please the indoor man: "We like our apartment. We enjoy mixing up cocktails and an hors d'oeuvre or two, putting a little mood music on the phonograph and inviting a female acquaintance for a quiet discussion of Picasso, Nietzsche, jazz, sex." In 1953, Hefner wrote about cocktails, conversation and hors d'oeuvres. In the January 1993 issue, actor Eric Bogosian described the latest diversions in a piece called *Testimony of a Crazed Urbanite*: "There's a store that sells every record, every CD, every book, every magazine, every poster, every videotape, every computer program, every comic book. You can play pool, swim, play pinball, bowl, meditate, learn to box, work out, play ball, Rollerblade and mud-wrestle in the city. Every sexual kink and every spiritual sect is here. You can be damned or be saved, it's your choice. It's called freedom."

Just as the times had evolved, so had PLAYBOY. Through it all the magazine has been a moral compass, offering direction to men playing at the frontiers of freedom. It became an international publication with 18 foreign editions including Australia, Brazil, the Czech Republic, Japan, Germany, Greece, Turkey, Poland and South Africa. When the Iron Curtain fell, PLAYBOY became a symbol for the freedom long denied citizens of eastern Europe.

The decade began with the religious right waging an all-out campaign on the arts. In Cincinnati, a group of bluenose fundamentalists and prudish prosecutors tried to imprison the director of a museum for curating an exhibit of sexually explicit photographs. PLAYBOY covered the trial, at which a jury of ordinary citizens made a choice for art and liberty. Cincinnati was the original home of Citizens for Decent Literature, an anti-porn group founded in the Sixties by longtime PLAYBOY nemesis Charles Keating. The magazine exposed the corruption behind Keating's pious façade, charting the downfall of an S&L scoundrel.

As the religious right self-destructed, PLAYBOY looked at the tragic consequences of sexual repression. The nation, wracked with paranoia and prejudice, seemed all too willing to engage in a witch-hunt for nonexistent monsters. The magazine challenged stories of ritual child abuse in day-care centers, examined the excuses of serial killers and took a critical look at false memories of child abuse being manufactured by therapists. The Clarence Thomas–Anita Hill confrontation gave PLAYBOY an opportunity to help define and arbitrate the issues in the continuing battle of the sexes. Radical feminists chanted "Men just don't get it." But men did get it—in PLAYBOY. A few months after the Clarence Thomas hearings, the founder of modern feminism, Betty Friedan, appeared in a *Playboy Interview* to set the issue straight. And, as an antidote to seriousness, the magazine reduced the conflict to its essentials by publishing a guide to flirting with liberated women.

By the Nineties, the battle of the sexes had grown noisier and PLAYBOY added to the din with such articles as Glenn O'Brien's *Flirting with Feminists*, described as "the essential manual on how to pick up the enlightened woman." The tightrope on which the sexes wobble and trip was painted by Wiktor Sadowski.

While pictorials still celebrated the girl next door, increasing numbers of supermodels took time to create stunning pictorials. Cindy Crawford helped set the standard—a photo session with Herb Ritts is now an essential part of every world-class model's portfolio. Rachel Williams, Stephanie Seymour and Elle Macpherson revealed the figures behind the fashion. And, not for the first time, the magazine returned the favor. The ad director for Guess jeans noticed Anna Nicole Smith on the cover of PLAYBOY and contributed to her international celebrity, as she became the 1993 Playmate of the Year. The magazine continued to support its concern about the AIDS crisis by enlisting Hollywood stars to create a portfolio of safe-sex fantasies. The project, which placed Shannen Doherty on the cover, was a life-affirming look at love in the Nineties.

Hefner had become an elder statesman of the sexual revolution, but he didn't act like it. He was the subject of *Once Upon a Time*, a full-length documentary produced by Mark Frost and David Lynch. (One critic called it a cross between *Citizen Kane* and *Truth or Dare*.) He was hard at work on a long-awaited autobiography, a chapter of which appeared in the 40th Anniversary Issue. Lest he appear guilty of taking himself too seriously, Hefner put in guest appearances on *Fresh Prince of Bel Air* and the *Larry Sanders Show*.

In its fifth decade PLAYBOY continues to be the most popular men's magazine in the world—selling more copies every month than *GQ*, *Rolling Stone* and *Esquire* combined. One editor offered an explanation: "Hefner has been blamed for creating the permissive society. He did, and hundreds of writers, artists, photographers and models used that permission to create the best work of their lives."

Disenchanted voters who saw hope in the presidential candidacy of Ross Perot could have saved themselves their United We Stand America dues if they'd read Roger Simon's profile *See Ross Run* and CIA veteran Frank Snepp's sidebar *The Company He Keeps*, about Perot's ties to Oliver North. The illustration is by master caricaturist David Levine, whose work has accompanied the *Playboy Profile* series since April 1990.

Hugh Hefner: Once Upon a Time, the David Lynch and Mark Frost documentary of Hefner's life story, premiered at the 1992 Chicago Film Festival, where Siskel and Ebert gave it two thumbs up. It has been shown on cable television as well as at other fests from Berlin to Palm Springs, and is now available on video. Fashion magazines tried to make waiflike models the idols of the Nineties; PLAYBOY readers and admirers of Guess ads around the world preferred the amply endowed Miss May 1992, Anna Nicole Smith, soon to be named Playmate of the Year (opposite). As she herself put it, "Who wants to hug a skeleton?"

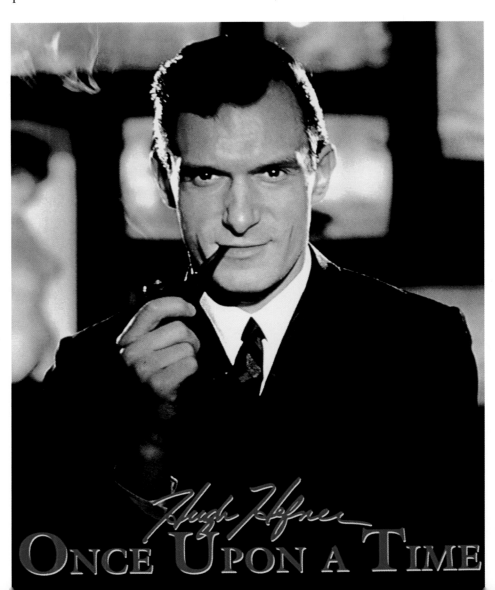

ONCE UPON A TIME

Playboy Advisor James R. Petersen covered the trial of Dennis Barrie, director of Cincinnati's Contemporary Arts Center, who was indicted on obscenity charges for exhibiting controversial photos by Robert Mapplethorpe. When the jury returned not-guilty verdicts, Petersen warned "it could just as easily have gone the other way." In his illustration for *Showdown in Cincinnati*, Rafal Olbinski pays homage to masterpieces that have also been blasted by would-be censors. Arthur C. Clarke, a PLAYBOY stalwart since 1958, kept seeing into the future with *Reach Out & Teleport Someone* (January 1992). In *Columbus, Go Home*, another valued contributor, Garry Wills, commented on the trash-Columbus boomlet of the 1992 Quincentennial. After 500 years as a hero, Columbus was no longer politically correct. His portrait is by Kinuko Y. Craft.

REACH OUT
& TELEPORT SOMEONE

THE MASTER OF FUTURISM LOOKS LONG-
DISTANCE AT THE NEXT WAVE IN COMMUNICATIONS

✳

AS THE CENTURY THAT SAW the birth of electronics and optoelectronics draws to a close, virtually everything we have wished to do in the field of telecommunications is now technically possible. The only limitations are financial, legal or political.

But, have we indeed reached the limits of communications technology? Men have always proclaimed that there is nothing more to invent, and they have always been proved wrong.

Electricity has been our most valuable and versatile tool for only a small fraction of human history—yet, see what it has done in its brief time. We are now uniting electron and photon to develop the science of optoelectronics, which will create devices whose names will be as familiar to our children as TV, video tape, CD, Comsat, laser and floppy disk are today—and as meaningless to us as those would have been to our grandparents.

Since the existence of radio waves would have been inconceivable just a few lifetimes ago, one cannot help wondering what other useful surprises nature has up her sleeve. The electromagnetic spectrum has been thoroughly explored—contrary to Edgar Rice Burroughs' hero John Carter, who discovered two new colors on Mars. But are there any other radiations and fields to be found, perhaps with properties that might make them even more valuable than radio waves?

It must have been 60 years since I encountered a story in *The Boy's Own Paper*—almost the only source of science fiction in my

ARTICLE BY ARTHUR C. CLARKE 151

ILLUSTRATION BY STEVE BOSWICK

COLUMBUS,

the 500th anniversary
of the european
discovery of america was
supposed to be a bash.
it's turning out to be
a bashing

article By Garry Wills

A CENTURY AGO, Christopher Columbus inspired what was arguably the greatest party ever thrown on this continent, the most visionary of all world's fairs, Chicago's World Columbian Exposition, which raised a gleaming White City on the shore line of Lake Michigan. Even the guarded and ironic Henry Adams said this vision had battered his defenses and left him "crushed flat" by revelations: "Chicago was the first expression of American thought as a unity." All that to celebrate the 400th anniversary of Columbus' arrival in the Americas.

One might have predicted an even grander bash for the 500th anniversary—that nice round number, half a millennium. A decade ago, Chicago itself was getting ready to repeat the fabled exposition, or even to top it.

But there was trouble from the outset. Environmentalists did not want any further tampering with Lake Michigan's shore line. Communities quickly mobilized to prevent incursions into their settled patterns. Much had changed in the intervening century—a fact made evident in the person of Mayor Harold Washington. A black man presiding over a new White City—that was something the planners of the Columbian Exposition, for all their visionary gifts, could never have foreseen. Mayor Washington had constituencies quite different from those addressed by Mayor Carter Harrison in the 1890s. The White City had been thrown up by the civic muscle and boundless money of the Gilded Age. Chicago's millionaires had income from rail, grain and livestock deals that were hardly disturbed by Chicago's cyclonic Great Fire of 1871.

But in the 1980s, planning for a new fair required government money at all levels, and competitors for that money thought there were better uses for it than in throwing a large party on the lake front. Some $10,000,000 was allotted to the planning and selling of the fair, but community groups opposed it

PAINTINGS BY KINUKO Y. CRAFT

GO HOME

the 500th anniversary
of the european
discovery of america was
supposed to be a bash.
it's turning out to be
a bashing

article By Garry Wills

A CENTURY AGO, Christopher Columbus inspired what was arguably the greatest party ever thrown on this continent, the most visionary of all world's fairs, Chicago's World Columbian Exposition, which raised a gleaming White City on the shore line of Lake Michigan. Even the guarded and ironic Henry Adams said this vision had battered his defenses and left him "crushed flat" by revelations: "Chicago was the first expression of American thought as a unity." All that to celebrate the 400th anniversary of Columbus' arrival in the Americas.

One might have predicted an even grander bash for the 500th anniversary—that nice round number, half a millennium. A decade ago, Chicago itself was getting ready to repeat the fabled exposition, or even to top it.

But there was trouble from the outset. Environmentalists did not want any further tampering with Lake Michigan's shore line. Communities quickly mobilized to prevent incursions into their settled patterns. Much had changed in the intervening century—a fact made evident in the person of Mayor Harold Washington. A black man presiding over a new White City—that was something the planners of the Columbian Exposition, for all their visionary gifts, could never have foreseen. Mayor Washington had constituencies quite different from those addressed by Mayor Carter Harrison in the 1890s. The White City had been thrown up by the civic muscle and boundless money of the Gilded Age. Chicago's millionaires had income from rail, grain and livestock deals that were hardly disturbed by Chicago's cyclonic Great Fire of 1871.

But in the 1980s, planning for a new fair required government money at all levels, and competitors for that money thought there were better uses for it than in throwing a large party on the lake front. Some $10,000,000 was allotted to the planning and selling of the fair, but community groups opposed it

PAINTINGS BY KINUKO Y. CRAFT

Warren Farrell, a former board member of New York's chapter of the National Organization for Women, broke with NOW and began critiquing feminism in his best-seller *Why Men Are the Way They Are*. PLAYBOY published a two-part excerpt from his next book, *The Myth of Male Power*, in 1993. Kinuko Y. Craft recalls Gulliver's plight in her illustration for part one, while Wiktor Sadowski chose the imagery of a cat-and-dog fight the following month. Georganne Deen's artwork for Denis Boyles' *The Thinking Man's Guide to Talking With Women* (opposite) depicts the seemingly harmless phrases that can turn relationships awry.

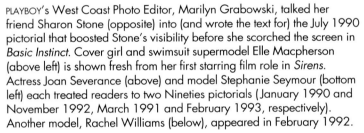

PLAYBOY's West Coast Photo Editor, Marilyn Grabowski, talked her friend Sharon Stone (opposite) into (and wrote the text for) the July 1990 pictorial that boosted Stone's visibility before she scorched the screen in *Basic Instinct*. Cover girl and swimsuit supermodel Elle Macpherson (above left) is shown fresh from her first starring film role in *Sirens*. Actress Joan Severance (above) and model Stephanie Seymour (bottom left) each treated readers to two Nineties pictorials (January 1990 and November 1992, March 1991 and February 1993, respectively). Another model, Rachel Williams (below), appeared in February 1992.

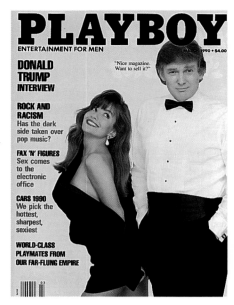

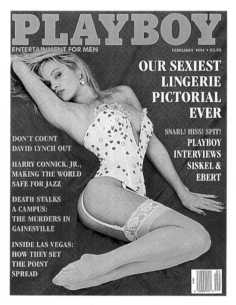

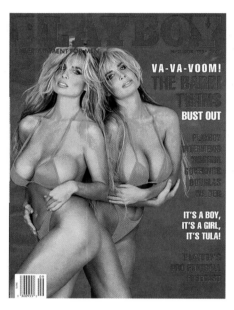

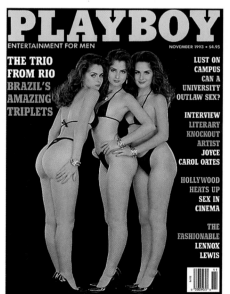

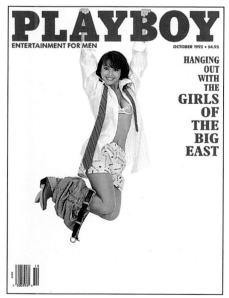

Feminists howled when Old Milwaukee beer commercials introduced a sexy but spurious Swedish Bikini Team. PLAYBOY's January 1992 Bikini Team cover (middle row, right) rode the crest of the resulting publicity wave. Her pose as a deb on the March 1992 cover (opposite) caught the eye of Guess director of advertising Paul Marciano, who chose the busty blonde known as Anna Nicole Smith to head his company's ad campaign.

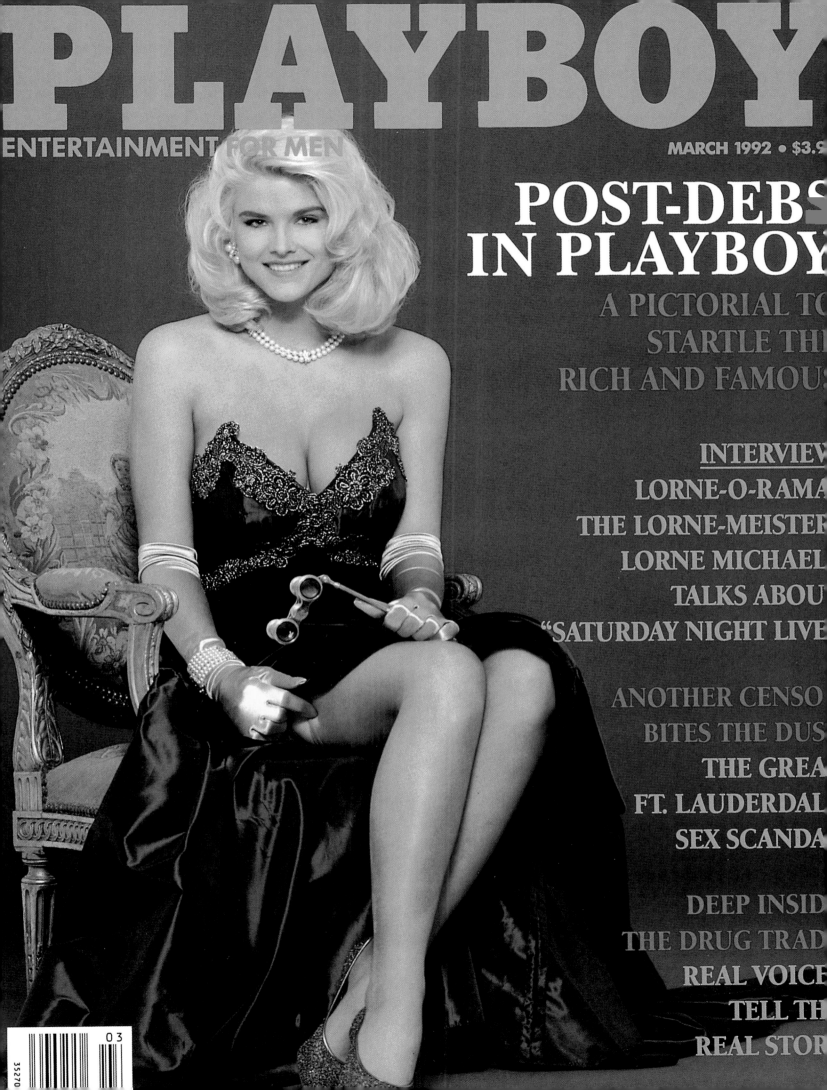

PLAYBOY

ENTERTAINMENT FOR MEN

MARCH 1992 • $3.9

POST-DEBS IN PLAYBOY

A PICTORIAL TO
STARTLE THE
RICH AND FAMOUS

INTERVIEW
LORNE-O-RAMA
THE LORNE-MEISTER
LORNE MICHAEL
TALKS ABOUT
"SATURDAY NIGHT LIVE

ANOTHER CENSO
BITES THE DUS
THE GREA
FT. LAUDERDAL
SEX SCANDA

DEEP INSID
THE DRUG TRAD
REAL VOICE
TELL TH
REAL STOR

After she was named 1993 Playmate of the Year, Anna Nicole Smith (above) visited Hong Kong—where her appearance at a shopping mall touched off a near riot by 1500 fans. Hollywood also took note, and she won roles in *The Hudsucker Proxy* and *Naked Gun 33⅓*. The Barbi Twins (top right) got readers' attention in 1991—so much so that they were asked to welcome in the New Year in January 1993. Also called back for encores were Jessica Hahn (right) and *The Price Is Right*'s Dian Parkinson (opposite), both of whom also made best-selling *Playboy Celebrity Centerfold* videos. Jessica reappeared in PLAYBOY in 1992, while Dian—who still had an eight-month backlog of fan mail dating from her pictorial in December 1991—came back for an encore in May 1993.

The Nineties brought a new generation of film and sports heroes to PLAYBOY's pages. If he'd been born white, actor Wesley Snipes (opposite) reckoned in his October 1993 *20 Questions*, "I'd own this magazine by now." Mario Van Peebles (right), who directed and starred with Snipes in *New Jack City*, was photographed by famed lensman George Hurrell for the December 1991 fashion spread *Hollywood Hot Shots*. And all-time hockey scorer Wayne Gretzky went formal for Fashion Editor Hollis Wayne in January 1991.

GREAT GRETZKY

when it comes to winter formal-wear, hockey's hottest star goes the great white way

fashion
By HOLLIS WAYNE

The winter-weight white tuxedo is the new alternative to the basic-black penguin look. Stick with a traditional shawl-collar single- or double-breasted model updated with a lower button stance—as the great Wayne Gretzky has done here. Then accessorize with a white or off-white wing-collar formal shirt and a black bow tie or a jewel-toned formal vest and a colored bow tie. If you do go back to black, the brocade dinner jacket—as Gretzky wears overleaf—is an elegant look that we especially like. Wear it tieless with a banded-collar shirt and some great studs.

Even off the ice, number 99 is on the cutting edge of fashion in a white wool-crepe dinner jacket, $1450, wool-blend tuxedo pants, $650, rayon pocket square, $30, all by Piero Dimitri; silk Jacquard vest, $275, silk Jacquard shirt, $250, bow tie, about $50, all by Paul Lester for Mark Christopher; and 14-kt.-gold mother-of-pearl cuff-link/stud set, from Peter Elliot, $130.

PHOTOGRAPHY BY MARIO CASILLI

In *Blundering Toward Waco* (illustrated by Wilson McLean, above), former Manhattan Assistant District Attorney David Heilbroner inspected FBI training facilities and discovered the mindset that led to the Branch Davidian fiasco. PLAYBOY had first run into Charles Keating decades earlier when, as founder of Citizens for Decent Literature (later Citizens for Decency Through Law), he sought to squelch all forms of erotica, including those appearing in men's magazines. His unmasking as the man behind the biggest savings-and-loan ripoff in history is the subject of Joe Morgenstern's *Profit Without Honor* (the diabolic portrait is by Steve Boswick). Meanwhile, over at the White House, George Bush and friends had been *Fighting the Wrong War* in their drug-busting efforts, which author Robert Stone found alarmingly close to the myopia that resulted in the debacle of Vietnam: lack of insight into the situation and a belief that piling on enough weaponry can solve anything.

TOM CRUISE: *"Where do I get my seriousness? You can't help but grow up fast when your parents get divorced. You see your mother go to get food stamps and she's making $50 too much to get them, with four kids to support."*

DONALD TRUMP: *"There has always been a display of wealth and always will be, until the depression comes, which it always does. And let me tell you, a display is a good thing. It shows people that you can be successful."*

QUINCY JONES: *"I say it takes a strange kind of mind to find fault with a project that raised $50 million to feed the hungry. Anybody who wants to throw stones at that can get up off his ass and go do something better."*

THE PLAYBOY

LEE IACOCCA: *"[The Japanese] are aggressive. When you hurt them commercially, they fight back. It's a war. If we get too thin-skinned about it, then this country's got a problem. I'm a red-blooded American. I fight back."*

MARTIN SCORSESE: *"Random violence perplexes me. Violence in films today is so abstract. Horror films and the disemboweling of people. I don't know what's happened to our society. I don't know why we have to see our entrails being dragged out."*

SPIKE LEE: *"I've never seen black men with fine white women. They be ugly. And you always see white men with good-looking black women. I just don't find white women attractive. And it's way too many fine black women out there."*

Interviewees of the Nineties found PLAYBOY a terrific platform for exchanging barbs as well as ideas. Real estate mogul Donald Trump charged in March 1990: "Leona Helmsley is a truly evil human being." Helmsley, interviewed that November, retorted: "Donald Trump is a snake." Japanese politician Shintaro Ishihara criticized Lee Iacocca in October 1990; the Chrysler chief barked back in January 1991.

DARYL GATES: *"Our people are not perfect; we don't sign them up on some far-off planet and bring them into police service. They are products of society, and let me tell you, the human product today often is pretty weak."*

BETTY FRIEDAN: *"When women are not people, when they are full of impotent rage, sex is not going to be fun—for their partners or for them. The erotic experiences of many women were twisted by their self-images, and men played along."*

SHARON STONE: *"The sex scenes were ludicrous. Do you have sex like that? Do you know women who have orgasms from these anatomically impossible positions? Please. In two minutes? Send them over to my house so I can learn."*

INTERVIEW

RALPH NADER: *"The Republicans and Democrats are converging into a single party: the Power Party. I once said to my father when I was a boy, 'Dad, we need a third political party.' He said, 'I'll settle for a second.' He was ahead of his time."*

FRANK ZAPPA: *"There's this ludicrous fear of the power of music manifesting itself in the corruption of the youth of America. There are more love songs than anything else. If songs could make you do something, we'd all love one another."*

HOWARD STERN: *"What is this bugaboo about sex? What is this hang-up? To me a penis is like your arm. You know? Just another part of your body. But as adults we're so freaked out by it. We're so fucking uptight, fucking crazy. We've gone mad."*

L.A. chief Daryl Gates defended his cops after the Rodney King beatings; Sharon Stone revealed other parts of her personality; Frank Zappa made one last appeal for freedom of expression; Ralph Nader became the 15th individual interviewed twice by PLAYBOY; an *Interview* with Betty Friedan marked the feature's 30th anniversary; and Howard Stern decried sexual paranoia.

Playboy's History of Jazz & Rock, a sweeping series on American popular music, made its debut in 1990 and continues under the authorship of David Standish. For the March 1992 installment, *Swing, Brother, Swing*, Kinuko Y. Craft painted Billie Holliday (above), and Wilson McLean portrayed Frank Sinatra in the surrealist style of Salvador Dalí. In her illustration for the chapter *Hot Jazz from Storyville* (January 1991, opposite), Craft took a leaf from the sketchbook of Twenties cartoonist John Held. Cab Calloway wielded the baton in March 1992; Steve Boswick painted Duke Ellington in the style of Miguel Covarrubias (right) for July 1991's *Some Like It Hot*.

Reneé Tenison (left), Miss November 1989, thrilled citizens of her tiny Idaho hometown by becoming Playmate of the Year for 1990. She was the first woman of African American heritage to win the title. Pamela Anderson (above), the centerfold for February 1990, made her mark in showbiz as the Tool Girl for TV's *Home Improvement* and then starred in the syndicated hit *Baywatch*.

Las Vegas' Corinna Harney (opposite, bottom) became not only Miss August 1991 but PMOY for 1992. Lisa Matthews (above)—the April 1990 Playmate who (along with Kimberley Conrad Hefner) was a leader in the Operation Playmate letter-writing campaign during Operations Desert Shield and Storm—was named PMOY for 1991. Even though it was her first modeling job, Chicago's Jenny McCarthy (right) became Miss October 1993 and Playmate of the Year for 1994. (Jenny even played a centerfold in her acting debut, on TV's syndicated *Silk Stalkings*.)

"*The sky looks blue because your protective lenses are tinted, dear.*"

"Let's sample the splendid '69 vintage—that was the year they added the pubic hair."

"Daddy, there's something I have to tell you."

"I just noticed you're sitting all alone."

"Pay no attention. It's just part of the neighborhood watch."

Linda & Harry & Bill & Hillary

article by
MICHAEL LEAHY

the first friends are tv moguls
and multimillionaires. so why don't
they get any respect?

WHEN IT LOOKED as if the whole thing might die in the snowdrifts of New Hampshire, when Gennifer Flowers and the specter of the Oxford draft dodger threatened to kill him off, when he had been gripped by the flu and seemingly eaten every fast-food burger in New England while metamorphosing into an indulged doughboy, it had been Harry who had simply gone out and bought him bigger suits. It had been megamillionaire and TV emperor Harry who, working on three hours' sleep, got down on his hands and knees to lay color-coordinated carpet in a television studio for the candidate's live call-in show before New Hampshire voters. It had been Linda, ten days before the primary, who had directed the gathering of filmed testaments from Arkansans, film to be used in New Hampshire advertising in order to dispel the image of the Oxford draft dodger. It had been Linda, in July, who had written, produced and edited *The Man from Hope*, a moving 14-minute bio-pic on her friend, which rival Republican strategist Mary Matalin would later call "the single most important visual in turning around the preconvention image of Clinton as a pampered, spineless guy and in sending him out of Madison Square Garden in first place, when he had arrived in third."

After defeating George Bush, whom Harry and Linda had supported four years earlier, Bill Clinton emotionally acknowledged his debt to Harry at a November party for the producer on his 52nd birthday. "He was there when I got sick and I was under siege and I got so fat I could hardly walk," said the president-elect during a toast. There were hugs. Hillary Clinton and Linda led everyone in singing *That's What Friends Are For*.

By the following May it felt like ancient history.

Just four months after they had celebrated the first full day of their friend's new administration by sleeping in the Lincoln bedroom, the First Friends had become the headache of the week inside the White House, the latest culprits in a series of public-relations gaffes that threatened to imperil the president's image and governing ability. The charges were serious. Television producer and aircraft entrepreneur Harry Thomason, who had been the Inauguration impresario, had abused his friendship with the president by wasting his time about a matter of importance to no one but Harry Thomason and some of his friends. He had called Clinton and a White House staff member, interceding on behalf of

Among the staff's favorite illustrations of the early Nineties: Anita Kunz' portraits of the Clintons and their showbiz friends the Thomasons from November 1993's *Linda & Harry & Bill & Hillary*. Martin Hoffman's painting of a nude woman in a doorway had been hanging in PLAYBOY's offices for years; Robert Silverberg's January 1992 tale *It Comes and Goes* fit it perfectly. Pat Andrea's painting (opposite) illustrated May 1990's *A Midsummer Daydream*, one in the popular series of yarns by award-winning novelist Donald E. Westlake—who for 26 years has been contributing fiction to PLAYBOY—featuring a comically inept crook named John Dortmunder.

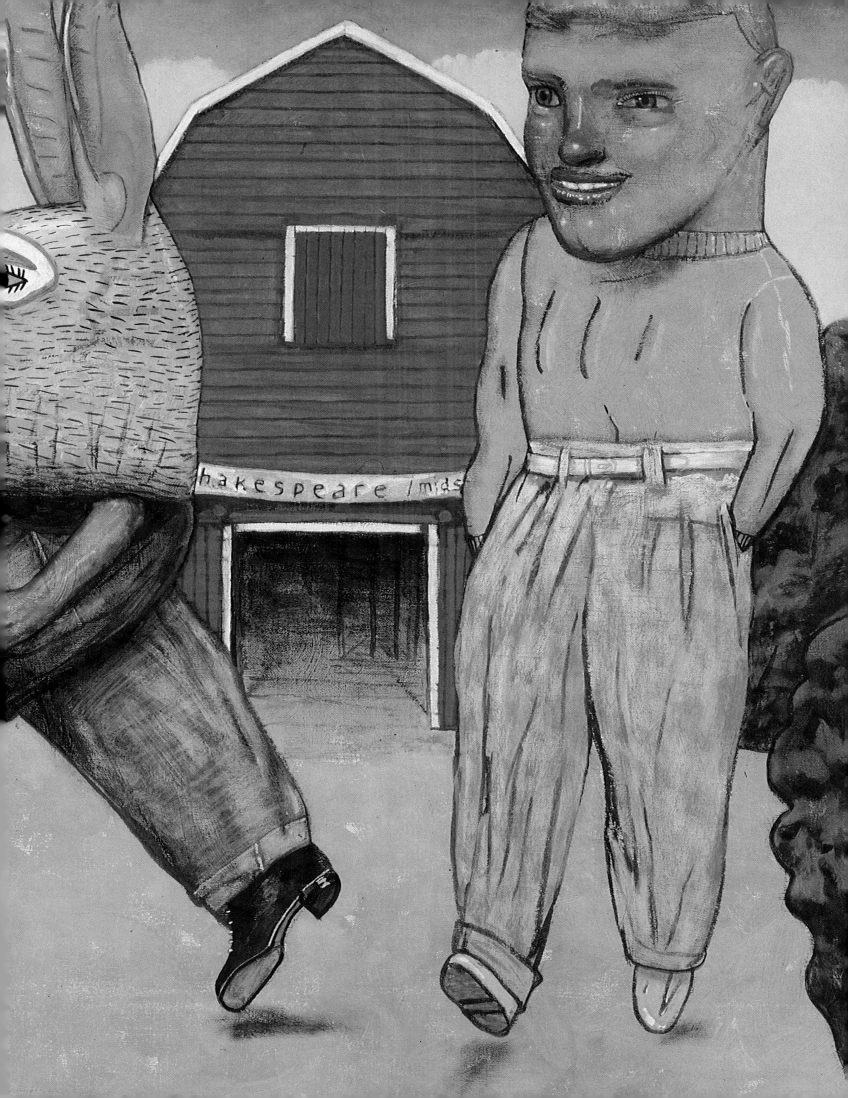

Beginning life all over again at 40, PLAYBOY celebrated four decades of publishing history with another special issue and a 40th Anniversary Playmate, Anna-Marie Goddard (left), an import from Holland. In what the New York fashion world excitedly declared a triumph, clothing designer Laura Whitcomb showcased her "postfeminist empowerment" collection inspired by the Rabbit logo (above). Explaining that her mission is to redefine female power, Whitcomb repositioned the iconic Bunny as a sexy strongwoman. As proof that figures from PLAYBOY's past have retained their appeal, artist Olivia De Berardinis' 1992 fantasy portrait featured Miss January 1955, pinup queen Bettie Page (opposite).

PLAYBOY

COLLECTOR'S EDITION   JANUARY 1994 • $5.95

FORTIETH
ANNIVERSARY ISSUE

THE
PLAYMATES

1953

A-1 Marilyn Monroe, December

1954

A-2 Margie Harrison, January
A-4 Margaret Scott, February
A-5 Delores Del Monte, March
A-6 Marilyn Waltz, April
A-8 Joanne Arnold, May
A-9 Margie Harrison, June
A-10 Neva Gilbert, July
A-11 Arlene Hunter, August
A-13 Jackie Rainbow, September
A-14 Madeline Castle, October
A-15 Diane Hunter, November
A-17 Terry Ryan, December

1955

A-18 Bettie Page, January
A-19 Jayne Mansfield, February
A-21 Marilyn Waltz, April
A-22 Marguerite Empey, May
A-23 Eve Meyer, June
A-25 Janet Pilgrim, July
A-26 Pat Lawler, August
A-27 Anne Fleming, September
A-28 Jean Moorehead, October
A-30 Barbara Cameron, November
A-31 Janet Pilgrim, December

1956

A-32 Lynn Turner, January
A-34 Marguerite Empey, February
A-35 Marian Stafford, March
A-36 Rusty Fisher, April
A-37 Marion Scott, May
A-38 Gloria Walker, June
A-39 Alice Denham, July
A-40 Jonnie Nicely, August
A-41 Elsa Sorensen, September
B-1 Janet Pilgrim, October
B-2 Betty Blue, November
B-3 Lisa Winters, December

1957

B-4 June Blair, January
B-5 Sally Todd, February
B-6 Sandra Edwards, March
B-7 Gloria Windsor, April
B-8 Dawn Richard, May
B-9 Carrie Radison, June
B-10 Jean Jani, July
B-11 Delores Donlon, August
B-12 Jacquelyn Prescott, September
B-13 Colleen Farrington, October
B-14 Marlene Callahan, November
B-15 Linda Vargas, December

1958

B-16 Elizabeth Ann Roberts, January
B-17 Cheryl Kubert, February
B-18 Zahra Norbo, March
B-19 Felicia Atkins, April
B-20 Lari Laine, May
B-21 Judy Lee Tomerlin, June
B-22 Linné Nanette Ahlstrand, July
B-23 Myrna Weber, August
B-24 Teri Hope, September

B-25 Mara Corday, October
B-26 Pat Sheehan, October
B-27 Joan Staley, November
B-28 Joyce Nizzari, December

1959

B-29 Virginia Gordon, January
B-30 Eleanor Bradley, February
B-31 Audrey Daston, March
B-32 Nancy Crawford, April
B-33 Cindy Fuller, May
B-34 Marilyn Hanold, June
B-35 Yvette Vickers, July
B-36 Clayre Peters, August
B-37 Marianne Gaba, September
B-38 Elaine Reynolds, October
B-39 Donna Lynn, November
B-40 Ellen Stratton, December*

1960

B-41 Stella Stevens, January
C-1 Susie Scott, February
C-2 Sally Sarell, March
C-3 Linda Gamble, April*
C-4 Ginger Young, May
C-5 Delores Wells, June
C-6 Teddi Smith, July
C-7 Elaine Paul, August
C-8 Ann Davis, September
C-9 Kathy Douglas, October
C-10 Joni Mattis, November
C-11 Carol Eden, December

1961

C-12 Connie Cooper, January
C-13 Barbara Ann Lawford, February
C-14 Tonya Crews, March
C-15 Nancy Nielsen, April
C-16 Susan Kelly, May
C-17 Heidi Becker, June
C-18 Sheralee Conners, July
C-19 Karen Thompson, August
C-20 Christa Speck, September*
C-21 Jean Cannon, October
C-22 Dianne Danford, November
C-23 Lynn Karrol, December

1962

C-24 Merle Pertile, January
C-25 Kari Knudsen, February
C-26 Pamela Anne Gordon, March
C-27 Roberta Lane, April
C-28 Marya Carter, May
C-29 Merissa Mathes, June
C-30 Unne Terjesen, July
C-31 Jan Roberts, August
C-32 Mickey Winters, September
C-33 Laura Young, October
C-34 Avis Kimble, November
C-35 June Cochran, December*

1963

C-36 Judi Monterey, January
C-37 Toni Ann Thomas, February
C-38 Adrienne Moreau, March
C-39 Sandra Settani, April
C-40 Sharon Cintron, May
C-41 Connie Mason, June
D-1 Carrie Enwright, July
D-2 Phyllis Sherwood, August

D-3 Victoria Valentino, September
D-4 Christine Williams, October
D-5 Terre Tucker, November
D-6 Donna Michelle, December*

1964

D-7 Sharon Rogers, January
D-8 Nancy Jo Hooper, February
D-9 Nancy Scott, March
D-10 Ashlyn Martin, April
D-11 Terri Kimball, May
D-12 Lori Winston, June
D-13 Melba Ogle, July
D-14 China Lee, August
D-15 Astrid Schulz, September
D-16 Rosemarie Hillcrest, October
D-17 Kai Brendlinger, November
D-18 Jo Collins, December*

1965

D-19 Sally Duberson, January
D-20 Jessica St. George, February
D-21 Jennifer Jackson, March
D-22 Sue Williams, April
D-23 Maria McBane, May
D-24 Hedy Scott, June
D-25 Gay Collier, July
D-26 Lannie Balcom, August
D-27 Patti Reynolds, September
D-28 Allison Parks, October*
D-29 Pat Russo, November
D-30 Dinah Willis, December

1966

D-31 Judy Tyler, January
D-32 Melinda Windsor, February
D-33 Pat Wright, March
D-34 Karla Conway, April
D-35 Dolly Read, May
D-36 Kelly Burke, June
D-37 Tish Howard, July
D-38 Susan Denberg, August
D-39 Dianne Chandler, September
D-40 Linda Moon, October
D-41 Lisa Baker, November*
E-1 Sue Bernard, December

1967

E-2 Surrey Marshe, January
E-3 Kim Farber, February
E-4 Fran Gerard, March
E-5 Gwen Wong, April
E-6 Anne Randall, May
E-7 Joey Gibson, June
E-8 Heather Ryan, July
E-9 DeDe Lind, August
E-10 Angela Dorian, September*
E-11 Reagan Wilson, October
E-12 Kaya Christian, November
E-13 Lynn Winchell, December

1968

E-14 Connie Kreski, January*
E-15 Nancy Harwood, February
E-16 Michelle Hamilton, March
E-17 Gaye Rennie, April
E-18 Elizabeth Jordan, May
E-19 Britt Fredriksen, June
E-20 Melodye Prentiss, July
E-21 Gale Olson, August

E-22 Dru Hart, September
E-23 Majken Haugedal, October
E-24 Paige Young, November
E-25 Cynthia Myers, December

1969

E-26 Leslie Bianchini, January
E-27 Lorrie Menconi, February
E-28 Kathy MacDonald, March
E-29 Lorna Hopper, April
E-30 Sally Sheffield, May
E-31 Helena Antonaccio, June
E-32 Nancy McNeil, July
E-33 Debbie Hooper, August
E-34 Shay Knuth, September
E-35 Jean Bell, October
E-36 Claudia Jennings, November*
E-37 Gloria Root, December

1970

E-38 Jill Taylor, January
E-39 Linda Forsythe, February
E-40 Christine Koren, March
E-41 Barbara Hillary, April
F-1 Jennifer Liano, May
F-2 Elaine Morton, June
F-3 Carol Willis, July
F-4 Sharon Clark, August*
F-5 Debbie Ellison, September
F-6 Mary & Madeleine Collinson, October
F-7 Avis Miller, November
F-8 Carol Imhof, December

1971

F-9 Liv Lindeland, January*
F-10 Willy Rey, February
F-11 Cynthia Hall, March
F-12 Chris Cranston, April
F-13 Janice Pennington, May
F-14 Lieko English, June
F-15 Heather Van Every, July
F-16 Cathy Rowland, August
F-17 Crystal Smith, September
F-18 Claire Rambeau, October
F-19 Danielle de Vabre, November
F-20 Karen Christy, December

1972

F-21 Marilyn Cole, January*
F-22 P.J. Lansing, February
F-23 Ellen Michaels, March
F-24 Vicki Peters, April
F-25 Deanna Baker, May
F-26 Debbie Davis, June
F-27 Carol O'Neal, July
F-28 Linda Summers, August
F-29 Susan Miller, September
F-30 Sharon Johansen, October
F-31 Lenna Sjooblom, November
F-32 Mercy Rooney, December

1973

F-33 Miki Garcia, January
F-34 Cyndi Wood, February*
F-35 Bonnie Large, March
F-36 Julie Woodson, April
F-37 Anulka Dziubinska, May
F-38 Ruthy Ross, June
F-39 Martha Smith, July
F-40 Phyllis Coleman, August
F-41 Geri Glass, September

Became Playmate of the Year

1973 (cont.)

G-1 Valerie Lane, October
G-2 Monica Tidwell, November
G-3 Christine Maddox,
December

1974

G-4-5 Nancy Cameron, January
G-6 Francine Parks, February
G-7 Pamela Zinszer, March
G-8 Marlene Morrow, April
G-9 Marilyn Lange, May*
G-10 Sandy Johnson, June
G-11 Carol Vitale, July
G-12 Jean Manson, August
G-13 Kristine Hanson, September
G-14 Ester Cordet, October
G-15 Bebe Buell, November
G-16 Janice Raymond, December

1975

G-17 Lynnda Kimball, January
G-18 Laura Misch, February
G-19 Ingeborg Sorensen, March
G-20 Victoria Cunningham,
April
G-21 Bridgett Rollins, May
G-22 Azizi Johari, June
G-23 Lynn Schiller, July
G-24 Lillian Müller, August*
G-25 Mesina Miller, September
G-26 Jill De Vries, October
G-27 Janet Lupo, November
G-28 Nancie Li Brandi, December

1976

G-29 Daina House, January
G-30 Laura Lyons, February
G-31 Ann Pennington, March
G-32 Denise Michele, April
G-33 Patricia Margot McClain,
May
G-34 Debra Peterson, June
G-35 Deborah Borkman, July
G-36 Linda Beatty, August
G-37 Whitney Kaine, September
G-38 Hope Olson, October
G-39 Patti McGuire, November*
G-40 Karen Hafter, December

1977

G-41 Susan Lynn Kiger, January
H-1 Star Stowe, February
H-2 Nicki Thomas, March
H-3 Lisa Sohm, April
H-4 Sheila Mullen, May
H-5 Virve Reid, June
H-6 Sondra Theodore, July
H-7 Julia Lyndon, August
H-8 Debra Jo Fondren,
September*
H-9 Kristine Winder, October
H-10 Rita Lee, November
H-11 Ashley Cox, December

1978

H-12 Debra Jensen, January
H-13 Janis Schmitt, February
H-14 Christina Smith, March
H-15 Pamela Jean Bryant, April
H-16 Kathryn Morrison, May
H-17 Gail Stanton, June
H-18 Karen Morton, July
H-19 Vicki Witt, August
H-20 Rosanne Katon, September
H-21 Marcy Hanson, October
H-22 Monique St. Pierre,
November*
H-23 Janet Quist, December

1979

H-24 Candy Loving, January
H-25 Lee Ann Michelle, February
H-26 Denise McConnell, March
H-27 Missy Cleveland, April
H-28 Michelle Drake, May
H-29 Louann Fernald, June
H-30 Dorothy Mays, July
H-31 Dorothy Stratten, August*
H-32 Vicki McCarty, September
H-33 Ursula Buchfellner,
October
H-34 Sylvie Garant, November
H-35 Candace Collins,
December

1980

H-36 Gig Gangel, January
H-37 Sandy Cagle, February
H-38 Henriette Allais, March
H-39 Liz Glazowski, April
H-40 Martha Thomsen, May
H-41 Ola Ray, June
I-1 Teri Peterson, July
I-2 Victoria Cooke, August
I-3 Lisa Welch, September
I-4 Mardi Jacquet, October
I-5 Jeana Tomasino, November
I-6 Terri Welles, December*

1981

I-7 Karen Price, January
I-8 Vicki Lasseter, February
I-9 Kimberly Herrin, March
I-10 Lorraine Michaels, April
I-11 Gina Goldberg, May
I-12 Cathy Larmouth, June
I-13 Heidi Sorenson, July
I-14 Debbie Boostrom, August
I-15 Susan Smith, September
I-16 Kelly Tough, October
I-17 Shannon Tweed, November*
I-18 Patricia Farinelli,
December

1982

I-19 Kimberly McArthur,
January
I-20 Anne-Marie Fox, February
I-21 Karen Witter, March
I-22 Linda Rhys Vaughn, April
I-23 Kym Malin, May
I-24 Lourdes Estores, June
I-25 Lynda Wiesmeier, July
I-26 Cathy St. George, August
I-27 Connie Brighton,
September
I-28 Marianne Gravatte,
October*
I-29 Marlene Janssen,
November
I-30 Charlotte Kemp, December

1983

I-31 Lonny Chin, January
I-32 Melinda Mays, February
I-33 Alana Soares, March
I-34 Christina Ferguson, April
I-35 Susie Scott, May
I-36 Jolanda Egger, June
I-37 Ruth Guerri, July
I-38 Carina Persson, August
I-39 Barbara Edwards,
September*
I-40 Tracy Vaccaro, October
I-41 Veronica Gamba,
November
J-1 Terry Nihen, December

1984

J-2 Penny Baker, January
J-3 Justine Greiner, February
J-4 Dona Speir, March
J-5 Lesa Ann Pedriana, April
J-6 Patty Duffek, May
J-7 Tricia Lange, June
J-8 Liz Stewart, July
J-9 Suzi Schott, August
J-10 Kimberly Evenson,
September
J-11 Debi Johnson, October
J-12 Roberta Vasquez,
November
J-13 Karen Velez, December*

1985

J-14 Joan Bennett, January
J-15 Cherie Witter, February
J-16 Donna Smith, March
J-17 Cindy Brooks, April
J-18 Kathy Shower, May*
J-19 Devin DeVasquez, June
J-20 Hope Marie Carlton, July
J-21 Cher Butler, August
J-22 Venice Kong, September
J-23 Cynthia Brimhall, October
J-24 Pamela Saunders,
November
J-25 Carol Ficatier, December

1986

J-26 Sherry Arnett, January
J-27 Julie McCullough,
February
J-28 Kim Morris, March
J-29 Teri Weigel, April
J-30 Christine Richters, May
J-31 Rebecca Ferratti, June
J-32 Lynne Austin, July
J-33 Ava Fabian, August
J-34 Rebekka Armstrong,
September
J-35 Katherine Hushaw,
October
J-36 Donna Edmondson,
November*
J-37 Laurie Carr, December

1987

J-38 Luann Lee, January
J-39 Julie Peterson, February
J-40 Marina Baker, March
J-41 Anna Clark, April
K-1 Kym Paige, May
K-2 Sandy Greenberg, June
K-3 Carmen Berg, July
K-4 Sharry Konopski, August
K-5 Gwen Hajek, September
K-6 Brandi Brandt, October
K-7 Pam Stein, November
K-8 India Allen, December*

1988

K-9 Kimberley Conrad, January*
K-10 Kari Kennell, February
K-11 Susie Owens, March
K-12 Eloise Broady, April
K-13 Diana Lee, May
K-14 Emily Arth, June
K-15 Terri Lynn Doss, July
K-16 Helle Michaelsen, August
K-17 Laura Richmond,
September
K-18 Shannon Long, October
K-19 Pia Reyes, November
K-20 Kata Karkkainen,
December

1989

K-21 Fawna MacLaren, January
K-22 Simone Eden, February
K-23 Laurie Wood, March
K-24 Jennifer Jackson, April
K-25 Monique Noel, May
K-26 Tawnni Cable, June
K-27 Erika Eleniak, July
K-28 Gianna Amore, August
K-29 Karin & Mirjam van
Breeschooten, September
K-31 Karen Foster, October
K-32 Reneé Tenison, November*
K-33 Petra Verkaik, December

1990

K-34 Peggy McIntaggart, January
K-35 Pamela Anderson, February
K-36 Deborah Driggs, March
K-37 Lisa Matthews, April*
K-38 Tina Bockrath, May
K-39 Bonnie Marino, June
K-40 Jacqueline Sheen, July
K-41 Melissa Evridge, August
L-1 Kerri Kendall, September
L-2 Brittany York, October
L-3 Lorraine Olivia, November
L-4 Morgan Fox, December

1991

L-5 Stacy Arthur, January
L-6 Cristy Thom, February
L-7 Julie Clarke, March
L-8 Christina Leardini, April
L-9 Carrie Yazel, May
L-10 Saskia Linssen, June
L-11 Wendy Kaye, July
L-12 Corinna Harney, August*
L-13 Samantha Dorman,
September
L-14 Cheryl Bachman, October
L-15 Tonja Christensen,
November
L-16 Wendy Hamilton,
December

1992

L-17 Suzi Simpson, January
L-18 Tanya Beyer, February
L-19 Tylyn John, March
L-20 Cady Cantrell, April
L-21 Anna Nicole Smith, May*
L-22 Angela Melini, June
L-23 Amanda Hope, July
L-24 Ashley Allen, August
L-25 Morena Corwin, September
L-26 Tiffany Sloan, October
L-27 Stephanie Adams, November
L-28 Barbara Moore, December

1993

L-29 Echo Johnson, January
L-30 Jennifer Leroy, February
L-31 Kimberly Donley, March
L-32 Nicole Wood, April
L-33 Elke Jeinsen, May
L-34 Alesha Marie Oreskovich,
June
L-35 Leisa Sheridan, July
L-36 Jennifer Lavoie, August
L-37 Carrie Westcott, September
L-38 Jenny McCarthy, October*
L-39 Julianna Young, November
L-40 Arlene Baxter, December

1994

L-41 Anna-Marie Goddard,
January

PLAYBOY TRIVIA

Playboy Interviews

Subjects have included:

> One Princess—Monaco's Princess Grace
> One Prince—Cambodia's Norodom Sihanouk
> Five Kings—Billie Jean, Don, Larry, Martin Luther Jr. and Stephen

Number of individuals who have been *Playboy Interview* subjects twice: 15—Muhammad Ali (once as Cassius Clay), Mel Brooks, Fidel Castro, Cher, Bill Cosby, Bob Dylan, Jackie Gleason, Jimmy Hoffa, Jesse Jackson, Steve Martin, Ralph Nader, Paul Newman, Ted Turner, Gore Vidal and Robin Williams

Number of couples who have been *Playboy Interview* subjects: 6—Jane Fonda and Tom Hayden, John Lennon and Yoko Ono, Julie Andrews and Blake Edwards, Paul and Linda McCartney, Imelda and Ferdinand Marcos, Roseanne and Tom Arnold

Number of sports figures: baseball 11, football 6, basketball 5, tennis 1, boxing 3, Olympian 1, hockey 1, auto racing 1, sports journalism 2

Number of writers: 36

Number of film directors: 22

Number of actors: 58

Number of actresses: 18

Number of musicians: 34

Number of heads of state: 8—Jimmy Carter, Fidel Castro, José Napoleón Duarte, Ferdinand Marcos, Jawaharlal Nehru, Daniel Ortega, Norodom Sihanouk, Lech Walesa

Number of men: 343

Number of women: 59

Number of transsexuals: 1—Wendy/Walter Carlos

Writer with the most *Playboy Interview*s to his credit: Lawrence Linderman (28)

Pictorials

Mothers and daughters who have posed for PLAYBOY:
> Jayne Mansfield (Miss February 1955) and daughter Jayne Marie (*Jayne's Girl*, July 1976)
> Carol Eden (Miss December 1960) and daughter Simone (Miss February 1989)
> Tamara Davis and daughters Dawn and Shannon (*Like Mother, Like Daughters*, August 1993)

Fathers and daughters who have posed for PLAYBOY:
> Peter Sellers (April and September 1964) and daughter Victoria (April 1986)

Number of wives photographed for PLAYBOY by John Derek: 3—Ursula Andress, Linda Evans and Bo Derek

Number of wives photographed for PLAYBOY by Russ Meyer: 2—Eve Meyer and Edy Williams

Number of wives photographed for PLAYBOY by Joe Hyams: 1—Elke Sommer

Photographers who have shot the most Playmates: Arny Freytag (69), Richard Fegley (68), Pompeo Posar (65)

Sets of twins who have been Playmates: 2—Mary and Madeleine Collinson (October 1970) and Karin and Mirjam van Breeschooten (September 1989)

Other sisters who have been Playmates: Janice (May 1971) and Ann (March 1976) Pennington

Cousins who have been Playmates: Elaine (June 1970) and Karen (July 1978) Morton

Number of transsexuals who have been featured in PLAYBOY pictorials: 1—Tula Cossey (September 1991)

First issue with staples removed: October 1985

Playmate fee in 1964: $1000

Playmate fee in 1994: $20,000

Playmate of the Year fee in 1964: $250

Playmate of the Year fee in 1994: $100,000

The first black Playmate: Jennifer Jackson (March 1965)

The largest number of photos taken to create a centerfold: 743 sheets of 8" x 10" film to get the right photo of the Collinson twins (October 1970)

The first centerfold to show pubic hair: Liv Lindeland (January 1971)

The only Playmate to marry Hugh Hefner: Kimberley Conrad (January 1988)

The girl who everyone thinks was a Playmate but wasn't: Barbi Benton, who appeared on covers and in pictorials but was never a Playmate

The only issue that featured two nonrelated Playmates: October 1958 (Mara Corday and Pat Sheehan)

Most appearances as a Playmate: Janet Pilgrim has appeared as a Playmate three times (December 1955, July 1955 and October 1956)

Only front and back centerfold: Playmate Nancy Cameron (January 1974)

Playboy Clubs

Actresses who once worked as Playboy Bunnies: Lauren Hutton, Julie Cobb, Lynne Moody, Sherilyn Fenn, Susan Sullivan, Jackie Zeman, Maria Richwine, Barbara Bosson

Musician who once worked as a Playboy Bunny: Deborah Harry

Writer who once worked as a Playboy Bunny: Gloria Steinem

Some TV personalities who dressed up as Playboy Bunnies: Steve Allen, Bill Dana, Barbara Walters, Cher, Flip Wilson, Bob Hope, the Smothers Brothers, Carol Channing, Johnny Carson, Farrah Fawcett, Sally Field

Entertainers who got a start on the Playboy Club circuit: Dick Gregory, Pat Morita, Gregory Hines, George Carlin, Flip Wilson, George Kirby, Slappy White, Jackie Gayle, Danita Jo, Rob Reiner, Nipsey Russell, Irwin Corey, Peter Allen, Steve Martin, Lainie Kazan, Don Adams, Joe Williams, Richard Pryor and Rich Little

Opening Dates of Playboy Clubs, Hotels and Casinos

Chicago	1960	Ocho Rios, Jamaica	1965	Bahamas	1978
Miami	1961	Boston	1965	Nagoya, Japan	1979
New Orleans	1961	London	1966	Sapporo, Japan	1980
St. Louis	1962	Montreal	1967	Miami Plaza	1980
New York	1962	Denver	1967	Atlantic City	1981
Phoenix	1962	Lake Geneva, Wis.	1968	Buffalo	1981
Detroit	1963	Playboy Towers, Chicago	1970	St. Petersburg	1981
Manila	1964	Great Gorge, N.J.	1971	San Diego	1981
Baltimore	1964	Clermont, U.K.	1972	Lansing	1982
Cincinnati	1964	Portsmouth, U.K.	1972	Columbus, Ohio	1982
Kansas City	1964	Manchester, U.K.	1973	Omaha	1984
Los Angeles	1965	Tokyo	1976	Des Moines	1984
Atlanta	1965	Dallas	1977		
San Francisco	1965	Osaka, Japan	1978		

The Magazine

Playboy's international editions:

Germany	August 1972	Spain	November 1978	Hungary	December 1989
Italy	November 1972	Australia	February 1979	Taiwan	April 1990
France	November 1972	The Netherlands	May 1983	Czechoslovakia	May 1991
Japan	July 1975	Greece	April 1985	Poland	December 1992
Brazil	August 1975	Argentina	June 1985	South Africa	December 1993
Mexico	November 1976	Turkey	December 1985		

First issue to sell more than 1 million copies: October 1959

Biggest selling issue ever: November 1972 (7,161,561)

The missing issue: March 1955 wasn't finished by deadline and became the April issue

First Playmate to autograph her centerfold photo in the magazine: Jill DeVries (Miss October 1975)

First *Year in Sex* feature: February 1977

Cover price of first issue of PLAYBOY: $.50

Cover price of 40th Anniversary Issue: $5.95

Cabinet member who once posed for a Playboy fashion show: former Defense Secretary Les Aspin

Some PLAYBOY stories that became movies:
- *Fahrenheit 451* by Ray Bradbury (March–May 1954) became 1966 film starring Julie Christie and Oskar Werner
- *How to Succeed in Business Without Really Trying* by Shepherd Mead became 1967 movie and Broadway musical
- *The Hustler* by Walter Tevis (January 1957) became 1961 film starring Paul Newman and Jackie Gleason
- *The Fly* by George Langelaan (June 1957) became two films, first starring David Hedison (1958), second starring Jeff Goldblum (1986)
- *On Her Majesty's Secret Service* by Ian Fleming (April–June 1963) became 1969 film starring George Lazenby as James Bond
- *You Only Live Twice* by Ian Fleming (April–June 1964) became 1967 film starring Sean Connery as Bond
- *The Man With the Golden Gun* by Ian Fleming (April–July 1965) became 1974 film starring Roger Moore as Bond
- *Red Ryder Nails the Hammond Kid* by Jean Shepherd (December 1965) became 1983 film *A Christmas Story* starring Peter Billingsley
- *Octopussy* by Ian Fleming (March–April 1966) became 1983 film with Roger Moore as Bond
- *Dealing* by "Michael Douglas," a.k.a. Michael and Douglas Crichton (December 1970–February 1971) became 1972 film *Dealing: Or the Berkeley-to-Boston Forty-Brick Lost-Bag Blues* starring Barbara Hershey
- *The Terminal Man* by Michael Crichton (March–May 1972) became 1974 film starring George Segal
- *Semi-Tough* by Dan Jenkins (September 1972) became 1977 film starring Burt Reynolds
- *The Best Little Whorehouse in Texas* by Larry L. King (April 1974) became 1982 film starring Burt Reynolds and Dolly Parton
- *I Lost It in the Second Turn* by "Stroker Ace," a.k.a. Bill Neely and Bob Ottum (October 1973) became 1983 film *Stroker Ace* starring Burt Reynolds
- *All the President's Men* by Carl Bernstein and Bob Woodward (May–June 1974) became 1976 film starring Robert Redford and Dustin Hoffman
- *Jenny and the Ball Turret Gunner* (June 1976) and *Garp's Night Out* (February 1977) by John Irving became 1982 film *The World According to Garp* starring Robin Williams
- *Falling Angel* by William Hjortsberg (October–November 1978) became *Angel Heart* starring Mickey Rourke (1987)
- *Sexual Perversity in Chicago* by David Mamet (March 1977) became 1986 film *About Last Night…* starring Rob Lowe and Demi Moore
- *Nine and a Half Weeks* by Elizabeth McNeill (April 1978) became *9½ Weeks* starring Mickey Rourke and Kim Basinger (1986)
- *2010* by Arthur C. Clarke (September and December 1982) became 1984 movie starring Roy Scheider and John Lithgow
- *The Little Drummer Girl* by John le Carré (March 1983) became 1984 film starring Diane Keaton
- *Texasville* by Larry McMurtry (May 1987) became 1990 film starring Jeff Bridges and Cybill Shepherd

Some PLAYBOY stories that became television movies or miniseries:
- *Thomas in Elysium*, *Rudolph in Moneyland* and *Rich Man's Weather* by Irwin Shaw (January, March and July 1970) became 1976 miniseries *Rich Man, Poor Man* starring Peter Strauss and Nick Nolte
- *Duel* by Richard Matheson (April 1971) became 1971 TV movie (Steven Spielberg's first directing job)
- *Roots: The Mixing of the Blood* by Alex Haley (October 1976) became part of January 1977 miniseries telecast on eight consecutive nights on ABC
- *The Executioner's Song* by Norman Mailer (October–December 1979) became 1982 TV movie
- *Beauty & the Badge*, May 1982 pictorial on Ohio policewoman Barbara Schantz, became 1983 TV movie *Policewoman Centerfold*
- Stories of three women who appeared in PLAYBOY pictorials inspired the 1991 TV movie *Posing*, which in turn inspired the magazine's August 1992 pictorial on housewives
- *Hush Puppies* by Stephen Randall (September 1986) became the HBO movie *New Homeowner's Guide to Happiness*, first telecast November 27, 1987

The largest issue ever of PLAYBOY: December 1979 (414 pages)

Date of the first braille edition of PLAYBOY: July 1970

First issue of PLAYBOY to announce that it was "Now printing 1 million copies": June 1956

The only men who've appeared on the cover of PLAYBOY: Peter Sellers, Burt Reynolds, Steve Martin, Jerry Seinfeld, Donald Trump and Dan Aykroyd

First major advertiser in PLAYBOY: Springmaid sheets (February 1955, back cover)

Question from the first column of *The Playboy Advisor:* "What do you think of those martinis and manhattans that come in little plastic bags?" Answer: "We think they should remain in those little plastic bags."

The most frequent concerns posed to *The Playboy Advisor*:
1) I come too quick.
2) How do I increase the size of my penis?
3) My girl friend doesn't reach orgasm through intercourse.
4) How do you pick up the third person in a ménage à trois?
5) My lover and I have different levels of desire.
6) What do the stripes in the lining of a tie really mean?
7) Is it true John Dillinger's penis is at the Smithsonian?

Most famous put-on that backfired: *The Playboy Advisor* suggested that John Dillinger was actually Johanna Dillinger, a woman with a 19-inch clitoris. For the next few years the *Advisor* received letters asking if it was true that John Dillinger was a woman.

Playboy Enterprises

Playmates appearing with Hefner on the Playboy Pinball Machine: Sondra Theodore (July 1977) and Patti McGuire (November 1976)

First Playboy Records single to hit number one on pop-music charts: *Fallin' in Love* by Hamilton, Joe Frank & Reynolds

Major awards won by Playboy artist Mickey Gilley at the 12th Annual Academy of Country Music Awards Show in 1977: 6

Number of Playboy Home Videos that went platinum in 1992 (signifying 50,000 copies sold and $2 million or more in sales): 3—*Playmates of the Year: The 1980s, Sexy Lingerie* and *Wet & Wild*

Only publisher honored with a star on the Hollywood Walk of Fame: Hugh Hefner, on April 9, 1980

Early job responsibility for Christie Hefner at Playboy Enterprises: Supervision of a boutique (called Playtique, of course) in the Playboy Building

Number of animal species named for Hugh Hefner: 1—*Sylvilagus palustris hefneri* (an endangered marsh rabbit).

First Playboy product: Rabbit Head cufflinks (1955)

Playboy radio: In 1964 PLAYBOY had a radio program in Chicago that aired late nights on WCFL called *Playboy Table Talk*

Date Playboy Enterprises went public: November 3, 1971

Some movies made by Playboy Productions:
> *Macbeth*
> *Saint Jack*
> *And Now for Something Completely Different*
> *The Crazy World of Julius Vrooder*
> *The Naked Ape*

Some TV movies made by Playboy Productions:
> *The Great Niagara*
> *The Death of Ocean View Park*
> *A Whale for the Killing*
> *Third Girl from the Left*
> *Deliver Us from Evil*

Year in which PLAYBOY stopped placing stars on the P of the cover logo: 1979

There was a widespread rumor that the stars on the cover signified the number of times Hefner had made love to that month's Playmate. Their real purpose was to distinguish regional editions, from one star on magazines going to the central U.S. to 12 on copies destined for military personnel.

The Playmates of the Year

1960	Ellen Stratton	1969	Connie Kreski	1978	Debra Jo Fondren	1987	Donna Edmondson
1961	Linda Gamble	1970	Claudia Jennings	1979	Monique St. Pierre	1988	India Allen
1962	Christa Speck	1971	Sharon Clark	1980	Dorothy Stratten	1989	Kimberley Conrad
1963	June Cochran	1972	Liv Lindeland	1981	Terri Welles	1990	Reneé Tenison
1964	Donna Michelle	1973	Marilyn Cole	1982	Shannon Tweed	1991	Lisa Matthews
1965	Jo Collins	1974	Cyndi Wood	1983	Marianne Gravatte	1992	Corinna Harney
1966	Allison Parks	1975	Marilyn Lange	1984	Barbara Edwards	1993	Anna Nicole Smith
1967	Lisa Baker	1976	Lillian Müller	1985	Karen Velez	1994	Jenny McCarthy
1968	Angela Dorian	1977	Patti McGuire	1986	Kathy Shower		

The Playboy Interview

Subject	Interviewer	Date

1962

Miles Davis	Alex Haley	September
Peter Sellers	Robert Miller	October
Jackie Gleason	Richard Gehman	December

1963

Frank Sinatra	Joe Hyams	February
Bertrand Russell	Norman MacKenzie	March
Helen Gurley Brown	Richard Warren Lewis	April
Malcolm X	Alex Haley	May
Billy Wilder	Richard Gehman	June
Richard Burton	Kenneth Tynan	September
Jawaharlal Nehru	PLAYBOY staff	October
James Hoffa	Mike Wallace	November
Albert Schweitzer	James Biddulph	December

1964

Vladimir Nabokov	Alvin Toffler	January
Ayn Rand	Alvin Toffler	March
Jean Genet	Madeleine Gobeil	April
Jack Lemmon	Richard Warren Lewis	May
Ingmar Bergman	Cynthia Grenier	June
Salvador Dali	Stirling McIlhany	July
Dick Gregory	Paul Krassner	August
Henry Miller	Bernard Wolfe	September
Cassius Clay	Alex Haley	October
George Wallace	Bern Keating	November
Ian Fleming	Ken Purdy	December

1965

Martin Luther King Jr.	Alex Haley	January
The Beatles	Jean Shepherd	February
Art Buchwald	Marvin Kitman	April
Jean-Paul Sartre	Madeleine Gobeil	May
Melvin Belli	Alex Haley	June
Marcello Mastroianni	Marika Aba and Curtis Pepper	July
Robert Shelton	Bern Keating	August
Peter O'Toole	Kenneth Tynan	September
Madalyn Murray	Richard Tregaskis	October
Sean Connery	David Lewin	November
Al Capp	Alvin Toffler	December

1966

Princess Grace	Jacob Baal-Teshuva	January
Federico Fellini	Curtis Pepper	February
Bob Dylan	Nat Hentoff	March
George Lincoln Rockwell	Alex Haley	April
Arthur Schlesinger Jr.	Alvin Toffler	May
Mike Nichols	C. Robert Jennings	June
Ralph Ginzburg	Nat Hentoff	July
H.L. Hunt	Fred J. Eckert	August
Timothy Leary	Bernard Gavzer	September
Mel Brooks	Larry Siegel	October
Norman Thomas	Nat Hentoff	November
Sammy Davis Jr.	Alex Haley	December

1967

Fidel Castro	Lee Lockwood	January
Mark Lane	Eric Norden and Stephen Tyler	February
Orson Welles	Kenneth Tynan	March
Arnold Toynbee	Norman MacKenzie	April
Woody Allen	Sol Weinstein	May
Michael Caine	David Lewin	July
F. Lee Bailey	Nat Hentoff	August
John Lindsay	Hunter Lewis	September
Jim Garrison	Eric Norden	October
Michelangelo Antonioni	Curtis Pepper	November
Johnny Carson	Alex Haley	December

1968

Norman Mailer	Paul Carroll	January
Jim Brown	Alex Haley	February
Truman Capote	Eric Norden	March
Charles Percy	Alan Otten	April
Masters and Johnson	Nat Lehrman	May
John Kenneth Galbraith	Michael Laurence	June
Paul Newman	Richard Warren Lewis and Roy Newquist	July
William Sloane Coffin	Nat Hentoff	August
Stanley Kubrick	Eric Norden	September
Ralph Nader	Eric Norden	October
Don Rickles	Sol Weinstein	November
Eldridge Cleaver	Nat Hentoff	December

1969

Lee Marvin	Richard Warren Lewis	January
Mort Sahl	Nat Lehrman	February
Marshall McLuhan	Eric Norden	March
Allen Ginsberg	Paul Carroll	April
Bill Cosby	Lawrence Linderman	May
Gore Vidal	Eric Norden	June
Rod Steiger	Richard Warren Lewis	July
Ramsey Clark	Tom Wicker	August
Rowan and Martin	Harold Ramis	October
Jesse Jackson	Arthur Kretchmer	November
Joe Namath	Lawrence Linderman	December

1970

Raquel Welch	Richard Warren Lewis	January
Ray Charles	Bill Quinn	March
Dr. Mary Calderone	Nat Lehrman	April
William F. Buckley Jr.	David Butler	May
Tiny Tim	Harold Ramis	June
Joan Baez	Nat Hentoff	July
Dr. Paul Ehrlich	Geoffrey Norman	August
Peter Fonda	Lawrence Linderman	September
William Kunstler	Nat Hentoff	October
Elliott Gould	Richard Warren Lewis	November
Robert Graves	James McKinley	December

1971

Mae West	C. Robert Jennings	January
Tom Murton	Geoffrey Norman	February
Dick Cavett	Harold Ramis	March
John Wayne	Richard Warren Lewis	May
Albert Speer	Eric Norden	June
John Cassavetes	Lawrence Linderman	July
George McGovern	Milton Viorst	August
Jules Feiffer	Larry DuBois	September
Charles Evers	Eric Norden	October
Allen Klein	Craig Vetter	November
Roman Polanski	Larry DuBois	December

1972

Germaine Greer	Nat Lehrman	January
R. Buckminster Fuller	Barry Farrell	February
Saul Alinsky	Eric Norden	March
Jack Nicholson	Richard Warren Lewis	April
Howard Cosell	Lawrence Linderman	May
Jackie Stewart	Larry DuBois	June
Anthony Herbert	Bruce Galloway and Robert B. Johnson Jr.	July
Sam Peckinpah	William Murray	August
Bernadette Devlin	Eric Norden	September
Meir Kahane	Walter Goodman	October
Jack Anderson	Larry DuBois	November
Yevgeny Yevtushenko	Michael Laurence	December

1973

Carroll O'Connor	Richard Warren Lewis	January
Milton Friedman	Michael Laurence and Geoffrey Norman	February
Joe Frazier	Carl Snyder	March
Tennessee Williams	C. Robert Jennings	April
Huey Newton	Lee Lockwood	May

Walter Cronkite	Ron Powers	June
Kurt Vonnegut Jr.	David Standish	July
David Halberstam	Ward Just and Gretchen McNeese	August
Pete Rozelle	Lawrence Linderman	October
James Dickey	Geoffrey Norman	November
Bob Hope	William Murray	December

1974

Hugh M. Hefner	Larry DuBois	January
Clint Eastwood	Arthur Knight and Gretchen McNeese	February
Groucho Marx	Charlotte Chandler	March
Jane Fonda and Tom Hayden	Ron Ridenour and Leroy F. Aarons	April
Henry Aaron	Carl Snyder	May
Admiral Elmo Zumwalt	Richard Meryman	June
Barry Commoner	Larry DuBois	July
Erich Von Däniken	Timothy Ferris	August
Anthony Burgess	C. Robert Jennings	September
Al Goldstein	Richard Warren Lewis	October
Hunter Thompson	Craig Vetter	November
Robert Redford	Larry DuBois	December

1975

John Dean	Barbara Cady	January
Mel Brooks	Brad Darrach	February
Billie Jean King	Joe Hyams	March
Dustin Hoffman	Richard Meryman	April
William E. Simon	Peter J. Ognibene	May
Joseph Heller	Sam Merrill	June
Francis Ford Coppola	William Murray	July
Philip Agee	Brad Darrach	August
Erica Jong	Gretchen McNeese	September
Cher	David Standish and Eugenie Ross-Leming	October
Muhammad Ali	Lawrence Linderman	November
Jimmy Hoffa	Jerry Stanecki	December

1976

Elton John	David Standish and Eugenie Ross-Leming	January
James Caan	Murray Fisher	February
Norman Lear	Barbara Cady	March
Jerry Brown	Robert Scheer	April
Abbie Hoffman	Ken Kelley	May
Sara Jane Moore	Andrew Hill	June
Karl Hess	Sam Merrill	July
Robert Altman	Bruce Williamson	August
David Bowie	Cameron Crowe	September
Roone Arledge	Sam Merrill	October
Jimmy Carter	Robert Scheer	November
O.J. Simpson	Lawrence Linderman	December

1977

Alex Haley	Murray Fisher	January
Keith Stroup	Patrick Anderson	February
Pat Moynihan	Richard Meryman	March
Gary Gilmore	Lawrence Schiller and Barry Farrell	April
Saturday Night Live cast	John Blumenthal and Lindsay Maracotta	May
Robert Blake	Lawrence Linderman	June
Andrew Young	Peter Ross Range	July
Henry Winkler	Lawrence Grobel	August
James Earl Ray	James McKinley and Laurence Gonzales	September
Barbra Streisand	Lawrence Grobel	October
Henry Kyemba	John Man	November
John Denver	Marcia Seligson	December

1978

Don Meredith	Lawrence Linderman	February
Bob Dylan	Ron Rosenbaum	March
David Frost	Lawrence Linderman	April
Anita Bryant	Ken Kelley	May
George Burns	Arthur Cooper	June
William Colby	Laurence Gonzales	July
Ted Turner	Peter Ross Range	August

Sylvester Stallone	Lawrence Linderman	September
Dolly Parton	Lawrence Grobel	October
Geraldo Rivera	Jim Siegelman	November
John Travolta	Judson Klinger	December

1979

Marlon Brando	Lawrence Grobel	January
Neil Simon	Lawrence Linderman	February
Ted Patrick	Flo Conway and Jim Siegelman	March
Malcolm Forbes	Larry DuBois	April
Wendy/Walter Carlos	Arthur Bell	May
Dennis Kucinich	Robert Scheer	June
Joseph Wambaugh	Lawrence Linderman	July
Edward Teller	Gila Berkowitz	August
Pete Rose	Maury Z. Levy and Samantha Stevenson	September
Burt Reynolds	Lawrence Linderman	October
Masters and Johnson	James R. Petersen	November
Al Pacino	Lawrence Grobel	December

1980

Steve Martin	Lawrence Grobel	January
Pat Caddell	Peter Ross Range	February
Terry Bradshaw	Maury Z. Levy and Samantha Stevenson	March
Linda Ronstadt	Jean Vallely	April
Gay Talese	Larry DuBois	May
John Anderson	Robert Scheer	June
Bruce Jenner	Jay Stuller	July
William Shockley	Syl Jones	August
Roy Scheider	Sam Merrill	September
G. Gordon Liddy	Eric Norden	October
Larry Hagman	David Rensin	November
George C. Scott	Lawrence Grobel	December

1981

John Lennon and Yoko Ono	David Sheff	January
Tom Snyder	Nicholas Yanni	February
James Garner	Lawrence Linderman	March
Ed Asner	Sam Merrill	April
Elisabeth Kübler-Ross	Marcia Seligson	May
Steve Garvey	Samantha Stevenson	June
Robert Garwood	Winston Groom	July
George Gilder	Michael Laurence	August
James Michener	Lawrence Grobel	September
Donald Sutherland	Claudia Dreifus	October
Oriana Fallaci	Robert Scheer	November
Henry Fonda	Lawrence Grobel	December

1982

George Carlin	Sam Merrill	January
Lech Walesa	Ania and Krysia Bittenek	February
Patricia Hearst	Lawrence Grobel	March
Edward Koch	Peter Manso	April
Billy Joel	David and Victoria Sheff	May
Sugar Ray Leonard	Lawrence Linderman	June
Bette Davis	Bruce Williamson	July
Akio Morita	Peter Ross Range	August
Cheech and Chong	Ken Kelley	September
Robin Williams	Lawrence Linderman	October
Luciano Pavarotti	Lawrence Grobel	November
Julie Andrews and Blake Edwards	Lawrence Linderman	December

1983

Dudley Moore	Nancy Collins	January
Gabriel García Márquez	Claudia Dreifus	February
Sam Donaldson	Peter Manso	March
Paul Newman	Peter S. Greenberg	April
Ansel Adams	David and Victoria Sheff	May
Stephen King	Eric Norden	June
Earl Weaver	Lawrence Linderman	July
Ted Turner	Peter Ross Range	August
The Sandinistas	Claudia Dreifus	September
Hill Street Blues cast	John Blumenthal and Betsy Cramer	October
Kenny Rogers	David Rensin	November
Tom Selleck	David Sheff	December

1984

Dan Rather	Tony Schwartz	January
Paul Simon	Tony Schwartz	February
Moses Malone	Lawrence Linderman	March
Joan Collins	Lawrence Grobel	April
Calvin Klein	Glenn Plaskin	May
Jesse Jackson	Robert Scheer	June
Walid Jumblatt	Morgan Strong	July
Bobby Knight	David Israel	August
Shirley MacLaine	David Rensin	September
David Letterman	Sam Merrill	October
José Napoleón Duarte	Marc Cooper and Greg Goldin	November
Paul and Linda McCartney	Joan Goodman	December

1985

Goldie Hawn	Lawrence Grobel	January
Steven Jobs	David Sheff	February
60 Minutes team	Morgan Strong	March
Wayne Gretzky	Scott Cohen	April
Boy George	David and Victoria Sheff	May
Sparky Anderson	Ken Kelley	June
Rob Reiner	David Rosenthal	July
Fidel Castro	Dr. Jeffrey M. Elliot and Mervyn M. Dymally	August
John Huston	Lawrence Grobel	September
John DeLorean	Robert Scheer	October
Sting	David and Victoria Sheff	November
Bill Cosby	Lawrence Linderman	December

1986

Dr. Ruth Westheimer	James R. Petersen	January
Michael Douglas	David and Victoria Sheff	February
Sally Field	Lawrence Grobel	March
Dr. Jeffrey MacDonald	Dr. Jeffrey M. Elliot	April
Kathleen Turner	David Sheff	May
Kareem Abdul-Jabbar	Lawrence Linderman	June
Arthur C. Clarke	Ken Kelley	July
Jackie Gleason	Bill Zehme	August
Carl Bernstein	Tony Schwartz	September
Phil Collins	David Sheff	October
Joan Rivers	Nancy Collins	November
Bryant Gumbel	David Rensin	December

1987

Don Johnson	David Sheff	January
Mickey Rourke	Jerry Stahl	February
Lionel Richie	Glenn Plaskin	March
Louis Rukeyser	Warren Kalbacker	April
Prince Norodom Sihanouk	Debra Weiner	May
Whoopi Goldberg	David Rensin	June
Wade Boggs	Lawrence Linderman	July
Ferdinand and Imelda Marcos	Ken Kelley and Phil Bronstein	August
John Sculley	Danny Goodman	September
General Richard Secord	Morgan Strong	October
Daniel Ortega	Claudia Dreifus	November
Gore Vidal	David Sheff	December

1988

Arnold Schwarzenegger	Joan Goodman	January
Oliver Stone	Marc Cooper	February
Billy Crystal	David Rensin	March
Tom Clancy	Marc Cooper	April
Don King	Lawrence Linderman	May
Chevy Chase	John Blumenthal	June
Paul Hogan	David Rensin	July
Harvey Fierstein	Harry Stein	August
Yasir Arafat	Morgan Strong	September
Roger Craig	Ken Kelley	October
Bruce Willis	Lawrence Grobel	November
Cher	David Standish and Eugenie Ross-Leming	December

1989

Robert De Niro	Lawrence Grobel	January
Bob Woodward	J. Anthony Lukas	February
Tom Hanks	David Sheff	March
The IRA	Morgan Strong	April
Susan Sarandon	Claudia Dreifus	May
Edward James Olmos	Marcia Seligson	June
Barry Diller	Kevin Sessums	July
John Mellencamp	Charles M. Young	August
Keith Hernandez	Lawrence Linderman	September
Keith Richards	Stanley Booth	October
Garry Kasparov	Rudolph Chelminski	November
Candice Bergen	David Sheff	December

1990

Tom Cruise	Robert Scheer	January
Eddie Murphy	David Rensin	February
Donald Trump	Glenn Plaskin	March
Stephen Hawking	Morgan Strong	April
Dave Barry	Fred Bernstein	May
thirtysomething cast	David Sheff	June
Quincy Jones	Alex Haley	July
Larry King	David Rensin	August
Rickey Henderson	Lawrence Linderman	September
Shintaro Ishihara	David Sheff	October
Leona Helmsley	Glenn Plaskin	November
Jay Leno	Dick Lochte	December

1991

Lee Iacocca	Peter Ross Range	January
Gene Siskel and Roger Ebert	Lawrence Grobel	February
M. Scott Peck	David Sheff	March
Martin Scorsese	David Rensin	April
George Steinbrenner	Jeffrey Kluger	May
Robert MacNeil and Jim Lehrer	Morgan Strong	June
Spike Lee	Elvis Mitchell	July
Daryl Gates	Diane K. Shah	August
L. Douglas Wilder	Peter Ross Range	September
Robert Maxwell	David Sheff	October
Sean Penn	David Rensin	November
Carl Sagan	David Sheff	December

1992

Robin Williams	Lawrence Grobel	January
Liz Smith	David Sheff	February
Lorne Michaels	David Rensin	March
Jonathan Kozol	Morgan Strong	April
Michael Jordan	Mark Vancil	May
Ralph Nader	Murray Fisher	June
Michael Keaton	Lawrence Linderman	July
Derek Humphry	David Sheff	August
Betty Friedan	David Sheff	September
Sister Souljah	Robert Scheer	October
William Safire	Claudia Dreifus	November
Sharon Stone	David Sheff	December

1993

Steve Martin	David Sheff	January
Danny DeVito	Lawrence Linderman	February
Anne Rice	Digby Diehl	March
Frank Zappa	David Sheff	April
Charles Barkley	Tom Boswell	May
Roseanne & Tom Arnold	David Rensin	June
Barry Bonds	Kevin Cook	July
Dan Aykroyd	David Sheff	August
Larry Kramer	David Nimmons	September
Jerry Seinfeld	David Rensin	October
Joyce Carol Oates	Lawrence Grobel	November
Rush Limbaugh	D. Keith Mano	December

1994

David Letterman	Tom Shales	January

Playboy Panels

Narcotics and the Jazz Musician	November 1960
Hip Comics and the New Humor	March 1961
Sex and Censorship in Literature and the Arts	July 1961

TV's Problems and Prospects	November 1961	Uses and Abuses of the New Leisure	March 1965
The Womanization of America	June 1962	Crisis in Law Enforcement	March 1966
Business Ethics and Morality	November 1962	Religion and the New Morality	June 1967
1984 and Beyond Part 1	July 1963	Student Revolt	September 1969
1984 and Beyond Part 2	August 1963	The Drug Revolution	February 1970
Jazz: Today and Tomorrow	February 1964	Homosexuality	April 1971
America's Cultural Explosion: Its Scope		New Sexual Lifestyles	September 1973
and Challenge	November 1964	UFOs	January 1978

Celebrity Pictorials

Maud Adams	October 1981	Maryam d'Abo	September 1987	Christine Keeler	May 1989
Woody Allen	August 1965	Arlene Dahl	December 1962	Jayne Kennedy	July 1981
Woody Allen	November 1967	Sybil Danning	August 1983	Margot Kidder	March 1975
Woody Allen	February 1969	Patti D'Arbanville	May 1977	Nastassja Kinski	August 1979
Woody Allen	July 1971	Catherine Deneuve	October 1965	Nastassja Kinski	May 1983
Woody Allen	September 1972	Bo Derek	March 1980	Sylvia Kristel	March 1976
Pamela Anderson (Playmate)	February 1990	Bo Derek	August 1980	Sylvia Kristel	February 1982
Pamela Anderson	July 1992	Bo Derek	September 1981	Kris Kristofferson	July 1976
Bibi Andersson	February 1970	Bo Derek	July 1984	Vikki La Motta	November 1981
Ursula Andress	June 1965	Pamela Des Barres	March 1989	Audrey Landers	January 1983
Ursula Andress	July 1966	Janice Dickinson	March 1988	Judy Landers	January 1983
Ursula Andress	November 1973	Diana Dors	April 1956	Phoebe Légère	June 1988
Ursula Andress	April 1976	Linda Doucett	September 1993	Barbara Leigh	May 1973
Ursula Andress	January 1982	Vikki Dougan	June 1957	Barbara Leigh	October 1975
Ann-Margret	October 1966	Anita Ekberg	October 1955	Charlotte Lewis	July 1993
Rosanna Arquette	September 1990	Anita Ekberg	August 1956	Fiona Lewis	October 1975
Tina Aumont	July 1969	Anita Ekberg	November 1961	Gina Lollobrigida	September 1954
Barbara Bach	June 1977	Erika Eleniak (Playmate)	July 1989	Gina Lollobrigida	November 1955
Barbara Bach	January 1981	Erika Eleniak	August 1990	Sophia Loren	November 1957
Carroll Baker	December 1964	Erika Eleniak	December 1993	Sophia Loren	August 1960
Carroll Baker	August 1968	Linda Evans	July 1971	Tina Louise	April 1959
Barbi Twins	September 1991	Linda Evans	January 1982	Tina Louise	October 1960
Barbi Twins	January 1993	Linda Evans	June 1986	Linda Lovelace	April 1973
Brigitte Bardot	March 1958	Lola Falana	June 1970	Linda Lovelace	February 1975
Brigitte Bardot	November 1958	Farrah Fawcett	December 1978	Carol Lynley	March 1965
Brigitte Bardot	December 1959	Sherilyn Fenn	December 1990	Lisa Lyon	October 1980
Brigitte Bardot	July 1964	Jane Fonda	October 1966	Elle Macpherson	May 1994
Brigitte Bardot	April 1969	Jane Fonda	March 1968	Madonna	September 1985
Brigitte Bardot	January 1975	Fanne Foxe	September 1976	Madonna	July 1992
Kim Basinger	February 1983	Zsa Zsa Gabor	March 1957	Jayne Mansfield (Playmate)	February 1955
Kim Basinger	January 1988	Antoinette Giancana	February 1987	Jayne Mansfield	February 1957
Stephanie Beacham	February 1987	Elizabeth Ward Gracen	May 1982	Jayne Mansfield	November 1957
Pamela Bellwood	April 1983	Melanie Griffith	December 1975	Jayne Mansfield	February 1958
Barbi Benton	February 1970	Melanie Griffith	January 1986	Jayne Mansfield	February 1960
Barbi Benton	December 1973	Dayle Haddon	April 1973	Jayne Mansfield	June 1963
Barbi Benton	December 1985	Jessica Hahn	November 1987	Jayne Marie Mansfield	July 1976
Marisa Berenson	October 1971	Jessica Hahn	September 1988	Pamela Sue Martin	July 1978
Marisa Berenson	February 1976	Jessica Hahn	December 1992	Elsa Martinelli	October 1963
Sandra Bernhard	September 1992	Jerry Hall	October 1985	Julie McCullough (Playmate)	February 1986
Jane Birkin	November 1970	Jenilee Harrison	June 1987	Julie McCullough	December 1987
June Blair (Playmate)	January 1957	Margaux Hemingway	June 1978	Julie McCullough	October 1989
June Blair	March 1959	Margaux Hemingway	May 1990	Barbara McNair	October 1968
Tiffany Bolling	April 1972	Mariel Hemingway	April 1982	Heather Menzies	August 1973
Barbara Bouchet	May 1965	Mariel Hemingway	January 1984	Felicia Michaels	October 1992
Ingrid Boulting	August 1985	Barbara Hershey	August 1972	Marilyn Michaels	August 1982
Sonia Braga	October 1984	Eric Idle	November 1976	Shelley Michelle	April 1992
Michael Caine	October 1969	Iman	January 1986	Sarah Miles	July 1976
Claudia Cardinale	February 1962	La Toya Jackson	March 1989	Donna Mills	October 1987
Claudia Cardinale	September 1963	La Toya Jackson	November 1991	Donna Mills	November 1989
Anne Carlisle	September 1984	Fran Jeffries	February 1971	Marilyn Monroe (Playmate)	December 1953
Barbara Carrera	July 1977	Fran Jeffries	September 1982	Marilyn Monroe	December 1960
Barbara Carrera	March 1982	Claudia Jennings (Playmate)	November 1969	Marilyn Monroe	January 1964
Rae Dawn Chong	May 1982	Claudia Jennings	June 1970	Marilyn Monroe	January 1984
Susan Clark	February 1973	Claudia Jennings	December 1974	Marilyn Monroe	January 1987
Joan Collins	March 1969	Claudia Jennings	September 1979	Dudley Moore	July 1980
Joan Collins	December 1983	Rita Jenrette	April 1981	Terry Moore	August 1984
Tai Collins	October 1991	Don Johnson	December 1975	Jeanne Moreau	September 1965
Teri Copley	November 1990	Don Johnson	January 1986	Morganna	June 1983
Barbara Crampton	December 1986	Grace Jones	July 1985	Morganna	September 1989
Cindy Crawford	July 1988	Janet Jones	March 1987	Martin Mull	July 1978
Linda Cristal	December 1959	Lainie Kazan	October 1970	Lillian Müller (Playmate)	August 1975
Denise Crosby	March 1979	Paula Kelly	August 1969	Lillian Müller	June 1976
Denise Crosby	May 1988	Paula Kelly	July 1972	Lillian Müller	March 1977

Lillian Müller	August 1986	Ola Ray (Playmate)	June 1980	Susan Strasberg	December 1963
Julie Newmar	December 1956	Ola Ray	May 1984	Susan Strasberg	September 1967
Julie Newmar	May 1957	Vanessa Redgrave	April 1969	Dorothy Stratten (Playmate)	August 1979
Julie Newmar	May 1968	Tanya Roberts	October 1982	Dorothy Stratten	June 1980
Brigitte Nielsen	September 1985	Mimi Rogers	March 1993	Dorothy Stratten	January 1984
Brigitte Nielsen	August 1986	Sydne Rome	December 1982	Swedish Bikini Team	January 1992
Brigitte Nielsen	December 1987	Mickey Rourke	June 1990	Sharon Tate	March 1967
Judy Norton-Taylor	August 1985	Dominique Sanda	March 1972	Elizabeth Taylor	January 1963
Kim Novak	October 1959	Maria Schneider	February 1973	Judy Norton Taylor	August 1985
Kim Novak	December 1963	Peter Sellers	April 1964	Angel Tompkins	February 1972
Kim Novak	February 1965	Victoria Sellers	April 1986	Shannon Tweed (Playmate)	November 1981
Carré Otis	June 1990	Joan Severance	January 1990	Shannon Tweed	June 1982
Susie Owens (Playmate)	March 1988	Joan Severance	November 1992	Shannon Tweed	March 1985
Susie Owens	May 1993	Jane Seymour	July 1973	Shannon Tweed	May 1991
Bettie Page (Playmate)	January 1955	Jane Seymour	January 1987	Peter Ustinov	January 1965
Bettie Page	December 1992	Stephanie Seymour	March 1991	Mamie Van Doren	February 1964
Marisa Paré	October 1990	Stephanie Seymour	February 1993	Mamie Van Doren	June 1964
Barbara Parkins	February 1970	Omar Sharif	December 1968	Vanity	May 1985
Barbara Parkins	May 1976	Rhonda Shear	October 1993	Vanity	April 1988
Dian Parkinson	December 1991	Kathy Shower (Playmate)	May 1985	Brenda Venus	July 1986
Dian Parkinson	May 1993	Kathy Shower	June 1985	Veruschka	January 1971
Isabelle Pasco	December 1991	Kathy Shower	December 1987	Veruschka	January 1974
Pat Paulsen	April 1974	Kathy Shower	May 1988	Rachel Ward	March 1984
Janice Pennington (Playmate)	May 1971	Anna Nicole Smith (Playmate)	May 1992	Carol Wayne	February 1984
Valerie Perrine	May 1972	Anna Nicole Smith	June 1993	Raquel Welch	December 1979
Valerie Perrine	April 1975	Anna Nicole Smith	February 1994	Tuesday Weld	October 1960
Valerie Perrine	August 1981	Suzanne Somers	February 1980	Gwen Welles	November 1972
Bernadette Peters	December 1981	Suzanne Somers	December 1984	Gwen Welles	June 1975
Joanna Pettit	February 1968	Elke Sommer	September 1964	Vanna White	May 1987
Dana Plato	June 1989	Elke Sommer	December 1967	June Wilkinson	September 1958
Paulina Porizkova	August 1987	Elke Sommer	September 1970	June Wilkinson	August 1959
Victoria Principal	September 1973	Simonetta Stefanelli	March 1974	June Wilkinson	October 1960
Paula Pritchett	December 1970	David Steinberg	January 1979	June Wilkinson	November 1960
Paula Pritchett	July 1972	Dorit Stevens	September 1983	Edy Williams	March 1973
Melissa Prophet	May 1987	Stella Stevens (Playmate)	January 1960	Rachel Williams	February 1992
Roxanne Pulitzer	June 1985	Stella Stevens	May 1965	Wendy O. Williams	October 1986
Charlotte Rampling	March 1974	Stella Stevens	January 1968	Susannah York	June 1964
Tony Randall	January 1970	Sharon Stone	July 1990	Lana Wood	April 1971
Elizabeth Ray	September 1976	Tempest Storm	July 1955	Pia Zadora	March 1982

20 Questions

Subject	Interviewer	Month
1978		
Cheryl Tiegs	John Hughes	October
1979		
Dan Rather	Nancy Collins	May
Frank Langella	Marjorie Rosen	August
1980		
Shelley Hack	David Rensin	March
George Hamilton	John Calendo	July
Michael Douglas	Nancy Collins	November
Truman Capote	Nancy Collins	December
1981		
Lauren Hutton	David Rensin	March
John DeLorean	Warren Kalbacker	May
Jack Lemmon	Nancy Collins	June
Joan Rivers	Robert Crane	August
John Kenneth Galbraith	Warren Kalbacker	December
1982		
John Matuszak	Craig Modderno	January
Karen Allen	David Rensin	February
Louis Rukeyser	Warren Kalbacker	March
James Woods	Claudia Dreifus	April
SCTV cast (John Candy, Joe Flaherty, Eugene Levy, Andrea Martin, Rick Moranis, Catherine O'Hara and Dave Thomas)	Robert Crane	May
Brandon Tartikoff	Sam Merrill	June
Stevie Nicks	David Rensin	July
Mariette Hartley	Dick Lochte	August
Tom Petty	David Rensin	September
John LeBoutillier	Warren Kalbacker	October
Frank and Moon Unit Zappa	David and Victoria Sheff	November
1983		
Herschel Walker	Anson Mount	January
Yakov Smirnoff	David Rensin	February
Arthur Jones	Warren Kalbacker	March
Al McGuire	Bill Zehme	April
Charlton Heston	David Rensin	May
Debra Winger	David Rensin	June
Carrie Fisher	Robert Crane	July
Jan Stephenson	Robert Crane	August
Randy Newman	David Sheff	September
Joe Piscopo	David Rensin	October
Bubba Smith	Craig Modderno	November
1984		
Shelley Long	Robert Crane	February
Martin Mull	David Rensin	April
Gene Siskel and Roger Ebert	Bill Zehme	June
Fran Lebowitz	E. Jean Carroll	July
Kurt Russell	David Rensin	August
Jack LaLanne	David Rensin	October
Leigh Steinberg	David and Victoria Sheff	November
1985		
Diane Lane	David Rensin	January
Brian DePalma	Jim Jerome	February
Bob Giraldi	Bill Zehme	March
Joel Hyatt	Bill Zehme	April

Name	Interviewer	Month
Marvin Hagler and Thomas Hearns	Lawrence Linderman	May
Tom Watson	Warren Kalbacker	June
Jamie Lee Curtis	David Rensin	July
Ron Howard	David Rensin	August
Billy Crystal	David Rensin	September
Rosanna Arquette	Claudia Dreifus	October
Don Johnson and Philip Michael Thomas	David Rensin	November
Huey Lewis	David and Victoria Sheff	December

1986

Name	Interviewer	Month
Jay Leno	Bill Zehme	January
Anthony Pellicano	Steve Oney	February
David Byrne	David and Victoria Sheff	March
Kim Basinger	David Rensin	May
Al Unser Sr. and Jr.	Peter Manso	June
Tom Cruise	David Rensin	July
Sigourney Weaver	David Rensin	August
Gregory Hines	Claudia Dreifus	September
Jim McMahon	Kevin Cook	October
David Horowitz	David Rensin	November
Koko	Bob Crane	December

1987

Name	Interviewer	Month
Max Headroom (Edison Carter)	PLAYBOY staff	January
Ed Begley Jr.	Bill Zehme	February
Bob Vila	Glen Rifkin	March
Rae Dawn Chong	David Rensin	April
Barbara Hershey	David Rensin	May
Michael J. Fox	David Rensin	June
Garry Shandling	David Rensin	July
David Lee Roth	David Rensin	August
Penn and Teller	Laura Fissinger	September
Bob Uecker	David Rensin	October
Kelly McGillis	David Handelman	November
Justine Bateman	Robert Crane	December

1988

Name	Interviewer	Month
Susan Dey	Dick Lochte	January
Harold Washington	Walter Lowe Jr.	February
Tom Waits	Steve Oney	March
Harrison Ford	Bill Zehme	April
Teri Garr	Robert Crane	May
Theresa Russell	Claudia Dreifus	June
Judge Reinhold	Bill Zehme	July
Harry Edwards	Robert S. Wieder	August
Tracey Ullman	Bill Zehme	September
Morton Downey Jr.	Al Goldstein	October
John Cleese	Dick Lochte	November
Gene Simmons	David Rensin	December

1989

Name	Interviewer	Month
Andrea Marcovicci	John Rezek	February
Fred Dryer	David Rensin	March
Mario Lemieux	Paul Engleman	April
Richard Lewis	Dick Lochte	May
Nicolas Cage	Robert Crane	June
William Shatner	David Rensin	July
John Candy	Robert Crane	August
Jeff Daniels	Bill Zehme	September
Geena Davis	David Rensin	October
Bonnie Raitt	Paul Engleman & John Rezek	November
Patti D'Arbanville	David Rensin	December

1990

Name	Interviewer	Month
Andrew Dice Clay	David Rensin	January
Dwight Yoakam	Trish Wend	February
Dennis Hopper	David Rensin	March
John Larroquette	David Rensin	April
Jennifer Tilly	David Rensin	May
Willy T. Ribbs	Walter Lowe Jr.	June
Matt Groening	Neil Tesser	July
Dana Carvey	Warren Kalbacker	August
Maury Povich	David Rensin	September
Kiefer Sutherland	Paul Engleman	October
Chuck D	Bill Wyman	November
Elizabeth Perkins	Bill Zehme	December

1991

Name	Interviewer	Month
Lena Olin	David Rensin	February
George Foreman	Lawrence Linderman	April
Whitney Houston	Nelson George	May
John Milius	David Rensin	June
Eric Bogosian	Warren Kalbacker	July
Robert Downey Jr.	David Rensin	August
Danny Glover	David Rensin	September
Camille Paglia	Warren Kalbacker	October
Julia Roberts	David Rensin	November
Joe Pesci	Julie Bain	December

1992

Name	Interviewer	Month
Woody Harrelson	David Rensin	January
Jennifer Jason Leigh	David Rensin	February
Forest Whitaker	Kevin Cook	March
Bob Goldthwait	Warren Kalbacker	April
John Leguizamo	Warren Kalbacker	May
Patrick Swayze	Larry Linderman	June
Nicole Kidman	David Rensin	July
Catherine Crier	David Rensin	August
Dennis Miller	Wayne Kalyn	September
Tim Robbins	Warren Kalbacker	October
Patrick Stewart	Neil Tesser	November
Helmut Newton	Margy Rochlin	December

1993

Name	Interviewer	Month
Sean Young	David Rensin	January
Tim Allen	David Rensin	February
Laura Dern	Margy Rochlin	March
Cindy Crawford	David Rensin	April
Giorgio Armani	Warren Kalbacker	May
Rebecca De Mornay	David Rensin	June
Rip Torn	Warren Kalbacker	July
Scott Turow	John Rezek & Paul Engleman	August
Sarah Jessica Parker	David Rensin	September
Wesley Snipes	David Rensin	October
Brian Dennehy	David Rensin	November
Branford Marsalis	Neil Tesser	December

1994

Name	Interviewer	Month
Shaquille O'Neal	Richard Lalich	January

INDEX

Picture Credits